Women's Writing

The later twentieth century saw a huge wave of academic interest in women's writing, which led to the rediscovery of neglected works from a wide range of genres, periods and languages. Many books that were immensely popular and influential in their own day are now studied again, both for their own sake and for what they reveal about the social, political and cultural conditions of their time. A pioneering resource in this area is Orlando: Women's Writing in the British Isles from the Beginnings to the Present (http://orlando.cambridge.org), which provides entries on authors' lives and writing careers, contextual material, timelines, sets of internal links, and bibliographies. Its editors have made a major contribution to the selection of the works reissued in this series within the Cambridge Library Collection, which focuses on non-fiction publications by women on a wide range of subjects from astronomy to biography, music to political economy, and education to prison reform.

Woman's Work and Woman's Culture

First published in 1869, this influential volume contains a compilation of essays written by prominent Victorian feminists and their supporters, both men and women, discussing a variety of issues which were considered of importance to the early feminist movement. Edited by campaigner Josephine Butler (1828–1906), the contributions from activists and supporters including Frances Power Cobbe (1822–1904) and Sophia Jex-Blake (1840–1912) challenge the widespread assumption that 'women's sphere is the home', through discussion of the contemporary attitude to and condition of women. Various aspects of the inequality which women experienced, including the need for female suffrage, the ending of women's legal non-existence, and the right of women to access higher education and careers including medicine and science, are explored and advocated, illustrating the central concerns of the early feminist movement and the areas in which the movement had success in later years. For more information on Josephine Butler, see http://orlando.cambridge.org/public/svPeople?person_id=butljo

Woman's Work and Woman's Culture

A Series of Essays

EDITED BY JOSEPHINE BUTLER

CAMBRIDGE
UNIVERSITY PRESS

CAMBRIDGE UNIVERSITY PRESS

Cambridge, New York, Melbourne, Madrid, Cape Town, Singapore,
São Paolo, Delhi, Dubai, Tokyo, Mexico City

Published in the United States of America by Cambridge University Press, New York

www.cambridge.org
Information on this title: www.cambridge.org/9781108021029

This edition first published 1869
This digitally printed version 2010

ISBN 978-1-108-02102-9 Paperback

WOMAN'S WORK

AND

WOMAN'S CULTURE.

ERRATUM.

Page 75. For "I would appeal to the theological writings of Miss Blunt," *read* "I would appeal to 'Readings on Morning and Evening Prayer,' by Miss Blunt."

WOMAN'S WORK

AND

WOMAN'S CULTURE.

A SERIES OF ESSAYS.

EDITED BY

JOSEPHINE E. BUTLER.

London:

MACMILLAN AND CO.

1869.

LONDON:

R. CLAY, SONS, AND TAYLOR, PRINTERS,

BREAD STREET HILL.

LIST OF SUBJECTS AND AUTHORS.

INTRODUCTION.

The following Essays have been collected with a grave and serious purpose. There is no aiming in them at novelty or piquancy. The writers have severally brought to the different branches of the subject treated the thought and practical experience of years: their motive has been to elicit and enforce truth, and to redeem the cause advocated, as much as may be, from the flippant and heartless treatment, and from the exaggerated and too passionate advocacy, to which it may have been subjected on the one hand and the other.

The Essays, including the following introductory remarks, were all written before Mr. J. S. Mill's book—"The Subjection of Women"—appeared. Most of them were already in print. The others were out of the writers' hands. They have been allowed to remain without alteration. In some of them the same lines of thought are pursued more in detail which are opened up in Mr. Mill's book, and a measure of agreement will be found with the general principles announced by him. As the effect of independent enforcement would be impaired if plagiarism were suspected, I think it desirable to say, on our first page, that the case is as I have stated it.[1] The writers have also been independent of each other, each in ignorance of what might be said by the others, and therefore only answerable for his or her own Essay.

I must, at the very beginning of this volume, enter a protest, in my own name and that of the other Essayists, against the questions treated herein being regarded as exclusively "women's questions," or the cause advocated as the cause, solely, of women. It has long been my conviction that the cause we advocate, though primarily and more immediately the cause of women, is secondarily in a yet graver and more weighty sense the cause of men; for I do not think that one can have read the Scriptures, or history, or human life, at all thoughtfully, without being struck with this—that wherever one class or set of human beings has been placed at a disadvantage as compared with another class, has been deprived of whatsoever just privileges or denied a legitimate share of God's endowment of the world, the class so treated is not always the one for whom our gravest fears admit of the most reasonable justification. If we look at the matter largely, taking spiritual as well as material consequences into account, and the moral retri-

[1] The only exception to this is the latter part of the Essay on the Education of Girls: those pages were kept back until after the 14th of June, when the Endowed Schools Bill was considered before a Committee of the House of Commons.

butions which are surely brought about by the avenging years as they roll on, we can scarcely fail to perceive that the class which suffers most eventually, is not the class which is deprived, oppressed, or denied, but that which deprives, oppresses, or denies.

I must distinctly declare, that I am not about to reiterate any accusations against the men of the present generation, nor yet against men of past generations, nor to charge any living being with a conscious and wilful participation in any existing social wrong. The evils in society to which public attention is now awakened may be said to be in a great measure the result of accident, and of the halting and unequal progress of society. To thank all those men whose justice, candour, and unselfish helpfulness is recorded in my heart each day of my life as among God's best gifts to our age, would be to me a more congenial task than the pointing out of anything that may seem yet to be wanting. But I believe that there is no truer kindness than to remind those who, themselves just, true, and generous, have been born to an inheritance of monopolized privileges, of the duties which such an inheritance entails. For wherever there is monopoly on the one hand, there is loss and waste on the other. A man born to the possession of a great neglected estate, on which he finds his labourers degraded, cottages in ruins, and fields which ought to be storehouses of sustenance for city populations going to waste, undrained, and untilled, will scarcely think he has done his duty to society if, having any available means of improving it, he dies, leaving his estate as he found it, content to charge the ruin and neglect upon his forefathers or upon a series of accidents. It would not be thought that an unjust accusation had been brought against such a landowner, if a friend were to take him by the hand, and lead him through the dwellings of his tenants and labourers, and bid him mark the moral as well as material harvest of misery which each year of continued neglect was preparing for a number of human beings; even if such a friend were to reason with him on "righteousness, temperance, and judgment to come," until he trembled in the waking sense of deep responsibility, it would not be thought to be a harsh or needless counsel. Similarly it will be believed, I trust, that it is with an equal regard for the happiness of all human beings alike, men and women, the highly favoured and responsible as well as the spoiled and neglected, that I venture to remind the men of the present generation, that there is an entail more grievous than that which spreads its blight over so many estates in our fair England—an entail which is injurious to those who are supposed to be benefiting by it, no less than to the human fields which it desolates. There is a moral deterioration which is the invariable attendant upon the habit of the careless and irresponsible enjoyment of possession at the expense of the happiness and good of others. No portion of the human family can continue from age to age in the enjoyment of advantages which are not justly shared with others, nor in an attitude of indifference to the disabilities of another and a dependent portion of the community,—even though a monopoly of such advantages may have been an heritage to which they were born—without suffering deterioration, gradual but sure, in the deepest part of their nature. For persons in such a case, whether they or their forefathers be chargeable with the blame of it, there is no certain moral health save in the awakened perception of existing wrong, and the conscious will to restore the balance to society, as far as it lies in their power to do so, by bringing a share of monopolized blessings into the lot of those classes who have suffered deprivation.

In the Bible, I find the labourer deprived of just wages, the wronged widow, the neglected orphan, the leper driven out of society, the uninstructed from whom the key of knowledge had been withheld, the Gentile stranger oppressed by the privileged Jew, each and all in their turn tenderly mentioned in those pathetic and paternal utterances, beginning with "Thus saith the Lord." Their cry, it is said, enters into the ears of God. They are cared for by Him, and we dimly trust that restitution awaits them somewhere hereafter for loss suffered on earth.

Not that the kindness of God can always be said, so far as we yet see it, to fill up the measure of the unkindness of man. God's kindness is in reserve, we believe, or how could we endure life, knowing what we know? But what shall we say of the broken hearts, the deep discouragement and dismay, the deadness of souls, the destruction of moral natures, which are in so large a degree the fruits reaped by the classes who are impoverished, deprived of light, hope, instruction, and freedom, while others, who could give, have enough and to spare? God only knows how many millions of these, maddened by life's mystery, have voluntarily plunged into darkness, from the earliest period of the world's history down to last night's suicide from London Bridge, pitied no doubt by our Father in heaven, but doubting, fearing, it may be cursing, that most pitiful God, whose love and justice the poor heart can discern no longer athwart the black cloud of earth's cruelty. Yet I maintain that this very despair is less of a moral poison affecting the eternal destiny of a human spirit than is that blind self-satisfaction, deepening and hardening from generation to generation, which is engendered by the monopoly of privilege, and all the more if it be privilege of the noblest and highest kind. Wherefore, if I were a man, I would call upon my fellow-men to hearken and consider seriously what may be the deeper meanings of the invocation which is coming up on all sides from women in all parts of the earth, and in self-defence to prepare to render back such measure of justice as may seen, through whatsoever cause or accident, to have been withheld. For to persons who have rested in their privileges, who, even if not wantonly robbing any man of any good thing, have passed by on the other side, and dreamed away their lives in a thraldom to conventions and customs which are eating the heart out of society, to these the language of prophets speaking in God's name is stern. The shadow of the Almighty's frown rests darkly on those pages of Scripture which speak of the carelessly secure and neglectful. The language used is sometimes that of entreaty, of a summons to wake up and behold, and repent: sometimes it is that of prophetic judgment; and that judgment our own eyes tell us, and the gloomy page of history tells us, is one which falls silently, scarcely recognised, generation after generation, upon the dominant and privileged family, state, race or nation, until, like the richly-endowed and privileged Jews who lived when Christ came into the world, they have become blind to their own blindness, and incapable of seeing light when light appears.

It is certain, then, that all who look upon this question of woman's interests from a grave and lofty point of view must behold it, as it is indeed, a question which concerns humanity at large, and that very vitally; and I wish it were felt that women who are labouring especially for women are not one-sided or selfish. We are human first; women secondarily. We care for the evils affecting women most of all because they react upon the whole of society, and abstract from the common good. Women are not men's rivals, but their helpers. There can be no antagonism that is not injurious to both. When women laying claim for women to certain privileges hitherto withheld are called self-seeking and self-asserting—terms applied to them by ladies living at ease, and ignorant of the facts of life, much more frequently than by men—it seems to be forgotten that the term "Women" is a large and comprehensive one. When men nobly born and possessing advantages of wealth and education have fought the battles of poor men, and claimed and wrung from Parliaments an extension of privileges enjoyed by a few to classes of their brother-men who are toiling and suffering, I do not remember ever to have heard them charged with self-seeking; on the contrary, the regard that such men have had for the rights of men has been praised, and deservedly so, as noble and unselfish. And why should the matter be judged otherwise when the eyes of educated and thoughtful women of the better classes are opened to the terrible truth regarding the millions of their less favoured countrywomen, and they ask on *their* behalf for the redress of wrongs, and for liberty to work and to live in honesty and self-reliance?

The question is too large to be fully examined here (it will be approached from other sides in other parts of this volume), of how far this present distress among women is an exceptional distress, an accidental and transitory state of things, and how far, on the other hand, men have altogether failed, up to the present day, to reach the standard to which the teaching of Christianity would have led them in their relations to their fellow-creatures. I cannot myself doubt that the great principles announced by Christ have hitherto remained very imperfectly recognised in the most important of their adaptations, and that a future generation will look back with wonder on the present state of women as an illustration of the slowness with which society has become leavened by those principles. Yet it is evident that there have been periods since the Christian era when the failure to recognise those principles did not entail such grave consequences as it does at this day, when circumstances and popular ideals of life were more favourable than now to the happiness and moral dignity of women. The present distress must to some degree be reckoned among the phenomena of a transition-period in society ; it is in part owing to the rapid advances in discovery, invention, expeditive processes, instruments of production, &c., which advances have been unequally yoked with our national conservatism of certain customs, conventions, and ideals of life and character. The great tide of an imperfect and halting civilization has rolled onward, and carried many triumphantly with it. But women have been left stranded, so to speak. Never was levity more out of place, or indifference less philosophical, than at such a crisis. It is a crisis which calls for action; for it is evident that a readjustment of man's and woman's fields of work, and in some degree of their manner of life, must take place in order to restore the equilibrium of society. A much greater number of women must support themselves now than has been the case at any other time. The agitation for the enlargement of woman's sphere of work has a real and pressing cause. It has been said that nothing short of hunger will drive a nation to rebellion ; but here we actually have a large measure of that ghastly element of rebellion—hunger and a lack of honestly-won food. The census taken eight years ago gave three and a half millions of women in England working for a subsistence ; of these, two and a half millions were unmarried. In the interval between the census of 1851 and that of 1861 the number of self-supporting women had increased by more than half a million. This is significant, and still more striking I believe, on this point, will be the returns of the next census two years hence. But the census does not tell how many of these two and a half millions are working for starvation wages, nor how many of them have declined from a position of respectability to which they were born to one in any class or rank, however low, in which they may have a chance of earning a piece of bread. Nor does the census include among these breadwinners the armies of women, counted by thousands in all our towns and cities, who are forced downwards to the paths of hell, by the pressure from above, through the shutting up of avenues to a livelihood by means of trade monopolies among men, and through the absence of any instruction or apprenticeship to qualify them for employment. Of this class of persons, and of this sorest of human griefs, we are never forgetful; no, not for a day. I speak for myself and for other *women* at least, my fellow-workers. The subject was thought too painful an one to be specially treated in a volume for general reading; therefore I think it the more needful to assert that these our fellow-women are not forgotten by us; on the contrary, we continually feel—and the public must be constantly reminded of it—*that there is no analogy whatever among men, however miserable certain classes of men may be, to the wholesale destruction which goes on from year to year among women*—destruction of bodies, of consciences, of souls; and the existence of this class would alone have been enough to urge us who are happier to raise our voices to claim what we claim now—freedom and power to reach and deal with great social evils in their beginnings, and not only in a limited degree in their dire effects. At present, and indeed ever since the world began, this class of people have been generally left out of account in all theories of life, and in the framing of legislative and social measures, except so far as society has had to be protected against them as against a public nuisance, and so far as individual missionary efforts have attempted to restore a few of the fallen. I think that any theory of life or of public arrangements is thoroughly unscientific, as well as unchristian, which leaves this mass of people out of account, which deals with it as a fact which must be endured, but which must be as much as possible pushed into a corner, and fenced round so as to annoy and hurt the rest of the community as little as possible. Such economy resembles that of an indolent housewife who is aware of a certain chamber in her house which is full of the accumulated dirt of years, but which she fears to look into, hopeless of any possible cleansing, and the door of which she keeps carefully closed, content so long as the rest of the dwelling is not fatally infected by the presence of the evil.

It has been well said, that "philanthropy and politics, now flowing apart, will unite in one stream when philanthropists become conscious of power to reach the *sources* of crime and misery, and when statesmen understand that their functions are assigned to them for none but a philanthropic end. How few of us will or can persevere in self-denial, if we seem to be striving for the impossible; if while we are painfully draining a small pool of misery, a new and full tide pours in! Under the crushing belief that, labour as we may, the result will be imperceptible, most of us turn away from a heartbreaking task, and try to forget other people's wretchedness. That mankind may reach a better state, philanthropy, like religion, must be the work and duty of all, not of a select few. With a view to this, women (whose heart is our great reservoir of tenderness) must have a hope of, not merely palliating, but uprooting national evils." Although there are in every town Refuges for the fallen, in which, and the missionary work of the streets, Christian women spend their lives for the restoration of their sisters, yet this work is but the draining of a pool into which a vast tide is continually pouring, which steadily swells the evil in spite of our utmost efforts. It is well known by all who have any practical experience of this subject, that want, the difficulty of obtaining work, friendlessness, and the absence of any technical or industrial education, are the main causes of this terrible destruction of human beings. It cannot be wondered at, then, that we confidently believe that the admission of intelligent and educated women to a participation in any social legislation which bears on this and kindred matters, and a share given to them in the necessary preventive as well as curative work which is required to be done, largely and wisely, would bring more light and hope into this dark portion of the world's history than has ever yet been brought into it. It is well known that all legislative and social enactments bearing on this class of women have been made hitherto by men alone, without the counsel or practical aid of women; and yet it is the present and eternal interests of women especially that this matter involves. I say women, but there are tens of thousands of these who can scarcely be called women. Among the 9,000 women who are pursuing this calling in one of our great seaports, a late inquiry showed that 1,500 were under fifteen years of age, and of these about a third were under thirteen years of age. It is much the same in other towns. Think of this, you mothers who are living at ease, in your pleasant drawing-rooms, with your tender darlings around you! You can feel with me the truth of the saying, that "God could not make anything sweeter than a little girl;" but you surely will not be content to preserve the holy sweetness of those whom God has given you, without a practical effort to lessen the power of those sinister social forces which are at present driving whole armies of little girls to madness and early graves.

And do not suppose that these children of the poor are of a different nature from your own sheltered children. Every one who has had any large experience and intimate personal knowledge of this class, must have felt as often astonished at the strength of virtue and the resisting power of innocence, among the poor, exposed to vice and temptation, as at the inherent and unconquerable tendency to evil that there is among some of all classes, even the most protected. Any one who i acquainted with the condition of women in the lower-middle classes,[1] as well as with the homes of the very poor, is inclined to be surprised that so many escape.

To mass all these women and children under one title as "infamous" is an indiscriminating philosophy, and betrays a great ignorance of human nature. A poor little French girl, bribed from her home by fair offers of honest employment and success in England,

[1] When Mr. Henley said in the House of Commons, on the 14th of June, that an extension of endowment funds to girls' schools was not pressingly needful, because "our girls are educated at home," I presume he was thinking of girls of the higher classes, the sisters of Eton and Harrow boys, &c. His words do not apply to girls of the class for whom a share of endowments has been requested: namely, the sisters of the boys who are at present benefiting from endowments in our provincial towns. These girls are *not* educated at home. They are the children of tradesmen, clerks, poor professional men, &c., who can just afford to educate their boys, and who *cannot* afford a governess at home for their daughters. These girls consequently go to inferior day-schools, if to any school, the teachers of which are among the foremost of those who are asking for a different state of things, feeling the unreality of their profession and the need of help. No one, I believe, proposes that the endowment of Eton should be extended to girls, while John Lyons' Will expressly forbids that girls shall have any share of the education provided at Harrow. Nor is it for the better classes, who can afford to have good governesses for their daughters at home, that we are at present concerned. Mr. Henley would probably be shocked himself if he were to consider certain statistics which I could bring before him about the recruiting of this great army of ruined women I have spoken of. Girls from this very class, for whom we are claiming education as their only salvation—humanly speaking,—frequently lapse into these ranks. I scarcely like to say what I know. It is not in their case a positive lack of a meal for to-day that drives them to this, but it is their generally exposed condition, the presence of temptation to frivolity, the absence of all mental resource, empty-headedness, love of dress, and the craving for some little affair of the heart to enliven the insipidity of their lives. And what, save a good education, can tend to the correction of all this? To say they can be educated at home, under mothers who are themselves uneducated, is to offer a stone to those who ask bread.

died in one of our great hospitals. She had endured an enforced life of the deepest ignominy for two years. In her illness her mind wandered, and to listen to her gentle ravings was like listening to some sweet, mournful song of an exile. She talked unceasingly of her dear home in France; she fancied herself wandering among the sunny, vine-clad hills of Burgundy, and her thoughts were all innocent, sweet, and lovely There was no word of any hope in God, for she was uninstructed; but her heart yearned for an earthly paradise—her father's vineyard, her mother's cottage; and her innocent smiles and gestures showed sometimes that she believed she had found them all again. Every memory of the horrors of the last two years was blotted out. When the delirium ceased, she said, suddenly, "Je me meurs," and her spirit passed away.

Many such examples have come before me of the indelibleness of the instinct of purity given by God to many women. I quote it as an illustration of the awful nature of those accidents of our social system which are diverting from their proper channels those gentle characteristics of womanhood which might bring so much blessing and happiness to society, and delivering them over to Satan, to work, through their own ruin, the ruin of others. The timid among us, both men and women, are glad to be allowed to forget the existence of this great shame in the midst of us; and there is no one fact of life which they more easily succeed in forgetting. Indeed, it is often considered needful for our own moral health, and a proper concession to the prevailing refinement of manners, to be ignorant, or to simulate ignorance, of it. But Christ's teaching in this particular does not seem to sanction such a measure of ignorance or of refinement. Kepler, the astronomer, speaking of the discoveries he had pursued, said, "I have thought God's thoughts after Him." Let any one consider, who believes that our social system can be securely maintained without taking into account the salvation of this class, whether he can apply the test of Kepler's words to his own conscience; has he thought God's thoughts after Him? What are God's thoughts? Was it not said, "It is not the will of your heavenly Father that one of these should perish?"

And by the salvation of this class I mean something more than the Refuge or Penitentiary, and something more than the application of sanitary measures for the protection of our army and navy, and of that portion of the respectable of all classes by whom in a measure these unhappy women are maintained, and to whom, no doubt, it is a present advantage to be able to sin with impunity. I would not speak lightly of any measures adopted by Government from motives of humanity and public necessity; but, considering that, in spite of all such measures, thousands of ruined women are, through want of employment, daily being huddled into workhouse graves—most of them *very* young women—I think it is not unreasonable, nor should it be considered "self-seeking," that women should say to those who have hitherto ruled all things for us, "Let us see if we can help you to reach a little nearer to the heart of this evil." Is it enough that we should be able to say with regard to this matter, as a Parisian gentleman said to me, "We take care of our *men*," while we deny to thousands of our women every chance of earning a livelihood in any other profession than this?

The demand of the women of the humbler classes for bread may be more pressing, but it is not more sincere, than that of the women of the better classes for work. And these two demands coming together, it seems to me, point to an end so plainly to be discerned, that I marvel that any should remain blind to it. The latter demand is the attestation of the collective human conscience that God does not permit any to live as cumberers of the ground, and that the very condition of their moral existence is, that efforts made and pains taken by them should answer to some part of the needs of the community. But their position also is, as I have said, that of people stranded. The wave has passed them by. Their work is taken out of their hands: their place—they know not where it is. They stretch out their hands idly. A readjustment is needed, but it only slowly comes about. The present generation must be content to suffer as the victims of a transitional period; but for the next generation there is hope. Already the earnest action initiated in some quarters, and the sincere and kindly co-operation of some men and some women for the improvement of the condition of women generally, has dispelled in a great degree the despondency and the bitterness of soul which settles and deepens, when as yet no voice has been raised, and the years go on without hope of redress.

In almost all important popular crises in history, it is evident that the two great parties which generally divide the actors in such crises have been possessed, in an almost equal degree, with one dread—the dread of Revolution. In the political crisis of 1832, for example, we read the speeches on the Conservative side, and find them full of gloomy forebodings of revolution, which revolution seems to minds so constituted the direct effect of the opening out of privilege to the many which has hitherto been the heritage of the few. There were sensible men who honestly believed that the Reform Bill of 1832 would revolutionize the country in a sense which, to them, foreboded much evil. On the other hand, if we read the letters and private utterances of those who were urging the extension of privilege, the leaders themselves of the great movement, we find them expressing a dread of the same evil, Revolution, but anticipating it from a very different source, namely, the denial of extended privileges. What both these parties honestly deprecated was, no doubt, anarchy, confusion, the upsetting of law and order, and a general movement which could only be suicidal. I think history contains few more useful lessons than may be learned from this agreement between contending parties, considered in relation to the wide disagreement between them as to the means of averting destructive change and maintaining the balance of society. Is there any one now living who doubts that revolution would have followed ere long the denial of that extension of popular privilege for which a patient people had waited long? To the facts alone we need to look for an answer to the question whether those were right or wrong who believed that the admission of a numerous class to a hitherto monopolized influence would avert revolution, and tend towards healthy self-government. I think there is no slight analogy between such a case and the present crisis. The majority of Englishmen have, I believe, at this day, a secret dread lest the granting of the claims which are just now put forward by women should revolutionize society. I wish particularly to notice the fear, or presentiment, which seems to me the most worthy of our serious consideration—namely, the fear that to grant what they are asking would revolutionize our *Homes*. This is indeed a serious question; for I believe that Home is the nursery of all virtue, the fountain-head of all true affection, and the main source of the strength of our nation. On this subject I may be pardoned, as one who has had experience to the full of all the sacredness and blessedness of home, if I speak with warmth. It is sometimes supposed that the most fervent advocates of woman's cause are persons who have been pinched and starved in the matter of affection, disappointed in life, embittered by isolation, and therefore glad to exchange the exclusiveness of the domestic hearth for a communism in which they would not feel themselves left out, starved and solitary. It is no wonder if the sighs, and even the invectives, of some such isolated persons should be heard mournfully sounding through the general advocacy of a renewed social order. But let me be permitted to remind the public, if it needs such reminding, that many of those who are toiling, praying, and arguing for the promotion of this cause, are among the happiest ladies in the land. They are among those who might —if God had permitted such a hardening of the heart —have rested content, and more than content, with the sunshine which has fallen upon their path. But it is precisely this abundance of blessing bestowed on them which urges them to care for the less happy, and which becomes a weight hardly to be borne in the presence of the unloved, unapplied existences of some others, and the solemn awakening energy of demand for a place in God's order of society which is now arising from thousands of homeless women. Not but that the happiest among us have not observed and pondered with amazement, from our very childhood, on certain customs, laws, and maxims prevalent among us, which seem only to recognise the existence of one half of the human family. But we had not long to wait to compare our solitary conclusions with the awful revelations of actual life around us. To be very patient under the miseries of *others*, appeared to us, as we grew up to years of discretion, to be an easy virtue: we desired to practise some sterner virtue than this, and we saw that our own happiness was the very reason why we should speak out boldly for the unhappy; and it continues to be a reason determining us to labour on in the same course, through evil report and good report. It is from the heart of my beloved home, with my children around me, that I speak; wherefore I trust I shall be believed to be free from indifference to the fear that our homes may be revolutionized or destroyed. And let it be clearly understood, that the promoters of the cause for which I speak are generally no less afraid of the revolutionizing of our family life than those are who oppose us in the strength of this very argument. Where we differ, it is as to the means of averting such a consequence: and here we differ not a little.

The true spirit of Conservatism is shown in the adaptation of old and tried principles to new and varying circumstances; and there are ancient and honoured principles which I hold as tenaciously as the strongest Conservative. But I maintain that to hold tenaciously to the exact outward form in which those principles may have clothed themselves, simply on the ground of the antiquity of that form, is often the surest means of revolutionizing, in the most undesirable sense of the word, the society which we wish to strengthen. "He that *will* save his life, the same shall lose it;" and those who, at all costs to others, are determined to reserve to themselves, in the midst of a people whose hearts are already failing them for fear, and in a time of perplexity and distress, the too often selfish comforts and exclusive enjoyments of home and family life, are not unlikely to lose the very blessings which they are hugging, or carelessly enjoying, while the homeless are wailing outside.

I think I see that a great enlargement of hearts, and a free opening out and giving forth of the influences of homes, as reservoirs of blessing for the common good, would ultimately result in the restored security of all the best elements in our present ideal of Home, and that the saying would come true, "He that will lose his life for My sake" (for the sake of Him who taught that if a man have two coats he should give one to him that has none), "the same shall find it." Fair and happy homes would gather again, in larger groups, and their happiness would be placed on a surer foundation than that of the home-lovers of to-day, who are trembling lest they should be deprived of one particle of present comfort and enjoyment by the pressing case of those who have neither.

But before I continue this argument, I wish to say a word about that constantly reiterated assertion that "Woman's sphere is the home." The saying, as it is uttered now, in the face of the great facts of society as they lie confessed before us, is to a great extent wholly inapplicable, and assumes the character of a most ungentle irony. Many men who a few years ago echoed this cry, have had their eyes opened, and candidly confess that there was cruelty, though an unintentional cruelty, in the emphasis they gave to it before; yet there remain both men and women who continue solemnly to inform the women who are striving for some work or calling which will save them from starvation, and who have no human being but themselves to depend on, that their proper sphere is *home*,—that their proper function is to be wives and mothers, and their happiness is to be dependent on men! Alas! these women have learned a lesson which neither they, nor the generation which follows them, are likely to forget, on the subject of dependence on men.

Like Pharaoh, who commanded the Israelites to make bricks without the material to make them of, these moralizers command this multitude of inquiring women back to homes which are not, and which they have not the material to create. I trust that such mocking words as these will cease to be spoken. But to enter on a larger view of the subject; in a deeper sense than these moralizers conceive home *is* the sphere of woman, inasmuch as under circumstances in the smallest degree favourable, women instinctively create a home around themselves. The instinct is strong to gather into a circle a group, small or great, divided by a certain invisible boundary-line of united interests, and little aggregate of comforts, from the outer world:

> "An ear that waits to catch
> A hand upon the latch,
> A step that hastens its sweet rest to win:
> A world of care without,
> A world of strife shut out,
> A world of love shut in."

Such a vision dwells more or less in every woman's mind, except where poverty and misery have blotted it out. A poor woman before a magistrate, questioned why she and her family, one of whom had died of hunger, did not take refuge in the workhouse, replied, "We did not like to leave our home and our bits of comforts." Their bits of comforts were found to consist of one broken chair, and a board with some empty sacks upon it which served them as a bed. The tenacity with which women of all ranks naturally cling to home, or make a home of such elements as they find around them, might reassure the men who are at present so terrified lest domesticity should take flight from our land.

I dwell upon this tendency in women to call up domestic influences wherever they are, in order that I may indicate the direction of my hopes for the veering round again of some of the most difficult of our present circumstances towards the re-establishment, in various forms, of all that is good and healthful in our present ideal of family life. I plead that to grant the present demands of women will tend to the restoration of the true home ideals, and that the denial of those demands will hasten the day of disorganization and uprooting of sacred traditions, which is dreaded. How will the granting of them tend to this restoration? I can only briefly indicate, in the limits of this Essay, the hoped-for direction of feeling and practice under the supposed granting of the required conditions.

I think it would do so,

(1) Through the restored dignity of women;

(2) Through the opening out and diffusion of the home influence and character among the masses, by

the relegation to women of some of the more important work of dealing with our vast populations.

(1) At the present day women are cheap; their value in the great world's market has sunk to a very low ebb. Their attitude, speaking generally, is that of cringing for a piece of bread. What dignity can there be in the attitude of women in general, and toward men in particular, when marriage is held (and often necessarily so, being the sole means of maintenance) to be the one end of a woman's life, when it is degraded to the level of a feminine profession, when those who are soliciting a place in this profession resemble those flaccid Brazilian creepers which cannot exist without support, and which sprawl out their limp tendrils in every direction to find something—no matter what—to hang upon; when the insipidity or the material necessities of so many women's lives make them ready to accept almost any man who may offer himself? There has been a pretence of admiring this pretty helplessness of women. But let me explain that I am not deprecating the condition of dependence in which God has placed every human being, man or woman,—the sweet interchange of services, the give and take of true affection, the mutual support and aid of friends or lovers, who have each something to give and to receive. That is a wholly different thing from the abject dependence of one entire class of persons on another and a stronger class. In the present case such a dependence is liable to peculiar dangers by its complication with sexual emotions and motives, and with

relations which ought, in an advanced and Christian community, to rest upon a free and deliberate choice,—a decision of the judgment and of the heart, and into which the admission of a necessity, moral or material, introduces a degrading element. "Election makes not up with such conditions," Burgundy said to King Lear when he relinquished Cordelia to his nobler rival, who declared, "Love is not love when it is mingled with respects that stand aloof from the entire point." Truly, the present condition of society is one which does not favour election. It leaves little room for the heart's choice. It has often occurred to me that the nature of a man must differ considerably from that of a woman if he does not care to be loved for *his own sake*, and does not desire conditions of life which allow of his knowing whether he is or not the deliberately preferred, the elect of the person whose companionship for life he solicits. I have seen a woman meet with an indignant rejection the offer of a man whom she knew had for his object simply *a wife*, and marriage in general. "If it is only a wife you want," she replied, "there are wives enough to be had. Seek one elsewhere. I am not the person you seek." I should be glad to see a greater degree of such self-respect both among men and women; but such a feeling can scarcely thrive in a society in which to act upon it would be for many women starvation and a wasted life, and in which it is not easy for a man to distinguish a genuine preference in a woman amidst the general scramble for husbands.

I am aware that many think that marriages of convenience, prudently arranged, are for the most part the happiest; and it is true that religious principle and kindliness of heart, where there is any basis for mutual esteem, serve to make such marriages frequently very happy. But we cannot read the history of mankind without seeing that the desire of worthiness in one who would win the heart of a worthy person has been at all times of the world's history one of the strongest incentives to a noble life. That worshipful love of a woman who continually holds communion with God while practising the perfection of a dutiful life on earth is, I believe the strongest incentive which a man can have, next to the love of Christ, to a life of purity, duty, and self-denial. All the most beautiful stories of noble lives and deeds are found in countries and in ages where such love as this was possible. I do not say that we need more of emotion and sentiment among us than we have; on the contrary, I hope that education, earnest work in trades and professions, and a share in grave national interests, will correct the foolish sentimental tendencies of the women whose chief literature at present is the sensation novel; but I do not hesitate to declare my belief that we need —together with other and higher influences—a revival of the grave and romantic ideas of love which have prevailed in happier periods of human history, and which can never wholly perish. We need, in fact, *love* tself,—the love which is based on a deep respect— instead of those mimicries and desecrations of the name of love which prevail. I doubt whether a man generally feels the best kind of attraction towards a woman who is socially worthless, though she may be in herself a good woman; he sees her not only with his own eyes, but reflected in the opinions of the persons around her. I have seen a lover's face kindle with a fresh glow of tenderness and admiration when some testimony came before him of the social worth of the woman he loved. I have marked also the grave efforts which young men have had to make when the women they wished to win were happy, industrious workers in some trade requiring skill and intense application, and possessed of that kind of beauty of face and mind which an earnest life imparts, and which is never seen in an idle or frivolous woman. In such a case the lover thought himself happy when he could for a moment arrest the work of the nimble fingers, and win a look from the watchful eyes intent upon the work in hand. The sense, as in this instance, of the reality and gravity of life on the one hand, and of the worth of the person to be won on the other, are no trifling elements in the moral progress of society. I give these slight instances, which the few steps already made in the direction of industrial openings for women enable me to note, in order to illustrate what I find it somewhat difficult to express in generalities. I believe that the opening out of a freer life for women would ultimately, though not very soon, tend to the increase of marriage, for the worth and therefore the attractiveness of women would be increased, and undoubtedly it would tend to the preservation of all that we wish to preserve in existing homes. On the question whether it is desirable that women should marry more than they do, I will only say, that while men continue to preach the doctrine—implicitly believed by most of them—that in marriage lies the only possible salvation for women, and while the thoughts of women continue to be directed to it as the one aim of life, marriage is likely to become less and less desired by the nobler portion of the community, and the marriages which are made will for the most part fail to be truly dignified and happy. I cannot believe that it is every woman's duty to marry, in this age of the world. There is abundance of work to be done which needs men and women detached from domestic ties; our unmarried women will be the greatest blessing to the community when they cease to be soured by disappointment or driven by destitution to despair.

There has been a divorce among us between usefulness and beauty; it is a separation which involves a real loss of worth and happiness; and it ought not to be: for the highest beauty will, I believe, everywhere be found to rest upon the greatest utility. Who has not felt that the attractiveness of our better-class women, who too often lead the life of butterflies, is spoiled by the vanity and egotism which so easily take possession of minds devoid of great thoughts, and deprived of the invigorating influence of work? Egotism is a poison before which beauty perishes. The divorce is not less injurious, on the other hand, where thousands of women are obliged to spend their lives in such unceasing drudgery and ill-paid or unpaid toil, that beauty and grace are meaningless as applied to them; and thus, as we descend to the poorest populations of our towns, we find, in place of marriage, loose and lawless intercourse, consciences becoming darker and more dead through the ever-accumulating weight of crime and misery which is passed on as a family heritage, and even the physical type degraded for successive generations, till finally our Prisons, Penitentiaries, and Workhouses are crowded to overflowing with worthless, unwholesome human weeds, low-browed apes, in whom intelligence is all but extinguished, and love has perished, and the instinct of hunger and the lowest animal instincts alone remain. In such a state of things—although there are yet many homes among us where simple manners and high aims prevail, and although some women have risen to an exceptional excellence by the strength of their sorrow for their country, and a noble anger—we cannot hope to find the dignity of woman, in general, more than an empty name.

(2) But I have said that the desired end will also be advanced by the extension beyond our homes of the home influence. In the present pretty general realization of the futility, if not the positive harm, of many forms of private philanthropy, and the often-repeated deprecation of meddling individuals who pauperize the community by their old-fashioned, Lady-Bountiful way of dispensing alms and patronage, we do not perhaps quite foresee the reaction which is setting in, with a tendency so strong in the opposite direction that it brings us into the danger of once more missing the philosophy of the whole matter.

The tendency at present is to centralization of rule, to vast combinations, large institutions, and uniformity of system. I have a doubt about any wholesale manipulation of the poor, the criminal, scholars in schools, &c. I believe it to be so far from founded on a philosophical view of human nature and of society, that, if carried to extremes, the last state of our poor will be worse than the first. For the correction of the extreme tendencies of this reaction, I believe that nothing whatever will avail but the large infusion of Home elements into Workhouses, Hospitals, Schools, Orphanages, Lunatic Asylums, Reformatories, and even Prisons: and in order to this there must be a setting free of feminine powers and influence from the constraint of bad education, and narrow aims, and listless homes where they are at present too often a superfluity. We have had experience of what we may call the feminine form of philanthropy, the independent individual ministering, of too mediæval a type to suit the present day. It has failed. We are now about to try the masculine form of philanthropy, large and comprehensive measures, organizations and systems planned by men and sanctioned by Parliament. This also will fail, if it so far prevail as to extinguish the truth to which the other method witnessed, in spite of its excesses. Why should we not try at last a union of principles which are equally true? "It is not good for man to be alone" was a very early announcement in the history of the world; neither is it good for man to *work* alone, in any matter whatsoever which concerns the welfare of the great human family: and the larger the work be which he undertakes, unassisted by her whom God gave to him for a helpmate, the more signal will be the failure in the end.

From the driest statistics we may deduce the lesson that everything worked on the elastic and varied principle of home-life thrives far better than the costliest Institution. In lying-in hospitals, under much greater apparent advantages, a larger average of poor women die than in their own humble homes. Workhouse girls brought up in masses never turn out well. Lunatics when boarded out, as at Gheel, or even in poor humble places, less clean and less well-fed, as in Scotland, are more apt to recover than in grand well-ordered Asylums. Everything lives and thrives better where there is the principle of play and freedom which home affords, and which is necessarily excluded where rule prevails, as it must do in enormous Institutions. And as in hospitals for fever or consumption the type of the disease becomes intensified by multiplication, so in conglomerations of beings of one character, the insane or the guilty, the mental or moral disease also becomes more intense. Nothing can supplement the true and needful educating process of individual freedom. The wholesale system tends to turn human beings into machines instead of training them to be self-depending responsible beings, possessing the self-restraint without which they have nothing; and all our labour is thrown away. The large and magnificently-ordered Institution is in danger of becoming as fatally a pauperizing influence as the Lady Bountiful; but the home develops freedom and energy.

We are told that judgment must *begin* at the household of God. Our English homes, which we continue to boast of as the strongholds of all virtue, might seem to be the least appropriate portion of the world to single out for warning. Doubtless there is goodness among them, and much wickedness outside. Yet I believe that a voice might justly say to them, as that of the angel of the Church of Thyatira, "Nevertheless I have somewhat against thee." A person conscious of innocence and every good feeling will hardly conceive that he has fulfilled his duty to his neighbours by simply being, without acting; nor does a whole family, however excellent, do its duty to society by simply existing. I believe we have flattered ourselves by thinking that our homes must have an influence for good, far and wide, if we simply continue good and pure, and keep within doors and enjoy our sacred seclusion. I think more is required of us than this, at least at the present age. The French speak of a selfishness *à deux*. I am sure that the prevailing character of many homes is only that of a selfishness of five or of ten, as the case may be. I do not deny that much good is done and sacrifices are made. I believe there are few families, not absorbed in money-getting or frivolity, who do not do good after their power; but with this there is often a conservatism of family comfort and life and warmth which approaches near to selfishness. We are stewards of the manifold gifts of God, and stewards are expected to dispense those gifts to others. The lives of happy people in happy homes are generally divided into two parts; a part of the day is given probably to the visiting of certain institutions or districts of poor people. But when that is done they return to a very different world, and the spirit of conservatism and exclusiveness triumphs when they enter within their own park-gates and cross their delicious lawns into their comfortable houses. I think means might be found, where there is a will, to break down in a measure such a separation, and to give forth more freely of the strength and comfort and sweetness of family life to the homeless and solitary and sinful. I have seen a family of children grow up all the more tender and considerate because their parents housed with them for years a harmless lunatic, a stranger, whose simple and happy belief that he was an important member of the family was often the subject of innocent mirth. I have seen a marked elevation of sentiment and growth of Christian feeling among a household of servants, dating from the reception into the house of a poor outcast who died among them, instead of in the hospital, tenderly waited upon by them in turns. I think I hear some exclaim of such things, that they are impossible in most families, and extremely undesirable if they were possible. Nevertheless I invite my readers to think whether short of such—which may seem extreme measures—there ought not to be a greater readiness to share with others, who have few or no privileges, the blessings and brightness of our homes, for the good of society. I would particularly ask of fathers, whether they are not conscious of some selfishness in the enjoyment of the family circle, and whether the present fear and uneasiness in regard to the stability of our long-established ideas about home may not be a permitted rebuke to them for that selfishness.

I wish to say a few words as to the relation to each other of the several claims which women are putting forward. There is a *dilettante* manner of viewing all these matters which prevails mostly in the drawing-rooms of the upper classes, which is unfavourable to a large view or sober judgment of them. Ladies, in the current slang of the day, will "go in" for female education, but reject all else; or they will practically sanction some one part of the movement which meets their taste or is not condemned as "unwomanly," while carelessly refusing even to look into the meaning or merits of any other part. I would not ask any one to approve of all that may be at present put forward, but it would be more praiseworthy in ladies if they were to leave the chatter of drawing-rooms more often, and commune with their own hearts,—if they were to endeavour to look at the whole matter more quietly, and see if there be not a necessary, a very significant connexion, among all the claims at present advanced. Growth may be imperfect if one part is pushed on and another, intimately related to it, is held back. The simultaneousness of the demand for industrial freedom and for higher education is based on a necessity. The education which most women need is one which will fit them for business in professions or in industries. With this latter is closely connected the degree of political freedom and responsibility which we seek in asking the parliamentary vote. I do not see how the spirit of monopoly in trades and industries is to be in any way overcome while the monopolists are alone represented in the country, and those who are excluded from work have no political existence; for upon justice more than upon chivalry must our hopes at this day rest.

But there is more than the outward necessity for a simultaneous urging of educational and industrial movements. However tardily the discovery may have been made in our Public Schools and Universities, women have seen from the beginning of this movement the great value of industry, educationally considered. I believe it begins to be confessed that one considerable blunder of many educational schemes has been in divorcing the two. I do not mean that the School can be the Workshop, or can give technical or industrial training. It cannot; but our ideas of Education, among the better classes, have hitherto implied that there must be some people who think and some who work, and that the functions of these two classes of people are altogether different. It is not yet fully understood that the richest thought is the product of action, and the best and most fruitful action the outcome of thought. In consequence of this unnatural divorce, our workers become more and more mere mechanics, and our thinkers prove themselves incompetent to cope with facts. I have much sympathy with those working men who think that theirs is the only true culture after all. No doubt they have only a part of truth, but no more have those who live exclusively in the region of ideas. It is well enough understood, that to make a nation truly great, thought must wed itself to fact; but it is not so fully recognised that this is equally true of the individual, and that it is indeed essential to the development of the noblest type of human character. Experienced teachers of girls have told me that they have often had occasion to notice the advantage enjoyed by those who have had some amount of industrial training over those of the same age and general culture whose lives have given them in this respect nothing to do. A girl, for instance, who has learned to use her hands and her faculties, through the need of her help at home in something which requires skill, will certainly make greater progress in intellectual pursuits than another girl of the same capacity who has had no such necessity. The general intelligence of the young Geneva watchmakers who help their fathers in the trade has often been remarked. Here I must recur to my former subject, and observe, that it is very probable that the home-bond, the good ideal of domesticity, would in a great degree be restored and strengthened by the admission of daughters to the family trade or profession. When fathers, brothers, and sisters are working at one art, a sort of pride in the family excellence grows up which is a wholesome bond of union. Miss Corlett, secretary to the Queen's Institute in Dublin, says, "In these times, the working-classes lose position and miss prosperity by cutting off their families from their avocations. That a return to the old system is possible I doubt; but the perfection of workmanship, the art of old trades, was in reality the tradition from father to son or daughter, the whole family working together in producing the specialty of the trade, whatever it might be. Among goldsmiths the daughters executed chasing, among furniture-makers carving, among stonemasons sculpture, among engravers drawing and graving. Possibly, now, books and apprenticeship replace the family tradition, but we are forced to see that our art is inferior to the old productions." [1]

The following letter will, I think, be interesting to many readers. As the writer of it is not so well known in England as in America, I may mention that she is a member of the Society of Friends, a venerable lady of much experience. I have heard of her refined and

[1] At a meeting of the Co-operative Association in London, a speaker adverted to the success which Madame Lemonnier has had in carrying out the union of industrial with general education in her schools in Paris, now under the management of Madame Sauvestre; in contrasting it with the limited success which has attended the same effort at the Cornell University in the State of New York, he spoke as follows:—"What a rebuke to the attitude of the Cornell professors was the victory patiently and quietly won by the schools organized by Madame Lemonnier in Paris, where female students had accomplished all that they proposed to do, which the youths of Ithaca had thus far failed to achieve! Were the Cornell University less ambitious, and were its rulers, instead of attempting to rival the older seats of learning in the Eastern States, content to devote their ample resources and magnificent endowments to practically inculcating the principles of co-operation, and preparing the way for the rapid regeneration of society by sending forth, year after year, bands of educated workmen, whose enlightened minds and well-skilled hands acting in concert would give dignity to labour—bands of workmen who would form the nucleus of co-operative industrial colonies, and occupy the lands which only waited to repay willing toil with bounteous harvests—the rank of the Cornell University might, it is true, be lower amongst other universities, but it would stand unrivalled amongst the instruments Heaven has ordained to liberate the struggling masses from the curse of poverty and ignorance."

gentle appearance at public meetings when a few words from her, much to the point and full of exquisite good sense, have been a touchstone by which the folly or wisdom of other speakers could be tested, as it were, instinctively by all. It is well known that the ladies among the Friends are of a refined and feminine character, and that this character is not the result of repression, but of the opposite :—

Roadside, near Philadelphia, 4 mo. 20th, 1869.

MY DEAR FRIEND,

Thy letter of Feb. 1st I would have answered immediately, as thou requested, if only to say that, unaccustomed to write for the press, I must decline, as I have done when urged to furnish articles for the Anti-Slavery or Woman's Rights' papers, to prepare an Essay on either of the subjects proposed, worthy such a work as your publisher, Macmillan, designs.

Still, on further reflection, my age and experience enabling me to state facts connected with the Society of Friends, and the Woman's Rights' movements, and desiring to give all the aid in my power, I venture to make some statements from which some one of your writers may produce an Essay.

The stand taken by George Fox, the founder of our Society, against authority as opposed to the immediate teachings of the "Light within," gave independence of character to women as well as men. Their ministry recognised, as a free gospel message, they went forth among the nations "preaching the Word," and spreading their principles. Adopting no theological creed, their faith was shown by their works in the everyday duties of life, "minding the Light" in little things as well as in the greater; thus keeping a conscience void of offence toward God and toward men.

In the executive department of the Society, the right conceded to woman to act conjointly with man has had its influence, not only in making her familiar with the routine of business relating to our "Discipline," but in giving her self-reliance in mingling with the various reformatory societies in the great movements of the age.

In the Marriage union, no ministerial or other official aid is required to consecrate or legalise the bond. After due care in making known their intentions, the parties, in presence of their friends, announce their covenant, with pledge of fidelity and affection, invoking Divine aid for its faithful fulfilment. There is no assumed authority or admitted inferiority; no *promise* of *obedience.* Their independence is equal, their dependence mutual, and their obligations reciprocal. This of course has had its influence on married life and the welfare of families. The permanence and happiness of the conjugal relation among us have ever borne a favourable comparison with those of other denominations.

The "Testimonies" of the Society against war, slavery, the forced maintenance of the ministry, and the extravagant and luxurious indulgences of the age, intoxicating drinks, &c., which are revived yearly and quarterly in our meetings of discipline, have prepared our members to unite in many reformatory movements of the day, demanding a "righteousness exceeding that of the Scribes and Pharisees." The restraint placed on the young from light and unprofitable reading has had a good effect also on the character in after-life.

Do not understand, however, that the Society is free from surrounding injurious influences. By birthright membership, without judicious training, and from other causes, many have "gone halting," as regards these testimonies, and our women themselves have much to learn from the more enlightened, as to their equal place in the community. [See Clarkson's Portraiture of Quakerism.] But not to dwell too long on our own Society,—The co-operation of women of all classes with men in anti-slavery, temperance, and other moral reform societies, has prepared woman to act more decidedly in her own behalf. In 1840, when the World's Anti-Slavery Convention was called in London, the American Society sent delegates of women with men (the greater number Friends). Our English abolitionists, afraid of the "ridicule of the morning papers," ruled us out, extending at the same time courtesy and flattery in lieu of right. Daniel O'Connell, William Howitt, Dr. Bowring, and others, pleaded our cause ably—in vain. Their appeals were published. If not easily obtained, I can furnish a copy. I might go on with a history of woman's advancement, from Mary Woolstonecraft, Frances Wright, and your own *Westminster Review*, down to our more recent efforts,—woman's journals, parliamentary action, and in this country woman's conventions, petitions, and appeals to our legislatures, reform in our state laws, public lectures, women entering the professions, schools of design, telegraph operations, &c. &c. Our woman's conventions originated with Elizabeth Cady Stanton, twenty years ago. They attracted much notice and no little opposition and misrepresentation; nevertheless, women were greatly encouraged to persevere in their work. Numbers travelled over our country, holding meetings, delivering lectures, inviting discussion on the Bible arguments, the laws, &c., maintaining that the time had come for woman to move in her proper sphere, no longer resting satisfied in the circumscribed limits with which corrupt custom and a perverted application of the Scriptures had encircled her. Thus has she been prepared intelligently to make application for her rights, until at last the ballot is demanded as a legitimate claim. We have several periodicals specially advocating woman's rights, some of them edited by women.

In the Social relations, the sacred duties of wife and mother are fulfilled with no less assiduity than where woman is kept in a subordinate position. The most refined of our sex are among its most able advocates. I hope to enlist one of these to write for you, Dr. Ann Preston, who, with many other women practitioners, is gaining recognition and respect every year. Thirty-five students were kindly welcomed this winter to the clinical lectures, delivered in Philadelphia by leading medical teachers.

In the Educational department also, woman holds her place. In *some* of our public schools her salary is equal to those of our best male teachers.

These mere facts are about all I feel able to write in compliance with thy request. It is with great reluctance I take the pen for more than family letters. Make such use of the foregoing as may be of any avail. If I can further aid in any way, save in a clever essay, my poor services shall be freely rendered.

Thine, for woman's elevation,

LUCRETIA MOTT.

If it is acknowledged that for the permanence of the true domestic ideal based upon real affection, equal marriage, and virtuous life, we need the elevation of the character, and a restoration of the dignity of woman; and if these Essays should serve in any degree to prove that that elevation and that restoration can be attained by the encouragement of a higher and a more diffused education, by the opening out of industries and professions, and by the granting of a larger share in social activity and public services, I trust that it will be perceived, possibly more clearly than it has yet been, that for the attainment of this end, and for the securing of these means, men as well as women must take up the matter in a practical manner and contribute acts as well as speech; and that very much will depend on the wise decisions and timely action of our legislators in regard to those portions of this great movement which are, or will come, under the consideration of Parliament.

It has long been a matter of surprise to me that writers on these subjects (Christian writers equally with those who do not profess Christianity) seldom refer to any higher authority than that of St. Paul. Persons of almost every shade of opinion professedly bring their theories, with more or less of respect for that standard, to the standard of Christian ethics; yet, from the earliest ages of the Church until now, we find them very rarely indeed bringing them to the test of the very words and acts of Christ himself. They appear to prefer to be guided by the earliest adaptations of the principles announced by Christ, rather than the pure principles themselves. Thus accepting, as if it were a necessary part of the principles themselves, the primitive form into which these principles were constrained by the circumstances of society, they have fallen into confusion and error, which they would have escaped by a faithful and constant reference to the pure principles themselves—to Christ, in short, and to none other. It seems as if there were a certain awe, a doubt perhaps, which keeps them at a distance from that Judge, while they continually appeal to and wrangle over the words and teachings of an apostle. This apostle spoke for the exigencies of a given period, and from the point of view of a man born under limitations of vision and judgment, but enabled by a divine insight to apply with wisdom the essential teaching of his Master to the accidents of the time and society in which he lived. It was thus, that, without revolutionizing society from the outside, or setting masters and slaves, men and women, at variance, by abruptly altering their relations, he promoted the most certain revolution and the deepest and only sure reformation, namely, that which begins in the conscience of men, chiefly in the conscience of those who are in a superior position, and who by freely granting freedom make it needless for the oppressed to snatch it. Mr. Lecky, and other modern writers, continually appeal to the teaching of "the Church," not as superstitious believers in the Church, but the contrary; yet it appears to me that their writings, as much as those of the superstitiously dogmatic, tend to keep up in the minds of men a confusion between essential Christianity and the teaching of a society—call it "the Church" or by whatever other name you please—which in a single generation departed from the simplicity of Christ, and whose dogmas, missing truth in the variousness of their corruption, have been by friends and enemies alike shouldered upon Christ, and, without sufficient examination, are supposed to have emanated from Him. When any one tells me that the Church or Christianity teaches this or that with respect to women and their social position, I go back to the words of Him who is acknowledged to be the Head of the Church and the Author of Christianity, and I frequently find very little likeness indeed in any of his teaching, whether of example or precept, to those views which, propounded by Councils, Fathers, or Decrees, have so greatly influenced the history of men and women, and nations, since Christ came upon the earth. If without a previous familiarity with the simple teaching of Christ in the Gospels I had read the last chapter of Mr. Lecky's "European Morals," I confess that I should thereby have been disgusted with essential Christianity as represented by him, and the more so because of the high and noble tone which pervades his writings. But it seems to me that he, like many others, mistakes the traditions of a vitiated Church for the essential ethics of Christ.[1]

[1] Since writing the above, my attention has been arrested by the following sentence in Mr. Mill's "Subjection of Women:"—". . . the practical feeling of the equality of human beings, which is the theory of Christianity, but which Christianity will never practically teach, while it sanctions institutions grounded on an arbitrary preference of one human being over another" (page 78). I cannot refrain from saying that I think even this most just, candid, and logical of writers is not perfectly clear in his discrimination between Christianity itself and the teaching and customs which

Among the ancient Jews, when perversions of principle and confusions of opinion resulted in some national crisis, the cry was "To the Law and to the Testimony!" A direct reference to the Law of Moses, a law which sometimes seems harsh enough, often revealed that the several regulations under it were inspired by an infinite tenderness; for that law took human institutions as they stood in a primitive state of the world, and by the introduction of a small and subtle principle sowed the seed of an emancipation which was to work from within. The social cruelties which came to be practised under the supposed sanction of Moses were not the fruit of his legislation, but of the traditions by which—Christ himself said—they had "made the Law of Moses of none effect." Something of the same kind has happened in Christian countries. In the midst of the present confusion which it seems to me there is among writers,

have adopted its name. If by the word Christianity he means here the truths and principles revealed and taught by Christ, then the above sentence is self-contradictory; for pure Christianity, in other words, CHRIST, could not at once teach the equality of all human beings and the justice of arbitrary preference of one over another. Sweet and bitter waters come not out of one fountain. Christ was the Light, and "in Him was no darkness at all." He never, either directly or indirectly, by word or by deed, sanctioned customs or institutions grounded on an arbitrary preference. Would it not be well if Mr. Mill were to define more clearly what he means by "Christianity?" If he means by it the teaching of Churches and Creeds claiming Christ as their originator, then I shall not be sorry to see him bring the weight of his logic to bear upon their inconsistencies and corruptions. But I am persuaded that a careful and candid examination of essential Christianity, apart from the errors that have been preached and practised by its professors, would convince a mind so candid and so generous as his, that that essential Christianity is itself the touchstone by which we must test the purity of Churches, as well as the morality of all our social theories.

Christian and materialist, with respect to the social direction of certain principles of Christianity, my appeal is to Christ, and to Him alone, not to any Church, or traditions, or Councils, or catechisms, nor yet even to an Apostle, who, I observe, while dealing with some matters of great social importance, says, "I speak this of permission and not of commandment." A greater than St. Paul is here; but we seem to have forgotten it. It is with hesitation and a deep awe that I approach this part of my subject. I must beg to be understood here to speak for myself alone. The several writers in this volume are agreed with me as to the moral law which we obey, and that He, whom we call the Founder of our religion, was the Example in its perfection of those virtues which we emphatically call Christian. But I imply no agreement with me farther than this,—although aware that in some cases the agreement goes farther,—when I record my own convictions in the first pages of this book. My words can be taken for what they are worth, but I am sufficiently convinced that it is well for men and women to say with courage and humility what they believe, and to witness with fidelity to what God and life has taught *them*. There is too much of an unconfessed timidity among the boldest of us. Even in writings which profess an indifference to what others think, there is sometimes an evident caution, and lack of courage to confess that we believe anything more than those whom we most esteem conceive to be true. The fashion of esteeming it childish to hold a strong objective faith is the cause of this timidity. It now needs some little courage to confess to a belief which many of the most thoughtful, and practically the most Christian among us, have been compelled to abandon. It is supposed that we have had it from the nursery, and that we have had neither the courage nor the intellect needful to search and see whether it be well founded and reasonable. Such an imputation must, I imagine, be somewhat hard for men to bear; for it appears that while many have so much courage as is required to announce the most radical sentiments, and to run counter to the superstitions of ages for the demolition of an established order, there are not so many who have that yet higher courage to confess before their fellow-men, whose acute intellects may have fathomed the heights and depths of philosophy, "I believe in the power of Prayer;" or "I believe that Jesus Christ is the Son of God." Women writers are peculiarly liable to subject the expression of their convictions to the promptings of a cowardly reference to the opinion of the public who will read them. For, indeed, in order to obtain a hearing at all, we are all but driven to degrading considerations of what will sell, and what will please or displease this or that class of thinkers who in turn hold rule over the literary market.

Once more I venture to say I appeal to Christ, and to Him alone, as the fountain-head of those essential and eternal truths which it is our duty and our wisdom to apply to all the changing circumstances of human society. Believing as I do that He is Very God, and that He was in human form the

Exponent of the mind of God to the world, I hold that His authority must be higher than that of any man or society of men by whom the Truth which we receive from them, so far as we receive Truth from them at all, can only be transmitted. I believe all His acts to have had a supreme and everlasting significance. The teaching of His great typical acts is not less profound than that of His words. His teaching was for all time; much of St. Paul's was for a given time. There has been at all times a silent minority who have held this belief, and gone back to this standard. In the darkest ages of the Church there have been women whose whole lives were a protest against the capricious and various teachings of the Church concerning women, and who consequently endured a life-long martyrdom. In the days of Luther and of the Puritans this silent minority maintained a similar protest against errors of a somewhat different tendency. I know not myself to what rightly to apply the name of Church, if it be not to such a company of faithful men and women who throughout all the ages have reflected the teaching of Christ himself in its integrity. These all asserted the equality of all men and women, and asserted it on Christ's teaching. I am not speaking here of any intellectual equality, about which more than enough has been said on both sides, and respecting which it seems to me that men are more anxious to retain a theory undisturbed, than to bring that theory to the test, which not the past, but a hoped-for future alone can supply. Of these subtle subdivisions, physical, intellectual, and moral, in which the inferiority or equality of women is so jealously defined and guarded in theory, I find no hint whatever in Christ's teaching. The equality He proclaimed is on a wider and deeper basis, and until the truth of *that* equality is felt and admitted by Christendom, and recognised in our laws, our customs, and our religion, there will continue to be the uncertainty and unhappiness which now exist, and the reiterated attack and defence on the subject of those intellectual and moral ranks which, when truly known, and then only, will incline us to praise the excellence of God's creation, instead of taunting each other. Among the dullest of the poor slaves, before their emancipation, there were some whose intellects were so quickened by the agony of the iron of slavery which had entered their souls, that they discovered for themselves that principle so dreaded by those who would maintain for themselves the monopoly of privileges. Crouching among the sugar-canes, they secretly searched throughout the Bible for arguments against slavery, and so keen, and so dangerous to the minds of their masters, were the arguments which those poor negroes drew from the Scriptures, (in spite of the sanction which on the surface and at first sight many parts of the Bible seem to give to slavery,) that the masters found it convenient to forbid the reading of the Bible to their slaves. I need scarcely say that it was through a steady gaze fixed on Christ himself, not on Moses or St. Paul, that these slaves discovered the truth that liberty and equality are the law of Christ for the world. Similarly, the same intense gaze, quickened by suffering and solitary questioning on a state of things that seems to us unjust, has led a silent minority of women in all times, and a greater number in these latter times, to conclusions which, had they been earlier expressed, would have been stamped as revolutionary.

The limits of this Essay are far too short to admit of more than the very slightest indication of Christ's teaching about women. In those beautiful pages of "Ecce Homo," which speak of Christ's dealings with certain women, and in which His acts are allowed to have a significance of which all ages hould have availed themselves for guidance, the writer is nevertheless deficient and one-sided. How could he but be so? for he is a man; and to bring the fulness of the reflected light of intelligent consciences to bear upon the principles announced by Christ's acts and words towards women, would need the combined thoughtfulness and wisdom of a man and a woman; and the writer is a man and not a woman, nor does he thoroughly know women. There are few men who can thoroughly know the minds of women in a state of society in which the reality of woman's nature is repressed, and it is especially difficult for those who are in a position of life which confines their intercourse to women of their own class, which is only one class among many. The author of "Ecce Homo" has set the example to those to whom it did not occur to do so for themselves, of venturing straight into the presence of Christ for an answer to every question, and of silencing the voice of all theologians from St. Paul to this day, until we have heard what the Master says. It may be that God will give grace to some woman in the time to come to discern more clearly, and to reveal to others, some truth which theologians have hitherto failed to see in its fulness; for from the intimacy into which our Divine Master admitted women with Himself it would seem that His communications of the deepest nature were not confined to male recipients; and what took place during His life on earth may, through His Holy Spirit, be continued now. It is instructive to recall the fact that the most stupendous announcement ever made to the world—the announcement of an event concerning which the whole world is divided to this day, and which more than all others is bound up with our hopes of immortality—the resurrection of Christ—was first made to women; nor can we wonder,—looking back over the ages since then, and seeing how any truths asserted by women, not at once palpable to the outward sense or proveable by logic, have been accounted as idle tales—that of the first apostles it should have been said, "the words of the women seemed unto them as idle tales," when they declared that Christ was risen. Among the great typical acts of Christ which were evidently and intentionally for the announcement of a principle for the guidance of society, none were more markedly so than His acts towards women; and I appeal to the open Book and to the intelligence of every candid student of Gospel history for the justification of my assertion, that, in all important instances of His dealings with women,

His dismissal of each case was accompanied by a distinct act of *Liberation.* In one case He emancipated a woman from legal thraldom: His act no doubt appeared to those who witnessed it as that of a dangerous leveller; for while He granted to the woman a completeness of freedom from the tyranny of law which must have electrified the bystanders, he imposed upon the men present, and upon all men by implication, the higher obligation which they had made a miserable attempt to enforce upon one half of society only, and the breach of which their cruel laws visited with terrible severity on women alone; they all went out convicted by conscience, while the woman alone remained free; but, be it observed (for this is sometimes perversely overlooked by persons who claim an immunity which is licentiousness, and who strike at the very root of equality, by separating self-restraint from the liberty which ought to be common to all), free in a double sense, free alike from the inward moral slavery and from the harsh, humanly-imposed judgment. The emancipation granted to another in the matter of hereditary disabilities was signal. In a moment he struck off chains which had been riveted by the traditions of centuries, and raised her from the position, accepted even by herself, of a "Gentile dog" to one higher than the highest of the commonwealth of Israel. In another case His "Go in peace," and words of tender and respectful commendation to one who had been exiled from society, contrasted solemnly with His rebuke to His self-satisfied host, who, while firmly holding his place among the honoured of this world, marvelled that Christ should not seem to be aware "what manner of woman" it was who touched Him. To another, before ever she had spoken a word, He cried, "Woman, thou art loosed!" and to objectors He replied, "Shall not this woman, being a daughter of Abraham, whom Satan hath bound lo these eighteen years, be loosed from this bond on the Sabbath day?" The tyrannies and infirmities from which He freed these persons severally, were various and manifold, and this does but increase the significance of his whole proceeding towards them. Search throughout the Gospel history, and observe his conduct in regard to women, and it will be found that the word liberation expresses, above all others, the act which changed the whole life and character and position of the women dealt with, and which ought to have changed the character of men's treatment of women from that time forward. While in His example of submission to parents, of filial duty and affection, in His inculcation of the sacredness of marriage, and of the duty of obedience to laws which *ought* to be obeyed, His righteousness far exceeded the righteousness of the Pharisees of His own or of the present day, it seems to me impossible for any one candidly to study Christ's whole life and words without seeing that the principle of the perfect equality of all human beings was announced by Him as the basis of social philosophy. To some extent this has been practically acknowledged in the relations of men to men; only in one case has it been consistently ignored, and that is in the case of that half of the human race, in regard to which His doctrine of equality was more markedly enforced than in any other. It is no wonder that there should be some women whose love for *this Saviour* exceeds the love which it is possible for any man to feel for Him, and that, retiring from the encounter with prejudices which are apt to lurk even in the minds of the most just and most generous of men, they should be driven to cast themselves in a great solitude of heart before *Him*,—for He only is just—He only is holy—He only is infinitely tender.

In conclusion, I have only to say one word to my fellow-workers, and to those who have the cause we advocate at heart. I would counsel them to repress impatience by considering well the nature of an organic change. Organic growth cannot be healthy except under conditions of freedom from constraint; from the pressure, on the one hand, of the swaddling clothes of the past, in the shape of bad or worn-out laws or customs, which must be torn off and put away before there can be any free growth; from the pressure, on the other, of too great an urgency. Growth cannot be hurried or forced, any more than it can be cramped, without injurious consequences. In respect to the first-named condition of healthy growth, I am inclined to echo the words of the late Lord Durham, who, when taunted with too strong a desire to get rid of ancient abuses, replied, "I frankly confess I am one of those persons who see with regret every hour which passes over the existence of recognised and unreformed abuses." And among such abuses I reckon one that is now before

Parliament for reformation—I mean the state of the law bearing on the property of married women, and some other recognised evils which do not come so directly within the province of legislation. On the other hand, we who have waited long, hoping for the dawn of a better state of things, are under a temptation to regard the present necessity with an intensity which precludes a calm and clear survey of questions lying all around, and less immediately connected with the matter in hand. There is a danger of working with unripe material. If, perchance, an opportunity is presented to me of using persuasion or the power of private friendship, in order to win some influential person to give a nominal adhesion to our cause, I hesitate; for the mere adhesion of a few names, however great or honourable those names may be, appears to me utterly worthless, unless the will and conscience of the persons bearing the names are sincerely and unmistakeably with us. I dislike to see any one yield to the gentle compulsion of friendship, so far as to commit himself to any course of action before his whole heart is in the matter; nay, I would rather that he should stand aloof entirely until the urgency of his own conscience makes neutrality no longer bearable, and he exclaims to himself, "Woe is me if I do not this thing!" Then alone are his services of any true value. The use of unripe material is, I am convinced, very damaging to a good cause: for men need all the strength of a deep conviction to enable them to stand firm in the midst of the innumerable and recurring reactions which every little practical failure so readily brings about in that public opinion which is based upon mere fashion rather than on a deep belief. And there will be failures enough to try our faith. Let no one suppose that we are unprepared for some measure of that disorganization and suffering, which must ever accompany a change from a worse to a better state. There will be suffering, and there will be evil too; for never in the whole history of the world, has the healthy action of any progressive principle been unaccompanied with suffering and misery, especially in its beginnings, and never was there a good cause which had not its enemies within its own bosom, worse than those which attack it from without.

The question is sometimes asked, in the midst of all this, What we hope for the future of the world? One word indicating that the light which I see before me is for the present a subdued light, and that my hopes are not those of an Utopian dreamer, may not be without its use. I cannot express my own convictions better than by using the words of a gentle philosopher,[1] quoted however only from memory: "There is an element in the economy of society which, from the day that it first made its appearance in the world down to the day when it shall have completely disappeared (if that day ever come), has affected and will affect profoundly the whole social mechanism; it will disturb, and to the extent of rendering them no longer recognisable, the laws of social harmony. This element is

[1] Bastiat.

Spoliation. It may be imagined that we have here to do with an accidental and exceptional fact, a transient derangement unworthy of the investigations of science. But in truth it is not so. On the contrary, Spoliation in the traditions of families, in the history of nations, in the occupations of individuals, in the physical and intellectual energies of classes, in the schemes and designs of governments, occupies nearly as prominent a place as property itself. Repair to the hut of the savage hunter, or to the tent of the Nomad shepherd, and what spectacle meets your eyes? The wife, lank, pale, disfigured, affrighted, prematurely old, bears the whole burden of the household cares, while the man lounges in idleness. What idea can we form of family harmonies? The idea has disappeared, for strength here throws upon feebleness the weight of labour. And how many ages of civilizing effort will be needed to raise the wife from this state of frightful degradation? Spoliation, in its most brutal form, armed with torch and sword, fills the annals of the world. Nor is it only on the limbs but on the consciences of men that she has imposed her yoke, realizing what would seem impossible—mental slavery! O Liberty, we have seen thee hunted from country to country, crushed by conquest, groaning under slavery, insulted in courts, banished from the schools, laughed at in saloons, caricatured in workshops, denounced in churches! It seems thou shouldest find in thought an inviolable refuge. But if thou art to surrender in this thy last asylum, what becomes of the hopes of ages and the boasted courage of the human race? Spoliation is a phenomenon too universal, too persistent to permit us to attribute to it a character purely accidental."

There is a mournfulness in these words to which my whole heart answers back. Not, perhaps, until we have tried every remedy possible for earth's ever-renewing maladies, and found them only very partially successful—not perhaps until the world confesses itself utterly defeated in its last and main endeavour, will the Supreme Interposition take place which we invoke when we say from our hearts, "Thy kingdom come." But of this I am sure, that every effort which is made in sincerity and truth, every life which is spent and yielded up in the cause of suffering humanity, is hastening the advent of the Day which we long for.

I.

THE FINAL CAUSE OF WOMAN.

BY FRANCES POWER COBBE.

Of all the theories current concerning women, none is more curious than the theory that it is needful to make a theory about them. That a woman is a Domestic, a Social, or a Political creature; that she is a Goddess, or a Doll; the "Angel in the House," or a Drudge, with the suckling of fools and chronicling of small beer for her sole privileges; that she has, at all events, a "Mission," or a "Sphere," or a "Kingdom," of some sort or other, if we could but agree on what it is,—all this is taken for granted. But, as nobody ever yet sat down and constructed analogous hypotheses about the other half of the human race, we are driven to conclude, both that a woman is a more mysterious creature than a man, and also that it is the general impression that she is made of some more plastic material, which can be advantageously manipulated to fit our theory about her nature and office, whenever we have come to a conclusion as to what that nature and office may be. "Let us fix our own Ideal in the first place," seems to be the popular notion, "and then the real Woman in accordance thereto will appear in due course of time. We have nothing to do but to make round holes, and women will grow round to fill them; or square holes, and they will become square. Men grow like trees, and the most we can do is to lop or clip them. But women run in moulds, like candles, and we can make them long-threes or short-sixes, whichever we please."

Now, with some exaggeration, there must be admitted to be a good deal of truth in this view. The ideal of each successive age, as Mr. Lecky has so admirably shown, has an immense influence in forming the character of the people by whom it is adopted, and the virtues of Patriotism, Fortitude, Self-sacrifice, Courage, Charity, Chastity, and Humility, have all prevailed in greater or lesser degree, according as the recognised heroic or saintly type of the age was a Theseus or Regulus; a Cato or Aurelius; a St. Simeon or St. Bernard; a Charlemagne or St. Louis; a Howard or Fénélon. Though the typical forms of female merit have been less clear than these, yet in their case also Miriams and Deborahs, the mothers of Coriolanus and of the Gracchi, St. Monica and St. Elizabeth, have had doubtless no small share in moulding the characters of many thousands of Jewish, and Roman, and Christian matrons and maids. How much of the ordinary Frenchwoman of to-day is the reflex of the shimmer left on the national mind by the glittering *grandes dames* of the Fronde, and of the age of Louis XIV. and Louis XV. (not to speak of other influences from the Dianes and La Vallières, the Pompadours and the Dubarrys), who shall say? Nay, again, how much of our domestic, religious, homely Englishwoman is the reproduction of seeds sown in the great Puritan age by Lady Hutchinson, Lady Fairfax, and Lady Rachel Russell? Even already the newer types are growing up which we may directly trace to Mrs. Fry and Florence Nightingale. To women, with their timidity and their social difficulties, such Exemplars are even of more importance than to men. They are both types with which, in their inner hearts, they sympathise and conform; and outward heralds and forerunners who clear the way for them through the jungle of prejudices, and leave palms in their pathway instead of thorns.

Nor is this all: There are instincts in us deeper than any conscious or unconscious imitation of a type. We do not take our place in the human family as adopted children, but as scions of the stock; inheriting, and not merely copying, what has distinguished the generations before us. The young foxhound which begins as soon as it can run to follow scent, the pointer puppy which stands at the sparrows it sees in the yard, obey no moral or intellectual impulse to imitate acts which they admire. They merely follow a dim inclination, the bent of their natures fixed through an ancestry, whose members have all followed foxes or pointed at birds. A beautiful instance of the instinct occurred recently in the case of a young St. Bernard dog, whose mistress guarantees the anecdote. The animal, which is of a very pure breed, was born in England last summer. When a few months old it seemed a stupid, heavy, good-natured brute, with very little of a puppy's pranks. One day, loitering about the cottage in Kent where it was out at walk, it spied a little baby seated alone in the middle of a road. Instantly the dog set off, took up the child gently by its clothes round the waist, and carried it bodily across a neighbouring field, and some way off, up a steep grassy bank. Arrived on the top, he deposited his burden, safe as it would have been on a rock above the snows of St. Bernard; and when the terrified owner of the baby came up with the kidnapper, the poor beast was found assiduously licking the little hands and face of the child, doubtless to "restore its animation."

Now this kind of instinct is by no means to be supposed to be peculiar to the lower animals. The "set" of mind, as Professor Tyndall well calls it, whether, as he says, "impressed upon the molecules of the brain" or conveyed in any other way, is quite as much a human as an animal phenomenon. Perhaps the greater part of those qualities which we call the characteristics of race, are nothing else but the "set" of the minds of men transmitted from generation to generation; stronger and more marked when the deeds are repeated, weaker and fainter as they fall into disuse. Thus the ferocity of the Malay may be held to be the outcome of a thousand murders; the avarice of the Jew, that of as many acts of usury divided between a score of progenitors. Tyndall says, "No mother can wash or suckle her baby without having a 'set' towards washing and suckling impressed upon the molecules of her brain; and this set, according to the laws of hereditary transmission, is passed on to her daughter. Not only, therefore, does the woman at the present day suffer deflection from intellectual pursuits through her proper motherly instincts, but inherited proclivities act upon her mind, like a multiplying galvanometer, to augment indefinitely the force of the deflection. *Tendency* is immanent even in spinsters, to warp them from intellect to baby-love."[1] Thus, if we could, by preaching our pet Ideal, or in any other way, induce one generation of women to turn to a new pursuit, we should have accomplished a step towards bending all future womanhood in the same direction. With men, in a civilized state, pursuits are so infinitely various, that the impetus which the son receives from his father is imperceptible. But women's lives are so monotonous, the possibilities of their divergence from the beaten track so soon exhausted, that the impression conveyed by a mother to her daughter is very often observable. The housewife has a housewifely child; the woman abandoned to pleasure bequeaths to her daughter propensities so notoriously dangerous that no wise man risks his domestic happiness by marrying her.

In a certain modified sense, then, the "mould" theory has its justification. It would undoubtedly be beneficial to have some generally recognised types of female excellence. But, on the other hand, we must not fall into the absurdity of supposing that all women can

[1] "Odds and Ends of Alpine Life," *Macmillan's Magazine*.

be adapted to one single type, or that we can talk about "Woman" (always to be written with a capital W) as if the same characteristics were to be found in every individual species, like "the Lioness" and "the Pea-hen." They would have been very stiff *corsets* indeed which could have compressed Catharine of Russia into Hannah More, or George Sand into the authoress of the "Heir of Redclyffe;" or which would have turned out Mary Carpenter as a "Girl of the Period."

To analyse the minor types of feminine character consecutively would occupy larger space than the present Essay must monopolize. If we can here approximately determine the relative value of the larger *genera* under which the subordinate species may be classified, we shall have advanced as far as can be hoped. I purpose, therefore, in the following pages to discuss these generic types as shortly as may be. They are of two Orders.

The first Order of types or conceptions of female character are those which are based on the theory that the final cause of the existence of Woman is the service she can render to Man. They may be described as "The types of Woman, considered as an Adjective."

The second Order comprehends those conceptions which are based on the theory that Woman was created for some end proper to herself. They may be called "The types of Woman, considered as a Noun."

In the first Order we find Woman in her Physical,

her Domestic, and her Social capacity: or Woman as Man's Wife and Mother; Woman as Man's Housewife; and Woman as Man's Companion, Plaything, or Idol.

In the second Order we find the two types of the woman who makes her own Happiness her end. and the woman who makes Virtue and Religion her end. The happiness-seeking theory we may call the Selfish, and the virtue-seeking the Divine theory of woman's life, since it alone recognises that God and not man is the end of existence to all His rational creatures, and that it is to His love that she, as well as man, must aspire as her eternal joy and reward.[1]

I shall commence by analysing the three leading types of the First Order.

The Physical theory of the purport of woman's life is common to all savages, and has been most bluntly enounced in modern Europe by the great Napoleon.

The Domestic theory is almost universally accepted by the civilized world, and is notably favoured by the English nation.

The Social theory is capable of vast variation, and commends itself to many earnest friends of women.

[1] In a dim way, and combined with fatal errors, this Divine theory of woman's mission has underlain all female monasticism. But though the ascetics have discovered the right *end*, they have constantly sought it by erroneous *means*; even the abnegation of those natural affections which God has made to be the angel-peopled ladder to Himself. By the sect of Quakers alone has the theory hitherto been fairly recognised and rationally applied to practice.

Its most elaborate development, however, is to be found in the writings of Auguste Comte, and to these we shall give careful consideration.

The theory about woman which we have called the Physical, is simply this: That the whole meaning and reason of her existence is, that she may form a link in the chain of generations, and fulfil the functions of wife to one man and mother to another. Her moral nature is a sort of superfluity according to this view, and her intellectual powers a positive hindrance. How such things came to be given her is unexplained. Her affections alone are useful, but the simpler ones of the mother-beast and bird would probably be more convenient. In a word, everything which enables a woman to attract conjugal love, and to become the parent of a numerous and healthful progeny, must be reckoned as constituting her proper endowment. Everything which distracts her attention or turns her faculties in other directions than these, must be treated as mischievous, and as detracting from her merits. The woman who has given birth to a son has fulfilled her "mission." The celibate woman,—be she holy as St. Theresa, useful as Miss Nightingale, gifted as Miss Cornwallis,—has entirely missed it.

This doctrine, of course, belongs properly to ages of barbarism, when the material always took precedence of the spiritual; and the first ambition of patriarchs and prophets was to have sons who should "speak with their enemies in the gate." It exists now, as regards women, only among the coarse and carnal-minded of both sexes, and Napoleon's brutal statement of it is but an instance of the judicial blindness to all nobler truths which falls on souls of such colossal selfishness. But it would be well if the whole train of thought concerning women which properly links itself to this base theory were wholly exploded, and that in no system of French or English education for young girls could a trace of such a conception of female life and its objects be found.

We may happily dismiss this disagreeable subject with a short remark. It is a sort of impiety against human nature ever to speak or think of it in its merely material and brutal part, without reference to its higher attributes. To admit that Woman has affections, a moral nature, a religious sentiment, an immortal soul, and yet to treat her for a moment as a mere animal link in the chain of life, is monstrous; I had almost said, blasphemous. If her existence be of no value in itself, then no man's existence is of value; for a moral nature, a religious sentiment, and an immortal soul are the highest things a man can have, and the woman has them as well as he. If the links be valueless, then the chain is valueless too; and the history of Humanity is but a long procession of spectres for whose existence no reason can be assigned.

Let it be added, that the same persons who treat womanhood as if all its purpose were exhausted in the bringing of children into the world, are precisely those who fail most completely to understand the true sacredness and dignity of wifehood and motherhood; and to whom it most rarely happens to exclaim, with poor Margaret Fuller, "I am the parent of an immortal soul! God be merciful to me, a sinner!"

The second theory we have to consider is the Domestic, or that of Woman as a Housewife. Very beautiful and true, but also very ugly and dull, are the ideas all confounded under this same head, and current side by side amongst us. That the Home is woman's proper kingdom; that all that pertains to its order, comfort, and grace falls under her natural charge, and can by no means be transferred to a man; that a woman's life without such a domestic side must always be looked on as incomplete, or at best exceptional: all this is very true. On the other hand, that, in the lower ranks, the cooking of dinners and mending of clothes; and in the wealthier class, amateur music and drawing, the art of ordering dinner, and the still sublimer art of receiving company, form the be-all and end-all of woman, is, assuredly, stupidly false.

A man can build or buy for himself a House, a Mansion, a Castle, a Palace; but it takes a woman to make a Home. The unhomelikeness of the abodes of the richest single men, or of women in whom the feminine element is lacking, is pitiable. The nest may be constructed, so far as the sticks go, by the male bird, but only the hen can line it with moss and down. The more womanly a woman is, the more she is sure to throw her personality over her home, and transform it, from a mere eating and sleeping place, or an upholsterer's show-room, into a sort of outermost garment of her soul; harmonized with all her nature, as her robe and the flower in her hair are harmonized with her bodily beauty. The arrangement of her rooms, the light and shade, warmth and coolness, sweet odours, and soft or rich colours, are not like the devices of a well-trained servant or tradesman. They are the expression of the character of the woman, as her touch on the instrument or her step in the dance is an expression of it; grave and dignified, or gay and playful; social or studious; calm or energetic. A woman whose home does not bear to her this relation of nest to bird, calyx to flower, shell to mollusk, is in one or other imperfect condition. She is either not really mistress of her home; or, being so, she is herself deficient in the womanly power of thoroughly imposing her personality upon her belongings.

Unhappily, as we all know, not only the inevitable vicissitudes of human affairs, but the special regulations of our social state, render home-making on the part of women a process continually interrupted. The domestic life and the passionate love of home are preached to a girl, even *ad nauseam*, as her special sphere and particular virtue; but in the ordinary career of every woman there are no less than three homes, to each of which she is called on in succession to transfer the most intransferable of sentiments. The home of childhood, with all its dear associations, she quits for the house of her husband; and when she has made this thoroughly her own, when every room in it has been identified with her joys and griefs, and her love seems to pervade it from end to end, she is called on, as a matter of course, in the sad hour of her widowhood, to go forth contentedly, as if the place had been only lent to her for her honeymoon; and to spend her old age in some unaccustomed abode, which no beloved memory hallows for her, and which in her failing strength she will never bring into harmony with her tastes. Yet with all these drawbacks, the instincts of women, the hereditary "set" of their minds towards home-making, is, at all events in our Anglo-Saxon race, of overpowering force. The true Englishwoman sets about making one home after another, as the bee whose comb is disturbed makes a fresh cell. Nine times out of ten she seeks and finds the way to do good on earth, more than in any other manner, by making for her family a dwelling whose atmosphere is full of peace and love, of order and beauty. The children who grow up in such a home come into the busy scene of later life "trailing clouds of glory," as if they descended from a better sphere; not as if they rose out of a pit of evil passions and disorder.

But when we have said everything that can be said of the beauty of the domestic life and its fitness for women, have we therefore proved that Martha of Bethany is the only patron-saint towards whom the sex can look as an exemplar? Nay, but in my humble judgment, no woman can be truly domestic who is *only* domestic. No woman can thoroughly order her house, make the wheels of daily life turn without creaking and grinding, adorn her rooms, nay, even design her table, without being a great deal else beside a housekeeper, a housemaid, and a cook. It is not by rolling three, or a dozen, servants into a mistress that a "lady of the house" can be manufactured. The habits of reason, the habits of mental order, the chastened and refined love of beauty, above all, that dignified kind of loving care which is never intrusive, never fussy, but yet ever present, calm, bright, and sweet; all this does not come without a culture which mere domesticity can never attain. The right punishment for those men who denounce schemes for the "Higher Education of Women," and ordain that women should only learn to cook and sew and nurse babies, should be to spend the whole term of their natural lives in such homes as are made by the female incapables formed on such principles. Existence with one of these fidgety, servant-abusing women, is like the toil of an Arab beside his water-wheel. The stupid machine creaks and grinds and jolts and clatters, and all the time carries up to the sky and down to the depths only a bucketful of mud.

But if the exclusive worship of St. Martha by wives thus defeats its own end, what is to be said for it among a whole family of grown-up daughters? Truly here lies a chapter of English life which had need to be carefully read by him who is inclined to talk as if all English interiors offered idyllic pictures of peace and joy. Paterfamilias at his office all day, and reading his newspaper all the evening; Materfamilias fuming about her servants; the young brothers all driven away to seek some less tiresome spot, and four or five hapless young women, from twenty to forty, without professions or pursuits, or freedom of time or money, and with only a few miserable make-believe accomplishments of pseudo-music, pseudo-art, pseudo-reading, to "improve the shining hours;"—truly it is a hateful sight! Only two things could be much worse for them, namely, being bronzed and lacquered into Girls of the Period, or deluded into the withering precincts wherein Starrs and Saurins are shrivelled from women into nuns.

Domesticity then as a theory of woman's life fails in this: that by placing the secondary end of existence (namely, the making of those around us happy) before the first end (namely, the living to God, and goodness), even the object sought for is lost. The husband and father and sons who are to be made happy at home, are not made happy there. The woman, by being *nothing but* a domestic being, has failed to be truly domestic. She has lost the power of ministering to the higher wants of those nearest to her, by over-devotion to the ministry of their lower necessities. To be truly the "Angel in the House," she must have kept, and ofttimes used, the wings which should lift her *above* the house, and all things in it.

Thirdly, the theory of Woman as a Social being is, as I have said, capable of many variations. The gifted woman who knows how to make her home a centre of intellectual and kindly intercourse; the artist, the woman of letters, the female philanthropist; all these have their place, and at one time or another, and in different coteries, stand forward as the admired types of woman in her Social capacity. In all of them there is right and reason, viewing the salon-keeping, or art, or literature, or philanthropy, as phases of life in its human aspect: the secondary purpose of existence wrought out as best may suit the woman's circumstances and abilities. In all there is wrong and error, if regarded as the ultimate ends of the existence of a human soul.

But regard for the limits of this Essay forces me to pass over these imperfectly defined theories of woman's social life, to the highly elaborate and very singular system which Comte has originated from the same basis. It demands our attentive study, both from its great peculiarity, and also because, although it is impossible to suppose that Positivism will ever supersede Religion properly so called, yet its action upon the thought of the age, albeit indirect, is already considerable, and may possibly become very extensive. I shall define Comte's conception of woman's office and duty as much as possible in his own words:

"Positivism encourages, on intellectual as well as moral grounds, full and systematic expression of the feeling of Veneration for women in public as well as in private life, collectively as well as individually. . . . Born to love and to be loved, relieved from the burdens of practical life, free in the sacred retirement of their homes, the women of the West will receive from Positivists (hereafter) the tribute of deep and sincere admiration which their life inspires. They will feel no difficulty in accepting their position as spontaneous priestesses of Humanity; they will feel no longer the rivalry of a vindictive Deity. . . . In a word, man will in those days kneel to woman, and to woman alône."[1]

"When the Mission of Woman is better understood, she will be regarded by man as the most perfect impersonation of Humanity. Prayer would be of little value unless the mind could form a clear conception of its object. The worship of woman satisfies this condition. True, the ultimate object of Positivist prayer is Humanity. But some of its best moral effects could hardly be realized if it were at once and exclusively directed to an object so difficult to conceive clearly. It is possible that women, with their stronger sympathies, may be able to reach this stage without intermediate steps; Men certainly would not be able to do so. The worship of Woman, begun in private and afterwards publicly celebrated, is necessary in man's case to prepare him for any effectual worship of Humanity. No one can be so unhappy as not to be able to find some woman worthy of his peculiar love, whether wife or mother; some one who in his solitary prayer may be present to him as a fixed object of devotion. Nor will such devotion cease at death."[2]

"The subject of the worship of Woman by Man raises a question of much delicacy; how to satisfy analogous feelings of devotion in the other sex? . . . . But my sex renders me incompetent to enter further into the secret wants of a woman's heart. Theory indicates a blank, but does not enable me to fill it."[3]

[1] "General View of Positivism," by Auguste Comte, trans. J. H. Bridges, p. 276. [2] Ibid., p. 278. [3] Ibid., p. 283.

Such being, according to M. Comte, the proper office of Woman, namely, as a sort of concrete Image of Humanity at large, suited to receive by proxy the worship due to that extremely vague and indeterminate deity, it follows that the lives and pursuits of these idols of flesh are to be regulated like those of Dalai Lamas, with a view to their service in the religion of Positivism. A woman driven by want to hard work of hand or head; a woman emulating man in the fields of political, or literary, or artistic, or commercial ambition, would ill serve to excite those religious emotions which have hitherto among mankind lifted themselves up (so far as poor human weakness and ignorance permitted) to the real unseen Ineffable Holiness above, and which M. Comte fondly conceived could be quite readily transferred without loss of fervour to his ideal of Humanity. In any case, he knew that men will never worship that which is on their own level, and whose weaknesses and limitations are exposed to their eyes. The idol of clay, if it is to be adored at all, must be lifted up and out of the jostling crowd, and placed in a niche where judiciously managed shadows may be thrown over it. The Lama must live shrouded in the recesses of his palace, not sit on the judgment-seat, nor mix in the throng of his worshippers. Accordingly, Positivism, having allotted to woman the position of Vice-goddess, proceeds logically to make her like all other idols, an image of Repose. "If women were to occupy themselves in the ordinary pursuits of men, they would be subject to competition, and, by rivalry, the affection of the sexes would be corrupted. Leaving all such subversive dreams," Positivism affirms the principle that man should provide for woman: "Each individual should consider himself bound to maintain the woman he has chosen for his partner. Women who are without husband or parents should have their maintenance guaranteed by society; and this not merely from compassion for their dependent position, but with the view of enabling them to render public service of the greatest moral value."[1] "Effectually to perform their Mission, they must abstain altogether from the practical pursuits of the stronger sex."[2] "Active life is injurious to delicacy of feeling," and power and wealth are ruinous to women. "From instances among the upper classes where wealth gives them independence, and sometimes, unfortunately, even power, we see but too clearly what the consequences would be."[3]

The only mode, according to M. Comte, in which women can safely participate in public life, will be by presiding over the great institution of the "Positivist Salon," where society will "entirely lose its old aristocratic character, and where women will promote active and friendly intercourse among all classes." In all other respects women will be (apparently) kept in entire idleness. They will be "removed from all industrial occupations, even those which might seem best suited to them." They will be "more rigidly excluded from royalty, and from every kind of political authority;"

[1] "General View of Positivism," by Auguste Comte, trans. J. H. Bridges, p. 265. [2] Ibid., p. 262. [3] Ibid., p. 263.

they will be "free in the sacred retirement of their homes;" and when they die, they will receive "from the organs of public opinion" the solemn promise to be buried with their husbands—an assurance regarding which M. Comte triumphantly remarks, "Such are the consolations which Positivist sympathy can give! They leave no cause to regret the visionary hopes held out by Christianity."[1]

Differing from M. Comte as to the proportionate comfort of lying,—two heaps of silent dust,—beside those whom we have loved, or dwelling with their glorified spirits in the holier life we look for beyond the grave; it is but natural to differ from him also in his estimate of what constitutes a happy and worthy existence for woman upon earth. While he has been exalting woman into an Idol, it seems to me he has utterly forgotten the effect on a human being of the double mischief of deprivation of wholesome work, and of such artificial, not to say blasphemous, elevation. What does history tell us of the character of saints and Stylites, and Lamas, and Kings adored as gods in their lifetime? Is the process of being worshipped, or canonized, or even honoured as silly women commonly honour their clergymen, a healthy one for the soul of the idol? Is it one to which the very strongest character can be safely subjected without liability to the development of insufferable pride and egotism? Not to speak of the essential evil of Positivism, the thrusting aside of that ONE who alone is

[1] "General View of Positivism," by Auguste Comte, trans. J. H. Bridges, p. 256.

worthy of the adoring love of His creatures, and who alone can make their prayers for light and strength something else than a self-acting spiritual heating apparatus—not to speak, I say, of the immeasurable, unutterable loss, in the Comtist system, of a GOD, there is in it the additional absurdity of substituting for Him creatures who *by that substitution* are almost inevitably deteriorated, and rendered unworthy of even their natural human share of honour and esteem. Can imagination conceive the vagaries of vanity and folly which would be developed among a nation of goddesses? The remedy for such a state of things would be found, I am assured, in the very speedy dethronement of the idols so preposterously set up for worship. Women would share the fate of Chinese Josses and Italian images of saints; and be beaten by their disappointed adorers, when found to lack the powers so idly credited to them. The last state of that sex would be considerably worse than the first, before M. Comte undertook to rehabilitate it.

Nor is the scheme of providing for women's sustenance at the public expense while forbidding them all employment, save the truly French one "*de tenir Salon,*" at all likely to counteract the evils of idolatry among them. Idleness, which is the root of all evil for men, is not particularly suited to be the root of all virtue for women. In truth, every woman of sense knows that it is precisely the want of suitable and hopeful work which is the great bane and peril of her sex. Women like the late Lady Byron or Miss Coutts, the distribution of whose wealth is itself a labour; and women who support themselves successfully, or aid their husbands practically by real work at home, are the happiest and most morally safe of their sex. The lady who is too rich to need to do anything, and yet not rich enough to find occupation in the regulation of her property, is she who is in most danger from every kind of temptation to discontent, to grievance-mongering, gossiping, slandering, extravagance, and finally to sinful passions born out of an idle and aimless existence. Yet this is the moral condition to which Positivism would reduce every woman in the land; the indolent and the restlessly energetic alike!

After all, M. Comte, with his even exaggerated estimate of the merits of women, has but planned for them like the apostles of the Physical and the Domestic theory. He has all along been thinking, *not* of what is Woman's own end and aim; how she can attain to Happiness or to Virtue, and what can she then do for all her fellow-creatures? But simply, like all the rest, he has thought, "What can Woman best do for *me?*" His scheme would probably drive her even farther away from the true end of her being than the Physical theory or the Domestic; while it would defeat its own purpose still more flagrantly, by bringing out every flaw in the idol's composition.

Turn we now from these theories of "Woman as an Adjective," to those which proceed on the ground that she is a Noun, and that the first end of her being must be an end proper to herself. Is that basis a truer one? Shall we be told it is much more beautiful, more elevated, more Christian, to contemplate life as only a service for others, and not a trust for ourselves? There is abundance of sentimental talk of this kind always to be heard where women are concerned, but is there reason or religion in it? Let us consider a little what we mean by our words.

Tennyson beautifully expresses the triumph of faith in trusting,

> "That not a moth with vain desire
> Is shrivelled in a fruitless fire,
> Or but subserves another's use."

A good man's conception, then, of even a moth's existence is not satisfied with mere subservience. The old hypothesis that the beasts were made chiefly for the use of man is as completely exploded as the parallel notion that the stars exist to add to our winter nights' illumination, and to afford guidance to our ships. Even the animals most completely appropriated by us would hardly be described by any one now as "made" for our use alone. The engineer who stated before a Committee of the House of Commons that "rivers were created on purpose to feed navigable canals" was less ridiculed than would be the clergyman who should teach the farmers of his congregation that their horses were created merely that they might carry them to market, or their cats that they might destroy the mice and save their cheese.

But, if it be admitted as regards horses and cats that they were made, first, for their own enjoyment, and only secondly to serve their masters, it is, to say the least, illogical to suppose that the most stupid of human females has been called into being by the Almighty principally to the end that John or James should have the comfort of a wife; nay, even that Robert or Richard should owe their birth to her as their mother. Believing that the same woman, a million ages hence, will be a glorious spirit before the throne of God, filled with unutterable love, and light, and joy, we cannot satisfactorily trace the beginning of that eternal and seraphic existence to Mr. Smith's want of a wife for a score of years here upon earth; or to the necessity Mr. Jones was under to find somebody to cook his food and repair his clothes. If these ideas be absurd, then it follows that we are not arrogating too much in seeking elsewhere than in the interests of Man the ultimate *raison d'être* of Woman.

From the standpoint of independent life, having some end proper to itself, two views, as I said before, are open: the Selfish theory of a woman's life, and the Divine.

Of course the Selfish theory, absolutely worked out, would be the conscious recognition by a woman that she took her own private Happiness for her "being's end and aim," and meant to live for it before all other objects. Actually, I presume it is very rare for any one consciously to adopt such a principle. But, without doing so to their own knowledge, many, nay, alas! perhaps a majority, do so in fact. And among those who, while repudiating Selfishness, are most profoundly selfish, are the women who loudly profess their allegiance to the Physical, or Domestic, or Social theories of woman's life. Those who are content to speak of themselves as only created to minister to the wants of their husband and children, are those oftenest to be seen sacrificing the welfare of both husband and children to their own pleasure, vanity, or ill-temper. The more basely they think of their own purpose of existence, the more meanly they are disposed to work it out.

If there be women, at once more logical and more hardened than these, who laugh in their sleeves at the notion that they exist for the sake of some man (perhaps vastly their inferior in ability), and who, with open eyes, and consciously to themselves, adopt their own Happiness as their chief end,—of course, to *them* more than to all the rest the false principle defeats itself. As the woman who lives only to be a Wife and Mother makes a bad wife and mother; as the woman who lives only to be Domestic, is never truly domestic; as the woman who is made a Social Idol becomes unworthy to be idolized; so the woman who seeks only her own Happiness, inevitably fails to attain Happiness. Whatever else may be uncertain concerning that mysterious thing,—felicity,—this at least is sure: to live for ourselves is to live for our own misery. Absolute Selfishness would create a hell in the midst of Paradise. The *happiest* of all beings is HE whose whole eternal existence is purely unselfish love.

Finally, for the Divine theory of Woman's life; the theory that she, like man, is created first and before all things to "love God and enjoy Him for ever;" to learn the rudiments of virtue in this first stage of being, and so rise upward through all the shining ranks of moral life to a holiness and joy undreamed of now: what shall we say to this theory? Shall Milton tell us that Man alone may live directly for God, and Woman only "for God in him"? I answer, that true religion can admit of no such marital priesthood; no such second-hand prayer. The founders of the Quakers, in affirming that both man and woman stand in direct and immediate relationship to the Father of Spirits, and warning us that no mortal should presume to come between them, struck for the first time a note of truth and spiritual liberty which has called forth half the life of their own sect, and which must sound through all Christendom before the right theory of woman's life be universally recognised. Let it not be said that this Divine theory will take Woman from her human duties. Precisely the contrary must be its effects; for it alone can teach those duties aright in their proper order of obligation. Just as the false theories always defeat their own ends, so the true one fulfils every good end together. The woman who lives to God in the first place, can, better than any one else, serve man in the second; or rather, live to God in the service of His creatures.[1]

[1] The exceptionally domestic habits and philanthropic pursuits of the Quaker women afford a curious illustration of this truth. According to current theories, they ought to be self-sufficient, wilful women, bad daughters, and worse wives: and Quaker homes, with no supreme master to rule them, ought to be scenes of discord ending in frequent separations. The fact that they are the contrary of all this might surely make the advocates of the "woman-made-for-man" system pause in their prophesyings of evil from female emancipation, which have thus for two hundred years been experimentally disproved.

It is she who may best rejoice to be a wife and a mother; she who may best make her home a little heaven of love and peace; she who may most nobly exert her social powers through philanthropy, politics, literature, and art. In a word, it is not till man gives up his monstrous claim to be the reason of an immortal creature's existence; and not till woman recognises the full scope of her moral rank and spiritual destiny, that the problem of "Woman's Mission" can be solved. When this has been done, the subordinate types of excellence to which in a secondary sense she may best aspire will not be hard to discover.

II.

HOW TO PROVIDE FOR SUPERFLUOUS WOMEN.

BY JESSIE BOUCHERETT.

THERE is a general impression that the difficulty now experienced in providing for single women in England is occasioned by a disparity in the number of the sexes caused by the emigration of a larger number of men than of women. This view is very forcibly expressed by Mr. Greg in his "Social Judgments," in an essay entitled "Why are Women Redundant?"

Although I attribute the distress prevalent among single women to a cause different from that assigned by Mr. Greg, I cannot, as a woman, refrain from expressing gratitude for the just and kindly spirit in which his essay is written. It contains a passage describing his belief that the evil we all deplore is within the possibility of remedy, which so well expresses my own conviction that I shall transcribe it: "We have never done the Creator the wrong of doubting (to use an expression we once heard from Dr. Chalmers) that the world is so constituted that if we were morally right we should be socially and physically happy; we are profoundly convinced that of all the evils which oppress civilization, and of all the dangers which menace it, none lie beyond the reach of human sagacity to analyse or of human resolve and compassion to avert and cure. If we thought otherwise, there would be little joy in living, and little comfort in looking forth on life."

I shall now endeavour to prove that the disparity in the numbers of the sexes is not the cause of the difficulty which single women experience in providing for themselves, by showing that the same difficulties exist in other countries from which there is little or no emigration, and in which the numbers of the sexes must therefore be nearly equal: also, that single women find it no easy matter to maintain themselves even in those parts of the world where the number of men is larger than the number of women. There is scarcely any emigration from France at the present day, yet M. Jule Simon, Mdlle. Daubie, and a host of other writers, proclaim the miserable condition of thousands of "Ouvrieres." New convents are constantly arising which are used as refuges for superfluous females. Mr. Bloomfield, in his interesting work on Brittany,[1] says, "In Brittany, the reason which oftentimes fills the convents is poverty, not religion. A man has a large family of daughters; what is he to do with them? Marriage is less easy in France than in England, *i.e.* marriage without fortune. Trade

[1] "Brittany," by James Bloomfield.

is distasteful, and besides, requires money. What is he to do with them ? The convent offers itself ; if he can only get them in there they are provided for life. There is an end of them. Thus reasons parental love, tinctured with prudence and embittered by many cares."

In Italy it is not denied that one use of convents is to provide a cheap and respectable maintenance for superfluous daughters, yet there is little emigration from Italy.

In countries where the men exceed the women in number, as in our own colony of Melbourne and in the United States, the women still find it difficult to live. Mr. Greg estimates the excess of men over women in the United States at 250,000 (a quarter of a million), yet it is stated by Dr. Channing, that in New York alone, in 1860, there were found 534 women who had to be their own bread-winners, and who could only earn a dollar (4*s.*) a week, and a very large number besides who could earn nothing. Mrs. Dall, and many other writers, fully bear out Dr. Channing's statement, and complain bitterly of the sufferings of American women from want of employment. The fact appears to be that the men from the Eastern side of the United States migrate towards the West, leaving a surplus number of women behind them.

In the Western States there are very few women compared to the number of men, but there is not even there what can properly be called a deficiency of women ; that is to say, there are as many as are wanted, and the small supply of an article does not constitute a deficiency, unless it is less than the demand.

However small the supply of an article may be, if there is as much as is wanted there is a sufficiency. In new countries, a due proportion of men and women does not mean an equal proportion, because in uncivilized regions there is a vast amount of rough hard work to be done that can only be done by men, and is better done by men unencumbered by wives. The most remote settlers in the backwoods, the gold-diggers and the other pioneers of civilization, must be single men. When the log-house is built and the farm cleared of timber, when the harvest has been sown and reaped, the squatter may begin to think of marrying; but to expose a woman with a young family to the hardships of a settler's early life would be cruel. A single woman might brave them, but to a young mother they would probably prove fatal.

Mr. Greg is mistaken, therefore, in speaking of a deficiency of women in the United States; for though there is an excess of men to the amount of a quarter of a million, it is probable that even a larger number are employed along the immense Western frontier of the States in bringing land into cultivation or in digging for gold. There may exist in the same country an excess of men, that is, more men than women, and a superfluity of women, that is, more women than can be provided for, either as wives or as workers; and this is precisely what has occurred in the United States, for in the Eastern States there are more women than can be provided for, and in the Western States there are as many as are wanted, although that number, compared to the number of the men, is so small.

Here and there in our own colonies there is a demand for maid-servants, and this demand ought to be regularly supplied; but the fastidiousness displayed by the colonists with regard to the quality of servant-girls sent out shows that the want of servants is not great: for instance, workhouse-bred girls cannot get situations, however humble, if it becomes known that they are workhouse-bred.

I deduct from these facts, that if Mr. Greg's plan for draughting off half a million of English women to the United States and our own colonies could be put into execution, it would be of no advantage to the women exported, as they would merely add to the numbers of superfluous women already existing there. Their departure would be an immense relief to the women remaining at home, but unfortunately there is nowhere to send them, for nobody wants them, either in the Old world or the New. It comes to this, that unless Heaven should send a new planet alongside for us to export our superfluous women to, we must make up our minds to keep them at home. Let us, then, proceed to consider by what means we can provide for the superfluous women in England, since it is evident we cannot hope to get rid of them.

It is sometimes useful, in order to perceive the effect of a system, to consider what would happen if it were carried out to the utmost length, and what the consequences would be of the opposite system.

This is what I propose to do. We have seen that a vast army of pioneers are employed all along the borders of civilization. Let us imagine what effect would be produced if these men were caught, brought back to the civilized countries they had left, and compelled to marry. Such a course would certainly tend to equalize the numbers of the sexes and diminish the number of single women; but would it increase or diminish the number of superfluous women? The competition among men for employment would bring down men's wages to so low a point that it would be impossible for men to maintain their wives. The wives of the men who had been brought back would probably have provided for themselves before marriage by some kind of work, so they would merely remain in their former employments; but many of the wives of the men who had always remained in England would have been maintained by their husbands; they would be thrown as extra-workers into the labour-market, and an increased number of superfluous women would be produced. It might also happen, that, in the struggle for subsistence which would ensue, men would invade women's employments; and as their superior strength and education would give them an advantage, they would probably succeed in taking possession of some trades, which would of course still further increase the number of superfluous women.

Now let us see what would happen if the opposite system were pursued, and every young man was compelled to emigrate as soon as he reached the age of twenty-one. The wages of the men who remained behind would immediately rise, there would no longer be any necessity for married women to go to work, and of those who are now in the habit of working many would be withdrawn from the labour-market.

In consequence of the scarcity of male labour women would be employed in many occupations now considered not to be women's work; and, if the system were persevered in, as years went by, and the men grew old and died off, women would be more and more employed in men's work. The country would at last contain a vast excess of women and a prodigious number of single women, but there would not be one superfluous woman, as every one would be valuable in the labour-market.

It is evident, that any approximation towards either system would cause an approach towards the consequences of the complete system. If emigration were unduly checked or not sufficiently encouraged, some of the effects of forbidding emigration altogether would ensue, and it appears to me that this is what has actually occurred in England. The reason of the distress among women is, that men have not emigrated as much as they ought to do. In consequence, the wages in almost all trades which are not protected by trades unions, and especially in agricultural labour, have been driven down so low by competition, that in several counties men cannot maintain their wives and families, and the wives are forced to go out to work to add to the men's earnings; numbers of men have also engaged in women's trades, and taken possession of them; thus the women's labour-market has been invaded from two sides, and crowds of women have been rendered superfluous.[1] The

[1] Married women have been forced into the labour-market far more than is necessary, for when a man earns quite enough to support his wife and family in comfort, it often happens that he spends so large a portion of his wages in drink, that the residue is insufficient for his family, and his wife is then obliged to go out to work, to provide food for herself and the children.

fault, however, is not in the constitution of the world, but in bad human arrangements. There is work enough for all if it were properly distributed; and until the whole world is brought into cultivation there will continue to be work enough for all. In new countries there is an unlimited amount of rough work which men only are capable of executing: in old countries there is a limited amount of easy work which either men or women are capable of performing. The men ought to go to the new countries in such a proportion as to leave easy work enough to employ the women. If, however, the men stay at home and do the easy work, the women have no resource; for it is quite impossible for them to go to the backwoods and do the work of men there.

If twice the number of men emigrated that emigrate now, the best consequences would ensue. Men's wages would rise, and consequently some wives would be withdrawn from the labour-market; a good many men would be withdrawn from the easier trades, and women would take their places. Thus many of our superfluous women would be enabled to find work.

It must not be supposed, moreover, that all emigrants remain single. Many of the emigrants settle in civilized parts of the country, and either marry one of the superfluous women of the country, or else some English girl who had gone out as a servant; and even the remote settlers often end by marrying: so the more men emigrate the faster the servant-girls who are sent out will marry off, and leave room for a fresh supply of maid-servants from England.

As it is now sufficiently clear that the emigration of men will enable our superfluous women to be provided for, I will proceed to the question of how men are to be induced to emigrate.

It is in the power of the Government to put facilities in the way of emigration; but something more than facility is required, because men who ought to emigrate very often prefer to remain in England.

How, for instance, are young men who are about to engage in trades suitable to women to be induced to leave the country? Unless the young men themselves should have scruples about engaging in women's work, the only means by which they can be induced to remove is to persuade the employers to take women in their stead, and the young men will then, finding themselves without employment, be obliged to go abroad.

But men have such great advantages over women in their natural superiority of strength and their artificial superiority of education, that employers are unwilling to exchange their services for those of women. How, then, are these advantages to be overcome?

The superiority in education may be destroyed by improving the education of girls, and the superiority in strength may be counterbalanced in various ways; but the chief counterbalance must be that the woman will undertake to work for less wages than the man.[1]

The objections commonly brought forward against introducing women into trades are, (1) That men would

1 Technical education for girls would probably be of great use in inducing employers to take them as apprentices.

be turned out of employment, and thereby reduced with their families to great misery; (2) That men's wages will be lowered by competition with women; that this will oblige them to send their daughters out to work, whom they would otherwise have maintained at home, and thus great inconvenience will be caused without in the least relieving the overcrowded state of the women's labour-market.

I propose to answer these objections one by one. The first objection has been ably stated in a Tract, entitled "Female Labour," by Bedford Leno, published by the Working-men's Social Science Committee:—

> "Benevolent ladies, well-intentioned clergymen, and philanthropic lawyers, have spent no end of time and money in trying to improve the conditions of life in which unmarried women are placed. Perceiving that the present mode of employing women is insufficient to keep half their number fully employed, they cast about for other fields of labour, and vainly conclude that by so doing they will effect a remedy. No remedy is worthy of the name that merely shifts the disease from one patient to another, and that such is the result of their endeavours we will satisfactorily prove.
>
> "These philanthropists, instead of asking themselves, 'Can woman perform such a task?' should first inquire whether she is required to perform it. If the latter question can be satisfactorily answered, then alone is her employment likely to prove efficacious. The introduction of woman-labour into an already overstocked trade is a positive crime, resulting in endless misery."

Mr. Leno then supposes the case of fifty women being taught to print, and that the amount of printing to be done remains the same:—

> "Does it not follow that the number of men out of employ will have increased to the same amount? What then is the result?

Remunerative employment will have been found for fifty young females, and fifty men will have been discharged."

I answer, that fifty new apprentices cannot take the place of fifty skilled workmen, and that the result of fifty girls being apprenticed to the printing trade would be that fifty fewer boys would be apprenticed to it; and as these boys would not be wanted in England, they would have to emigrate.

But it may be said, "Would it not be much better for the fifty boys to be apprenticed, and when they grow up, to marry? Fifty women would be equally maintained, and would probably be much happier as wives and mothers than as printers." I reply, that if the boys emigrate, a large part of them will marry all the same; thus eighty or ninety women will be provided for instead of fifty, and as the children of the emigrants will be born in some new country, England will be relieved of that amount of surplus population.

The second objection to the introduction of women into trades is that competition with women would lower men's wages, and oblige them to send their daughters out to work, whom they would otherwise have maintained at home. I reply, that the wages of workmen are not always lowered by the introduction of women into their trades; but even supposing that a workman's wages were lowered from this cause, I maintain that his position, if he has daughters dependent on him, will be positively improved, unless the fall in his wages is so enormous as to equal the amount of his daughters' earnings.

Thus if the wages of a printer were reduced by competition with women from thirty-five to twenty-five shillings a week, if his daughter earned but fifteen shillings a week he would be a gainer by five shillings; if he had two daughters, he would be a gainer by twenty shillings a week.[1]

We know exactly what the French printers lost and gained by the introduction of women into the trade at Paris. They said that their wages would have risen from four francs to five francs a day if it had not been for the competition with women.[2] Let us grant that this was so. The average earnings of the women were two francs a day. Thus a man with one daughter gained one franc a day; a man with two daughters gained three francs. Single men and men without daughters, or whose daughters were too young to be apprenticed, must have lost by the arrangement. It is to be regretted when any one under any circumstances sustains injury, however slight the injury may be; but it is better that a small number of workmen should be put to inconvenience than that a large number of women should be unable to earn an honest livelihood.

It must also be remarked, that the introduction of increased numbers of women into a trade does not always lower men's wages; for instance, the Census of 1861 shows that the proportion of women employed as shop-assistants had increased considerably since the

[1] Women printers earn from fifteen to twenty-five shillings a week.

[2] The wages of the printers were not positively lowered, but it is pretty clearly made out that they were prevented from rising.

Census of 1851, yet no complaints have been made of the lowering of the wages of male shop-assistants.[1]

I wish now to call attention to a very remarkable fact, which has never I believe been noticed before, that under some circumstances the employment of women in a trade has the effect of raising the wages of the men engaged in that trade, though it causes a smaller number to be employed.

When there are two descriptions of work to be done in a trade, one easy and moderately well paid, and the other difficult and highly paid, it is evident that a man who is employed the whole day in doing the difficult work will earn more than one who is engaged half the day on the easy work. If then women are employed to do the easy work, the men will be kept exclusively employed on the difficult work, and will earn more.

This appears to be the case to some extent in the law copying trade. The easy work is paid at a lower rate than the difficult work, and I have been told that there is an office in London where men are employed in one room in doing the difficult work and women are employed in another room in doing the easy work. If the men in that office are paid at the usual rate—and I have never heard anything to the contrary—it is clear that they must earn more than they would do in

[1] The number of men returned in the Census of 1851 as Drapers, Silk-mercers, Haberdashers and Hosiers, was 44,767. In 1861 the number was 46,969. The number of women in 1851 was 9,408; in 1861 it was 14,209. The proportion of women to men in 1851 was as 1 to $4\frac{1}{2}$; in 1861, 1 to $3\frac{1}{3}$. Women shop-assistants have increased at the rate of fifty per cent.; men shop-assistants at about four per cent.

an ordinary office, where men only are employed, and the easy work is divided among them.

The same thing occurs among the agricultural labourers in Northumberland. It appears, in Mr. Henley's Report on the employment of women and children in agriculture, that in the northern half of Northumberland, it is the custom to employ a woman-worker [1] with every labourer to do the lighter work.

Labourers' wages in that district vary, Mr. Henley tells us, from fifteen shillings to eighteen shillings a week, according to the labourer's ability, and the farmers engage them by the year, and pay them their wages all the same if they fall sick.

In Bedford and Buckinghamshire, Mr. Culley tells us in his Report, women are never employed, but that two men do the work which is performed in Northumberland by the man and woman, and men's wages vary from eleven shillings to fourteen shillings and sixpence a week, according to the labourer's ability, and cease when the labourer is unable to work from illness or bad weather. Mr. Culley specially informs us that the work is better done in Northumberland, in consequence of the superior strength of the Northumberland labourers, as the Northern women are nearly equal to the Southern men in strength, and the men are far superior. This superiority may be in some degree owing to climate or to race, but the abundant food which the high wages supply has also doubtless a good deal to do with it.

[1] The worker is always a single woman or a widow. Married women never go out to work. It often happens that the woman-worker is the daughter or sister of the labourer.

The advantages of the Northumberland system are considerable to all concerned. The woman-worker is glad to earn a shilling a day rather than get no employment,[1] the labourer and his family benefit by the higher wages, and the farmer pays less in wages than the Bedfordshire farmer.[2] The only person who loses by the arrangement is the second man, whose place is supplied by the woman; and if he should thereby be induced to emigrate, he also would prove a gainer in the end.

Now, without wishing to make too much of these instances, do they not lead one to think it possible that Selfishness has sometimes been shortsighted in excluding women from employments?

If women were employed to do the easy work in all trades, fewer men would be employed; but those employed would be better paid, and this would be a happier condition for men as well as for women. Nor ought the great advantage to the Colonies of obtaining more male labour to be overlooked.

In Queensland the demand for men is so great, that as the farmers cannot get Englishmen enough, they have imported South Sea Islanders to cultivate the land. What a strange spectacle does the great English empire present to the world! Savages doing Englishmen's work

[1] Women workers have also some extra advantages. In some cases they get a shilling a day, with a house rent-free, and a supply of potatoes. In other cases they are boarded and lodged, and get twelve pounds a year wages. It is said that many of them put money into the savings bank.

[2] Mr. Culley reckons that the savings in labour-wages amounts to seven shillings an acre.

abroad; men doing women's work at home; and women starving, begging, and sinning, because they can get no honest employment.

My belief is that it would be for the ultimate advantage of men to emigrate more, and so leave enough easy work to the women to enable them to live; but if I am mistaken in this opinion, and if it really is the fact that men are happier following easy trades in England than doing hard work in the Colonies, I still hold that they ought to go; for it cannot be denied that a man is less unhappy cutting down trees in Canada or tending sheep in Australia, than a woman is who has no means of earning an honest livelihood. If, then, it is recognised that the happiness of women is of as much importance as the happiness of men, it follows that men ought to encounter the minor evil of hard work rather than expose women to the greater evil of having no work at all.

The national plan at present adopted in England for providing for superfluous females, is that of shutting them up in workhouses.

It is not very unlike the mediæval one of convents, and presents many of the same defects; many women requiring relief being shut out, while the condition of those admitted is one of uselessness and unhappiness, and the waste of good working material is equally great in both cases. To me, the first defect appears the worst. It is no unusual thing for women in London to be refused admission to the workhouse on the ground—true enough, no doubt—that it is already full, and to be compelled to accept, instead, the insufficient outdoor allowance of a shilling a week and a loaf of bread; and it is probable the same thing occurs in all great towns. In country districts, however, it is easy to get into the workhouse; but when admission is gained, it is far from being a desirable place of abode, as it is purposely made uncomfortable, in order to deter people from entering, on the supposition that none lack work but the idle. As far as regards women, however, this supposition is untrue; every employment open to them being overstocked, while many easy occupations which they would be glad to enter are kept closed against them by the workmen; and it is manifestly unjust that women should be prevented from getting employment and yet be punished for not working.

If, as many people think, it is to the advantage of the community that women should be excluded from easy handicrafts for the sake of keeping more men in the country, then the community which profits by their enforced idleness ought to maintain them in comfort.

Here I must pause, because this is the very plan which is seriously recommended by a considerable number of benevolent persons; and as I do not believe it to be the true solution of the problem of how to provide for superfluous women, I must show the objections to this course.

These benevolent persons wish men to be the only workers, but they earnestly desire that men should not evade or shrink from the duty of maintaining women in comfort. They hold that fathers are morally bound to provide for their daughters until they marry, and brothers their sisters, and would not object to enforce this duty upon them by the law; and if a woman had no male relatives, they would be willing that the community should be taxed for her support in a comfortable public institution, on condition that women should be legally prevented from earning their own livelihood.

This plan is enforced by moral considerations, as well as economic arguments, on the ground that to send women out into the world to work is sure to injure their delicacy and modesty, which ought to be preserved in the sacred precincts of home, or, failing a home, in a public institution.

These amiable philosophers are evidently not believers in the old adage, "Satan finds some mischief still for idle hands to do;" yet the adage is true: and these unhappy girls, kept without useful occupation in their homes—narrow and dull as the homes of the poor necessarily must be—would soon become first miserable, and then wicked; and this objection applies with equal strength to the public institutions.

The "Girl of the Period" is an example of the bad effects of idleness. That girls of the period are confined to the wealthy classes is due to the circumstance that among the less rich middle classes girls are more generally permitted to earn money, and thus a healthy occupation is found for those who possess energy; while among the really poor, girls are required to earn their own livelihood. But condemn girls of the middle and working classes universally to a life of inaction, and the same type will make its appearance lower down in the social scale, but in a coarser and even more degraded form.

It may be said that women in the public institutions would be employed to nurse the sick, but it is not every woman who has a taste for sick nursing, or the capability of becoming a sick-nurse. These institutions would only be convents under another name, and every objection which applies to convents would apply to them with even more force, for women have, at least nominally, and sometimes in reality, the choice of whether they will enter the convent or not, a privilege which it does not appear certain they would enjoy with regard to these institutions, if the world was regulated as these philosophers desire.

The plan then which I advocate for providing for superfluous women is that of allowing them to engage freely in all occupations suited to their strength. The great merit of this plan is, that it would put an end to superfluous women altogether, by converting them into useful members of society. This is without doubt the plan intended by nature all along, and it is from failing to fulfil it that we have fallen into such difficulties.

But though the plan may be the right one, let it not be imagined that it is an easy one to carry out. The accomplishment of the plan requires no small amount of good feeling and generosity on the part of working men. Let us suppose that a ladies' hairdresser brings up his daughter to succeed him instead of his son. What is the son to do? There is no room for more men in other trades, so he will be obliged to emigrate; and if he loves ease, if he has no spirit of adventure, if he shrinks from leaving his friends,—if, in short, he is not a hero, he will prefer to remain at home dressing fine ladies' hair and manufacturing chignons, to roughing it in the bush with his axe in his hand and his gun on his shoulder. So, if he is not generous and manly, he will beg his father to leave the business to him, and to let his sister take her chance like other girls, and marry or starve, sink or swim, as chance may decide.

The same principle applies to all easy trades, but I select the example of a ladies' hairdresser, because the dressing of ladies' hair, and the making of hair chains and bracelets, are occupations which are specially suitable for women, yet this is one of the trades which are zealously defended against women, and into which it is not easy to introduce them.

It is from this system of exclusion that proceed most of the evils which press so heavily on single women; and as the system arises out of the natural selfishness of the human heart, it is confined to no country, to no particular era of time or stage of civilization, but is as old and as wide as the world itself. If Chinamen would admit women into their easy trades, there would be no necessity for drowning superfluous female infants; but then, so doing might lower men's wages, or force them to emigrate, and as they are not inclined to endure these hardships, perhaps the kindest thing they can do by the babies is to drown them.

We have all laughed at the story of the New Zealand chief who, when asked how he had provided for his second wife, from whom he had parted at the recommendation of the Missionary, replied, "Me eat her." It was but his way of providing for superfluous women, and, if it had the disadvantage of being disagreeable to the woman herself, the same may be said of other plans proposed by much better instructed men than the chief.

If he would have allowed his discarded wife a house and some land, as no doubt the Missionary expected, she might have provided for herself; but then, he wanted all the land for himself, and besides, he probably thought that to give women land and let them support themselves might raise up in them a dangerous spirit of independence, and quite destroy all their feminine charms and characteristics; so it seemed to him better to eat her, according to the ancient and venerable custom of the country. Is not the same principle acted on in England? Do not many people think it better that women should suffer than that professions and trades should be opened to them, on the ground that they would be "unsexed" by engaging in them?

It appears to me that our continuance in the present system can only be justified on the principle of the lady who said, "It is natural that *women* should suffer, but it is sad indeed when *men* have to endure privation."

If we consider it to be natural, and therefore not wrong, that women should be unable to earn an honest livelihood, then let us make no change; but if we agree with Dr. Chalmers' that "the world is so constituted, that if we were morally right we should be socially and physically happy," we must also admit that there is much moral wrong somewhere, which requires to be remedied, for it is certain that a great portion of those women who have to earn their own livelihood are neither socially nor physically happy.

III.

EDUCATION CONSIDERED AS A PROFESSION FOR WOMEN.

BY REV. G. BUTLER.

THE field of education is so vast, and the call for competent educators so great, that any endeavour to remove the barriers which have hitherto kept back a portion of the community from attempting to enter the field, ought, one would think, to be regarded with favour, as evincing, at least, a desire to supply a want which society feels, and to provide occupation for many deserving members of society.

To show that women, in regard to education, are labouring at present under unfair disadvantages, as compared with men; that justice and the common interests of all demand for them more ample recognition and encouragement, and that they are not only fitted for the work of education generally, but able to supply some special educational wants which are now apparent, will be the object of the following Essay.

Whatever professions, trades, or industries may be found by experiment to be unsuitable for women, we are justified in asserting that the profession of educators is suitable for them, and ought to be thrown open to them without restraint or fear.

At the Working Men's Congress at Lausanne, in 1865, a declaration was made that "all moral, physical, and economic arguments were against the employment of women as agents of production." Now this, if it be a truth, is in the stage of hypothesis only. Its establishment as a sound theory can only rest on experiment, and experiment can only be a sure guide under conditions of freedom in which the artificial disabilities of sex are removed, in which equal training and equal opportunities are given to women and to men. Under such conditions, the real ineradicable differences, be they what they may, between men and women, will assert themselves, and women will find out their proper work. Dogmatic assertions, therefore, are to be avoided, as to the unfitness of women for certain kinds of work, since the free experiment which would justify positive speaking is lacking. But this much I may venture to say, looking round on the experience of the present and the testimony of the past, that whilst in detail women are pre-eminently fitted for special departments of productive industry, yet, speaking of them broadly and as a whole, their functions appear to be distributive and administrative rather than productive, and, more markedly than all, perhaps, Educational.

This truth is recognised so far as the home education, the early training of the young child, is concerned. But the recognition of it has stopped short there, to the great disadvantage of society. In so far as women have engaged in education as a profession, beyond the maternal training of the earliest years of childhood, they have hitherto done so under great disadvantages. These may be classed under four heads: first, want of fitting preparation for the work; second, want of recognition of their position and services; third, want of proper pay; fourth, absence of anything like a system. A few words on each of these heads will make the facts clear.

I. When we consider the absence of Colleges and the non-existence of University degrees for women, the disadvantage under which they lie in comparison with men is very striking. It is a common complaint of male educators that they are not up to their work; that they have neither the intellectual training, nor the moral strength, nor the skilled aptitude for teaching which are needed. And this, be it remembered, is in spite of the Universities. There, at least, a high traditional standard of learning is kept up; the ablest instructors are secured, or, at least, invited; and the stamp affixed on acquirements gained under the Academic system is recognised by the world. Women are without these advantages. In many cases their education has been private—entrusted to one or two governesses in succession, with, perhaps, a drawing and music master; or, if they have gone to school, they have had an inferior class of teachers over them, whose influence cannot be compared to that of men who are confessedly at the top of their profession. Let it be understood that I am only speaking of instruction, not education. It would be unfair to depreciate the conscientious endeavours of teachers in ladies' schools to train the habits and mould the character. But no one can teach more than he has in his head. He must be a good teacher who can impart one half. Therefore I consider it is a plain truth, almost amounting to a truism, that private Establishments cannot vie, in teaching power, with public Schools and Universities. Something there is in large cities to supplement the home-training or school-teaching. Queen's College and Bedford College, in London, were started with a right and noble aim; and lectures at the Royal Institution and similar institutions have thrown open to the public the discoveries of Sir H. Davy, Faraday, Tyndall, Huxley, Owen, and Max Müller. By this means a great intellectual stimulus has been given to women as well as men. But the daily work, the patient correction of exercises, and essays, and examination-papers, which is part of the business of Professors and Tutors at the Universities, this has been relegated to inferior hands. It is wonderful to see how in many instances the instinct of teaching has overcome the want of training, and how some women, whose education has been scraped together in any available way, have taught both boys and girls. But this makes it all the more to be regretted that the admirable tact, and patience, and inventive power, which have been displayed in these attempts, should not have had a more complete and thorough training. The want of thoroughness and method, the tendency to a superficial treatment of subjects, of which many complain in women's teaching, are simply the result of insufficient training. Our female educators have not, as a rule, been brought into contact with minds of a superior order, and not only they, but society has suffered in consequence.

II. The want of recognition which female teachers meet with is another striking fact. How different is their position in society from that of men in the same sphere! How timidly even the Endowed Schools Bill of 18th February, 1869, recognised the existence of female teachers! We hunt through pages and pages for an instance of the feminine pronoun! Surely this ought not to be. Surely we ought to be ready to award "honour to whom honour is due."[1]

There is nothing in the position of female teachers like that which results from the combination of a Public School and University education in men. A master so educated feels that he is socially the equal of any one, noble or gentle. And he has the University stamp, if he has taken honours, pointing him out as a man of mark in his own profession. Hence, men who are well born, and well connected, do not scruple to take office as Assistant or Head Masters of schools. The instances of ladies by birth and education occupying the position of schoolmistresses are less common, and the influence they obtain is due rather to their own personal qualifications and force of character than to external circumstances. What we should wish to see is, that women who embark in

[1] Since the above was written, an amended copy of the Bill (date 11th May, 1869) has been printed, in which there is a clause (12 A) to extend the benefits of Endowments to girls.

education should meet with the same respect and consideration as that which is awarded to men. They cannot be imagined to be less sensitive to neglect, or less grateful for that cordial recognition and respect which the Schoolmaster commonly meets with, and which makes him feel that he is not merely a public servant, but a friend of the public. I feel sure that more public opinion is brought to bear upon the position of the Schoolmistress, the more her labours are appreciated, and the more her comforts are considered, the better her work will be done, and the more will solid fruits of education be reaped by the girls who are entrusted to her care.

III. Closely connected with this question is that of payment. Women teachers are, as a class, suffering from want of adequate salaries.

The Endowed Schools Bill could do much good, in an indirect way, by its influence on the judgment of society, in recognising, in the distribution of endowments and funds, the value of the work done by women as well as that done by men. Let us bear in mind the principle on which labour ought to be remunerated. Every sound political economist teaches that labour ought to be paid in proportion to its intrinsic worth and value, and not in proportion to the arbitrary ideas of the payers as to the necessities, or the supposed abilities, of the worker. Let the work done in teaching by Women be fairly compared with the work done by Men. If it be equally good, let their pay be equal. This is simple justice, and the practice of the opposite of this has produced a great amount of suffering and heart-burning on the one hand, and on the other the injurious tradition, so deeply rooted, that work done by women, though in every way equal to work done by men, needs to be, and ought to be, remunerated at a lower scale. Women, I imagine, only ask for equal pay when they can show that that which they bring into the educational market is equally good. This is, I repeat, simple justice and sound political economy. No doubt these matters are ultimately self-adjusting: that is to say, if the demand be abundant, the supply not overstocked, and the material offered be first-rate, the pay of women teachers must, in time, rise to its just level. Nevertheless, the experience of America, where these conditions are in a great measure fulfilled, shows how much evil a tradition or prejudice may work, by retarding indefinitely the self-adjustment of an economic principle. There female teachers are in request; their work is excellent, and still they are underpaid, as compared with men whose work is not superior to theirs, and they consequently suffer both in body and in mind.

Besides this, it is an error to suppose that the wants of women are fewer than those of men. They may not consume so much food; they drink less wine and beer, and they do not smoke. But they are more liable to break down, and therefore need medical advice more frequently, and certain comforts to enable them to carry on their arduous work. Where a man would require a ride, or some drastic exercise, a woman would be better for a drive. It is needless to go into details. The country where women are most employed in education is America. There female teachers preponderate in number over males. Mr. Fraser in his Report (Schools Enquiry Commission, p. 67) says:—

> "There is a trong preference in the United States for the employment of females as teachers, chiefly on the score of superior cheapness, but also, in the estimation of many, on the ground of superior efficiency."

The Tables which he gives show both the superior numbers of the female teachers, and their inferior pay: being in the ratio of about 1 to 2. The average of six States gives 444 dollars per annum as the salary for males, 210 dollars as that for females (Schools Enquiry Commission, p. 76). Mr. Fraser quotes (p. 77) a Philadelphian Report:—

> "Let us look at the salaries of our teachers, and make comparisons. We have in our schools about 1,300 female teachers, cultivated and intelligent ladies, who follow the profession of teaching after years of study. We demand and receive the highest order of talent, and what do we pay them? About 800 receive eighty cents a day; about 200 receive a dollar a day; about 200 receive a dollar and a quarter a day; about 100 receive less than two dollars a day. In other words, there are upwards of a thousand teachers, upon each of whom is lavished per diem a sum scarcely equal to the amount paid to the washerwoman, and about 800 of these obtain only two-thirds of a washerwoman's wages. A large proportion of the teachers receive less than the janitress who sweeps the school-house."

Madame Ankarsvârd, writing from Stockholm, says on this head, "When a man and a woman do the same amount of work, the woman may not, as a rule, look for the same remuneration. It is presumed that a woman has fewer wants than a man, but the injustice is glaring nevertheless. As the women themselves mostly are satisfied with these terms, I do not think the common-sense of justice will soon achieve the task of righting this."

Miss Jex-Blake mentions a notable instance of the principle of paying according to the sex of the worker, and not according to the work done. "Only one of the normal schools in Massachusetts has had a woman appointed as head. All the other principals are men. As soon as the lady was appointed the pay was cut down."

It is easy to say, this is in America, and not in England. But the reply is no less at hand : that in America women are more trusted, if not better treated, as educators, than in England. No one who is acquainted with the facts of the case can say that female teachers are adequately paid in this country. And where they are not well paid, they are not regarded with proper respect. The two are more closely connected than we care to acknowledge. We are too apt to despise people who are poorly clad, poorly housed, struggling, hard-working, pinched and careworn. In England a person who is left almost to starve, while doing ever so useful work, is likely to be somewhat looked down upon by moneyed parents who send their daughters to be educated by her. The rich middle-class parents will spend money upon furniture, upon house-rent, upon expensive dinners and equipages—upon anything, in fact, which cuts a dash and secures personal enjoyment—rather than on the education of their children, especially their daughters. The most precious treasure which money can purchase, a well-stored mind, is deemed of less importance than the most frivolous pleasures and most empty accomplishments, and this is almost universally the case throughout the civilized world.

A lady from North Italy says on the subject of Middle Class Schools: "La difficulté c'est la dépense d'argent. Jusqu'ici, le pere de famille italien qui depense de fortes sommes pour l'éducation de ses fils, hésite à en depenser la dixième partie pour celle de ses filles."

It is a very generally accepted axiom, and one which it seems has been endorsed by thoughtful men without a sufficiently minute examination into the truth of it, that a man—in the matter of maintenance—means generally a man, a wife, and children; while a woman means herself alone, free of dependants. A closer inquiry into the facts of life would prove that conclusions have been too hastily adopted on the latter head. I believe it may be said with truth, that there is scarcely a female teacher in England who is not working for another or others besides herself,—that a very large proportion are urged on of necessity in their work by the dependence on them of whole families, in many cases of their own aged parents,—that many hundreds are keeping broken-down relatives, fathers and brothers, out of the workhouse, and that many are widows supporting their own children. A few examples[1] taken at random from the lists of

[1] Miss Harriet Sophia Smith became a governess to assist her father, a wine merchant, in his declining health and business. Supported both parents for several years previous to their deaths, her mother having only recently died at the age of eighty-one.

Miss Frances Stone, father a surgeon. Left home on account of family difficulties. Aided a sister in keeping a home for her father, who became quite blind.

Miss Sarah Rippon has supported herself since the age of nineteen. Supported her stepfather for the last ten years of his life, and brought up and educated an orphan nephew, who is still young.

Miss Caroline Harriet Evans became a governess owing to the sudden death, by an accident, of her father, who was in business. Devoted her salary to two aged aunts as long as they lived, as a debt of gratitude for their care of her when left an orphan. Gave up a situation to nurse a brother in his last illness, and all her savings to pay his debts.

Miss Louisa D'Espourrin, father an officer in the French army. Began to teach when very young, owing to her mother's losses through revolutions in France and the West Indies. Devoted her whole earnings during twenty-five years to the support of her mother. Is now incapable of further exertion, from disease of the heart and exhausted nervous energy, consequent upon premature and long-continued exertion, and aggravated by constant and increasing anxieties.

Mary Charlotte Cramer became a governess owing to her parents' inability to support her. Gave up the greater part of her salaries to them, and to educate her seven sisters.

Miss Charlotte Emma Rhodes : father a lieutenant in the army. Became a governess for a maintenance, and has been teaching for thirty years. Assisted to bring up a brother to the medical profession, and also devoted some of her earnings to her mother.

Mrs. Mary Phelps, educated for a governess, and worked as such till her marriage, assisting her mother and brothers. On the death of her husband, who was a line-engraver, commenced a school for the support of herself and four daughters.

Miss Sarah Smith Jones was in affluence until her twentieth year, and became a governess owing to her father's loss of property by unfortunate speculations. Entirely educated a younger sister, and gave all she could earn to aid her parents in the support of an invalid sister at home.

Miss Catharine Crawford : father, a solicitor, left her mother and herself very ill-provided for. Became a governess to assist a brother, and to bring up and educate two orphan nephews. [Miss governesses applying to the Institution in Sackville Street, London, will illustrate this point; and let it be remembered that such cases are the rule, not the exception. Indeed, if the facts of life were better known, the hollowness of this defence of the inequality of payment would become manifest; for it is in theory alone that in families man is the only bread-winner, and it is false to suppose that single women have no obligations to make and to save money as sacred as those which are imposed on a man by marriage; while there is this difference, that a man may avoid such obligation if he pleases by refraining from marriage, while the poverty of parents or the dependence of brothers and sisters are circumstances over which a woman obliged to work for others has no control.

The consequences of underpaying female teachers in this country must be the same which Mr. Fraser remarks in America: in schools frequent changes; in private establishments breaks-down, owing to the wear and

Miss Elizabeth Burgess left home to support herself and help her family, upon her father, a manufacturer and merchant, losing everything by unfortunate speculations and the failure of a bank. Kept a school to make a home for him and her brothers.

Mrs. Jane Hall Bull became a governess to maintain herself and help her widowed mother, and subsequently, on becoming a widow, to support her five children.

Miss Eliza Bellars has been teaching more than thirty years; gave all she could spare from her salaries to her parents, and when keeping a school with a sister made a home for them, and helped two brothers and their families.

Mrs. Mary Wood became a governess to relieve her father of her support. Has worked forty years. Unable to save, from having to assist her parents, and subsequently her mother-in-law. For some years almost entirely supported her aged and invalid mother.

tear which continuous teaching involves. It is of great importance that sound principles of social economy should be adopted in this crisis of the history of education in England. If the new schools for girls, whether endowed, public, or private, start now with the proper recognition in money of the work of efficient teachers, then we may hope for much improvement in the education of the future. If a false start be made now, the education of the whole population, men and women, will continue to halt, or to walk on one leg only. "The standard of the education of the women in any country," says Mr. Mill, in his admirable letter to the women of Russia, "will be the measure of the education of the men of that country." Yet this is only partially recognised; and it is not in England alone that parents are unwilling to pay, for the education of their daughters, a sum in any degree commensurate with that which they pay for their sons.

IV. In his report on Lancashire Schools, Mr. Bryce (pp. 823—829) gives a sketch of the actual state of girls' education, from which it is clearly evident that there is no recognised system of female education; and that, although considerable teaching power exists in Governesses, and still more in Schoolmistresses, this is wasted, in a great measure, from the absence of system. The education of the teachers has, in most cases, been defective; they have had no special training for the work of teaching; they suffer from isolation, and ignorance of new methods of work, and they do not as a rule devote themselves to teaching as a permanent, but only as a temporary, occupation. It must be evident that under these circumstances, in spite of the marked natural capacity of women for teaching, to which Mr. Bryce bears testimony, they are working at a disadvantage, and they can neither do justice to their own powers, nor to those of their pupils.

Until our large towns recognise fully the importance of female education, and admit girls to the same advantages which are enjoyed by their brothers; until we see Colleges and Lecture-rooms open to girls, either simultaneously with boys, or at separate hours; until they have the intellectual advantages which are provided for boys in the way of first-rate instruction and the access to good libraries, we shall not see a large proportion of highly-educated women amongst us, nor consequently a large proportion of efficient women teachers.

Surely the experiment is worth trying on a large scale of Girls' Schools or Colleges, where a first-class or commercial education is given, in connexion with our public institutions—whether Colleges or Commercial Schools. This would ensure more thorough teaching, with a greater economy of means. The same staff of masters would be available for teaching boys and girls. The same system would prevail. The same library would be open to both. Common examinations might be held in common work. Excellence in any subject would be fairly tested by a recognised standard, and attested by a common authority. At present there is no such standard. Competent and incompetent teachers are alike employed in schools, and as private governesses.

In many cases there is no means of ascertaining incompetence. Take the case of a wealthy tradesman or manufacturer. He is probably a shrewd man of business; his wife may or may not be a good manager of her household. Well educated she has less chance of being. How can they judge of the capacities for teaching possessed by their daughter's governess? A Government Inspector or Commissioner might ascertain her qualifications in ten minutes; but they have not the requisite knowledge. Hence ignorance and superficiality flourish side by side with accurate and thorough knowledge, the employer of educational labour being unable to "take stock" of the mental qualifications of his daughter's governess. Every attempt, therefore, to introduce more uniformity of standard, more diffusion of knowledge of method, and more facility of testing the qualifications of female teachers, cannot fail to benefit girls' education.

In connexion with this last point is another, which deserves mention. I mean, the folly of the present day in people expecting women teachers and governesses to know and teach everything. One woman is expected to teach English, History, Geography, the rudiments of Science, Modern Languages and Literature, Arithmetic, Music and Drawing, and possibly Latin. How very few men are competent to teach so many subjects, even with the superior advantages of education that they have had! It certainly is assumed, or rather was assumed (for we are growing wiser and more modest), that a young College Tutor or Private Tutor could teach anything and everything. But in the best Colleges at Oxford and Cambridge, and doubtless at other Universities, the principle of division of labour is admitted. It is recognised that in order to teach well a man must select some branch or kindred branches of study; and women are surely entitled to the recognition of this principle. If, besides the extravagant claims made upon her in the way of accomplishments, the qualities of a good disciplinarian are sought, with perfect temper, gentleness of manner, &c. the wonder is, that Governesses are ever found. But the fact is, as every one knows, that there is a great deal of pretence in this department. For this parents are mainly responsible, and not the female teachers. Many a governess must despise herself secretly for the hollowness of the pretensions by which alone she can obtain a situation and bread to eat. And when she is employed, can we wonder that there should be a want of life in her work? Her intellect is like an ounce of gold, beaten out into a thin leaf enough to cover the dome of St. Paul's. What must be the result of her teaching on her young pupils? Nothing but a perpetuation of the same shallowness. But when a woman applies her whole energies to some particular subject or subjects which both by nature and education she has a right to teach, how invigorating is the process both to teacher and taught! It is so in the best boys' schools. No Master is called upon to teach subjects with which he is not either previously acquainted, or thoroughly competent to master, so as to conduct the teaching of his class. In some instances where this rule has been transgressed, opinion seems to veer round again. In the Public

Schools Report allusion is made to the late Dr. Arnold's theory, that every Rugby Master ought to teach modern languages, as well as ancient. Dr. Temple (Evidence, vol. iv. p. 248) points out the objection which lies against this, namely, that it practically limits the choice of Assistants, and compels the Head Master occasionally to put up with a second-rate man to the exclusion of one who is first-rate, but not a good modern linguist.

This view generally prevails in public schools. Masters are taken fresh from the University; and are not generally strong on all points, nor expected to teach every branch. Even in the case of Tutors in private families (an institution not much in vogue now), who has ever dared to require the omniscience in any man which has been demanded from poor women? Who ever heard of a Tutor being called upon to instruct his pupils in Latin Modern Languages, Arithmetic and Euclid, Music, Drawing, Dancing, the Use of the Globes, and Sewing-machine? Let us not require more in this way from women than we demand from men.

It is an opinion entertained by many competent judges, that the Public School Class system has unduly obtruded itself into other departments of education. By this system, boys who are nearly equal in Classics are required to do all their other subjects together. Thus, although the greatest inequality may prevail amongst them in respect of mathematics, modern languages, or natural sciences, they must all work together. Again, a class is limited by the powers of a Master to look over their work—especially their written exercises. From thirty to forty is a large number, which cannot be advantageously exceeded. In the highest classes, even this is too large for the care of one master. But there is another view of teaching, which ought not to be lost sight of. I mean the Professorial view. An able Professor can command the attention of 200 with no less ease than that of 20. The very numbers act as a stimulus to his exertions. A greater amount of teaching power is thus brought to bear upon a greater number of pupils. Individual aptitudes are hereby economised. Pupils feel that they are listening to some one who can teach them, not repeating words out of a book to a hearer of lessons. From this branch of teaching I see no reason why women should be excluded. On the contrary, I am convinced that they would succeed in it. They would have time allowed them to master a subject before beginning a course of lectures on it. Increased respect would be paid them by their intelligent pupils, and their own self-respect would be heightened by the feeling that they were doing their work thoroughly.

Let us imagine a Day School with 200 girls. Of course these would be of different ages—say from eight or ten to eighteen.

The senior girls, or those above fourteen, would be capable of being grouped together for such subjects as English History and Literature, Continental History and Literature, Greek and Roman History, Natural Science, Moral Philosophy, and its kindred sciences; the principles and history of Art, Mathematics, Physical and Political Geography. These groups of subjects, if taken in hand by seven or eight different teachers, might be adequately treated. If they were divided among three or four, the result would be better than what we now see and deplore—the superficial handling of a great number of subjects by individuals who ought to equal Alexander von Humboldt, or Mrs. Somerville, to cover all the ground mapped out for them.

Enough, and more than enough it may be thought, has been said on this head. Private governesses will still be wanted, and may be of great use when properly fitted to teach, and properly paid, with their powers concentrated on fewer subjects. But all they can do will require to be supplemented, and for this encouragement should be given to women to devote themselves to the profession of certain lines of study, for which their powers and inclinations may fit them.

It is time that I should say a word as to the capacity of women to teach both boys and girls. I believe it is not uncommon for boys to form their first acquaintance with Latin before they leave their mothers' side. As one of four brothers who began to learn Latin in this way, I cannot but regard it as natural and beneficial. And I know instances of married ladies who teach their boys, besides other very useful things, the elements of Latin. Some of the specimens of boys thus taught come before me officially, and I find that they generally know what they profess to know. Some years ago, at Cheltenham, I was in the habit of examining boys trained in ladies' schools in the place; and I am bound in justice to their teachers to say that they were distinguished above other boys of their age (under thirteen) for the intelligence and accuracy which they showed. They also distinguished themselves in athletics. I do not think it would be easy to find better schools for young boys than those kept by Miss Briggs, and the Misses Hills. There is another excellent preparatory school conducted by Mrs. Maclaren, Summerfield, Oxford, which I do not know personally, but from which two boys have recently, to my knowledge, been elected to scholarships at Eton and Uppingham. The thoroughness of the education received by the young Etonian was proved by his rapid rise in the school after his election, and by his gaining not only a double remove at Christmas—he had been elected in August—but the first prize for examination at Easter. Neither of these boys were so remarkable for their talent as for the thoroughness of their work; and I believe many more examples could be adduced of female teachers, who do not bear out the popular notion that women's work must be superficial, but prove that they are capable of giving a most thorough basis for literary or scientific training. "That most divine faculty, Patience," writes my informant, "the child of Love and Faith, is especially woman's. How should she be other than profound?" At Cheltenham there is a large and flourishing Ladies' College. I have conducted the yearly examinations there, and am therefore in a position to speak highly of the quality of the teaching given under the able Principal, Miss Beale. In some of the subjects in which I examined I may have traced a tendency to use the memory rather than the judgment: but the general impression left on my mind was highly favourable. At Liverpool College I frequently receive pupils from Ladies' Schools. These are not the least well taught of those who present themselves for admission. I could point to instances of the very reverse. As a rule, I believe there are fewer impostors among the female than among the male teachers. Schools are constantly being set up by discarded writing-masters, who know no one subject well, and profess to give a "sound classical and commercial education." I would much rather receive a boy from the hands of an intelligent schoolmistress than from one of these private schools. Mr. Bryce (Report, p. 596) says that he found these schools were generally better in proportion to their size, and that although "there was not perhaps so great a contrast among them as one finds between the head and the tail of a class of fifty in a great school, that is not because they were all as good as the head, but rather because they were all tail." Of course, there is a great difference between one private school and another. And it would be a gross injustice to the many able and highly conscientious men who devote themselves to private educational work, to ignore the good that they render to society. Only for their sakes, and for that of society, it is well that the truth should be known. They and education generally suffer much more from the existence among their ranks of unqualified pretenders, than they could from the larger employment in this country of women teachers.

That women should be deemed competent to undertake the very highest educational work, no reader of history will think strange. To pass over the names of Greek and Alexandrian ladies, who, like Diotima and Hypatia, taught not youths alone, but men, we find a goodly list of ladies in the Middle Ages, in fact down to the nineteenth century, who have been distinguished as professors.

In 1236 Betisia Gozzadini, having graduated at Bologna, lectured on the Institutes of Justinian to a large class of students at her own house.[1] In 1380 Maddalena Buonsignori lectured on Law at Bologna, and wrote a treatise "De legibus connubialibus."[2] In the same century Novella Andreas, daughter of the Professor of Canon Law at Bologna, lectured in his stead behind a curtain.[3] In 1400 Dorothea Bucca was Professor of Medicine in the University of Bologna.[4] In 1564 Elisabetta Losa received a legal degree, and held a Chair apparently in the University of Cordova.[5] In 1557 Bianca Borromeo was Professor of learned Languages in the University of Padua.[6] In 1733 Laura Caterina Bassi was Professor of Philosophy at the University of Bologna, a medal being struck in her honour,[7] with the inscription, "Soli cui fas vidisse Minervam."[8] In 1750 Maria Gaetana Agnesi was appointed Professor of Mathematics by Benedict XIV. She wrote treatises on "The Differential Calculus" and "Analytical Insti-

[1] Ghirardacci's "Hist. Bologna." [2] Mazzuchelli, "Gli scritti d'Italia."
[3] Bayle's Dictionary, "Cyte of Ladyes" (black letter).
[4] Finauer's "Allgemeine Hist. Erziehung." [5] Ibid. [6] Ibid.
[7] Biographie Universelle. [8] Biographie Universelle.

tutes," translated into French, and the latter into English by the Cambridge Professor of Mathematics.[1] In 1760 Anna Morandi Mazzolina was Professor of Anatomy at the University of Bologna. In 1780 Maria Petraccini, afterwards married to Feretti, took a degree in Medicine, and gave a demonstration and lecture on Anatomy before a Board of Professors at Ferrara. It is uncertain whether she taught.[2] In 1794 Clothilde Tambroni was Professor of Greek at Bologna; in 1790 she was deposed from her Chair on account of her political opinions, but reinstated by Napoleon.[3] In 1806 Maria delle Donne was appointed to a Chair of Midwifery by Napoleon Bonaparte at Bologna.[4]

Miss Jex-Blake, in her "Visit to American Schools and Colleges," mentions several lady-professors at Antioch College, Ohio, one of whom filled the Chair of Mathematics for several years. Mrs. A. S. Dean taught Natural Science and History from 1853 to 1859. Miss Hitchcock, now Mrs. E. Fay, taught Mathematics and French in 1853–4, and 1857–8. Mrs. H. C. Badger taught Modern Languages from 1859 to 1863. Lucretia Crocker was Professor of Mathematics and Astronomy in 1857–8. Lastly, Mrs. J. B. Weston has been instructor in Classics in the preparatory school at Antioch College, from 1860 to the present time. Miss Mitchell, in America, is said to be an able Astronomer; and there

1 "Macmillan's Magazine" for September 1868.

2 Fachini, "Donne illustre."

3 Biographie Universelle.

4 Fachini, "Donne illustre."

is no question that Mrs. Somerville would have adorned a Professorial Chair of Astronomy or Physical Science. There is a statement in a book in the British Museum called "Ballard's Memoirs," to the effect that one Mary Astell in the seventeenth century tried to found a Female College, and got a promise of 10,000*l.* for its support, when Bishop Burnet frustrated her plan; showing that Whig bishops can, on a pinch, be as intolerant as the Pope. And if it be asked, What are the qualities which women possess marking them as eminently qualified to conduct educational work, abundant answers will be furnished by the "Report of the Schools Enquiry Commissions," by Mr. Fraser. There we read (p. 67) that, in the opinion of the Commissioner of Rhode Island, "Women are succeeding better in that State than male teachers, even in the management of turbulent boys; while in the formation of the manners, and in the cultivation of the morals and tastes of the children, they are incomparably better teachers than men."

The State Superintendent of New York rises to the realms of poetry, and almost romance, in the following sentences:—

"It is impossible to over-estimate the value of the influence thus (by four-fifths of the teachers being females) brought to bear upon the daily-developing mind and character in our schools. To teach and train the young seems to be one of the chief missions of Woman. Herself high-minded, the minds of those with whom she comes in daily contact unconsciously aspire. Gentle herself, she renders them gentle. Pure herself, she makes them pure. The fire which truly refines the ore of character can be kindled only by her hand. Woman is more deeply read than man in the mysteries of human nature, at least of that of children. It might, perhaps, be nearer the truth to say that her superior knowledge in this respect is intuitive. Better her discipline of love than his reformatory theories, and austere rules, and stringent systems. Her touch conquers the rebelliousness which his but increases. Her persuasive reproofs far exceed his stern menaces and cold logic. Well may we be solicitous in regard to that pupil's course and destiny who does not pass from the scene of Woman's ministrations with his moral sense so delicately attuned as to render the discords of a vicious life impossible; with his tastes vitalized, and his perceptions quickened; with his sensibilities and sympathies all ready for action; with his conscience trained to unremitting vigilance, and the best impulses of his heart in full play. I am sure that the future will be grateful for these labours of women in our schools."—*Report for* 1865.

Mr. Fraser apologizes for coming down from this eloquent testimony to figures; and I feel a similar misgiving that anything that may be added to such glowing language will appear cold and lifeless. But it is not a bad thing to adduce one or two facts, such as the following, furnished by a report of an interview between some influential Advocates of Education and a Committee of the Legislature which sat on Education at Boston, Massachusetts, United States, April 2, 1869. Dr. Cornell related a striking instance of the refining effect of placing a rough young man in a school where both sexes were associated in study and social life, and Dr. Dio Lewis mentioned a case where an exceptionally unruly school had been restored to order in one week by placing one of each sex at the same desk for study. Mr. Bryce says (Report, p. 838) :—

"One cannot speak without admiration of the ability of many, of the zeal and earnestness of the great majority, among the ladies who are at the head of the girls' school in Lancashire."

In another part of his Report (p. 822) Mr. Bryce says:—

"Women are naturally skilful teachers, and they are, so far as my observation goes, zealous and conscientious teachers. Whenever I happened to hear the teaching of a lady of good ability who had herself been thoroughly educated, its merits struck me as at least equal, and probably superior, to those which would be found in the teaching of a man of the same general capacity and education. Women seem to have more patience as teachers, more quickness in seeing whether the pupil understands, more skill in adapting their explanations to the peculiarities of the pupil's mind, and certainly a nicer discernment of his or her character. They are quite as clear in exposition as men are, and, when well trained, quite as capable of making their teaching philosophical. I must confess myself to have been also impressed by the interest which they so often took in their pupils, and their genuine ardour to do the best for them."

"This makes it," he says elsewhere (p. 838), "the more a matter of regret that they should not have had the means which a systematic University course affords, of gaining a thorough and scientific knowledge of large subjects; and that the assistant teachers, to whom they must always have to entrust a large portion of school work, should so often be deficient in knowledge, in an intelligent comprehension of the nature of their duties, in mental cultivation, and literary interests."

Here we have the testimony of an acute observer, who has formed his conclusions on an acquaintance with a large number of schools, and who, while drawing attention to some of the deficiencies remarked above, bears emphatic testimony to the moral and intellectual qualifications for their work possessed by female teachers.

Indeed, a very small amount of reflection must make it evident that some of the most essential points in sound education are precisely those to which women have always directed their attention, and with respect to which their authority is at least as great as that of men.

The best male teachers are those who have some of the subtlety of mind, lively sympathy with the young, and versatility, which women possess. Women have one quality which is often overlooked in education, that of playfulness. This is a most valuable aid in guiding and managing, as well as interesting and encouraging, the young. They have also a tendency to study individual points of character, and adapt their teaching to each particular case. They are more disposed than men to take pains for an individual. And this is after the fashion of Christ's teaching: for He dealt closely with individuals, however humble, though He also taught the multitudes.

One of the great questions which will come before our statesmen shortly is, how to supplement the secular education which, and which alone, the State seems likely to give, by sufficient religious education. I earnestly hope that the aid of Women will here be called in. They seem to me to possess, more than men, the faculty of teaching the morality and spirit of Christ's religion without theology proper. But I would appeal to the Theological writings of Miss Blunt, and many excellent books by ladies, to show that they can exhibit the leading doctrines, as well as the moral precepts, of Christianity. No doubt there are some women who are too dogmatic; but these have not unfrequently been spoiled by an unfair advantage being taken of their devout and submissive tempers by male dogmatists, who have asserted their sacerdotal claims, to the extinction of female independence of thought and judgment. The best women are truly religious, and they make their religion pervade all their teaching, however secular.

The results of Quaker women's teaching, both of boys and girls, are said to be very good. It is their rule never to reprove in a voice louder or sharper than usual, which a child is apt to mistake for anger or peevishness: but their excellency probably lies deeper; in continuity of effort, in equability of temper, and impartiality of reproof, which, coming like a law of nature, will not irritate, but train.

It is of the utmost importance that boys should know at an early age what pain, toil, sleeplessness and exhaustion mothers go through for their infants. It tends first to gratitude, affection, and obedience to their mothers, and next to make them tender, considerate, and respectful towards the female sex. It opens their eyes to some of the responsiblities incurred by a father. Boys ought to be taught to understand the moral consequences of the union of marriage, before they are of an age to know of any other than the moral consequences. These are serious matters, which require delicate handling. When speaking of the influence of women on the moral training of boys, it seems not out of place to suggest them. Believing it to be of vital importance to the formation of character and the happiness, first of individuals, next of families, and eventually of nations, that boys should grow up with the knowledge which will make them tender, generous, and considerate in the most solemn relations of life, I venture to plead for such an admixture of Woman's influence, for such an extension beyond mere childhood of the sweet associations of a pure and happy home, as may furnish some countervailing antidote to the spirit of a public school, where none but male teachers are employed, where the boy's companions are exclusively of his own sex, where he is taught to regard all social matters from a purely boyish point of view, and whence he only comes among women when reserve has grown strong, and the passions are waking up, undisciplined by affection or reverence for womanhood. When that extension of Woman's influence takes place, society will be purer and happier, and I venture to think, not less adorned by manly virtues.

IV.

MEDICINE AS A PROFESSION FOR WOMEN.

BY SOPHIA JEX-BLAKE.

> " The universe shall henceforth speak for you
> And witness, She who did this thing, was born
> To do it ; claims her licence in her work.
> And so with more works. Whoso cures the plague,
> Though twice a woman, shall be called a leech."
>
> *Aurora Leigh.*

It is a very comfortable faith to hold that " whatever is, is best," not only in the dispensations of Providence, but in the social order of daily life ; but it is a faith which is perhaps best preserved by careful avoidance of too much inquiry into facts. The theory, if applied to past as well as to present times, would involve us in some startling contradictions, for there is hardly any act, habit, or custom, which has not been held meritorious and commendable in one state of society, and detestable and evil in some other. If we believe that there are eternal principles of right and wrong, wisdom and equity, far above and greater than the "public opinion" of any one age or country, we must acknowledge the absolute obligation of inquiring, whenever matters of importance are at stake, on what grounds the popular opinions rest, and how far they are the result of habit, custom, and prejudice, or the real outgrowth of deep convictions and beliefs inherent in the most sacred recesses of human nature. While the latter command ever our deepest reverence, as the true "vox populi, vox Dei," nothing can be more superficial, frivolous, and fallacious than the former.

In a country where precedent has so much weight as in England, it doubly behoves us to make the distinction, and, while gratefully accepting the safeguard offered against inconsiderate and precipitate change, to beware that old custom is not suffered permanently to hide from our eyes any truth which may be struggling into the light. I suppose that no thinking man will pretend that the world has now reached the zenith of truth and knowledge, and that no further upward progress is possible; on the contrary, we must surely believe that each year will bring with it its new lesson; fresh lights will constantly be dawning above the horizon, and perhaps still oftener discoveries will be re-discovered, truths once acknowledged but gradually obscured or forgotten will emerge again into day, and a constantly recurring duty will lie before every one who believes in life as a responsible time of action, and not as a period of mere vegetative existence, to "prove all things, and hold fast that which is good."

The above considerations arise naturally in connexion with the subject of this paper, which is too often set aside by the general public, who, perhaps, hardly appreciate its scope, and are not yet fully aroused to the importance of the questions involved in the general issue. We are told so often that nature and custom have alike decided against the admission of women to the Medical Profession, and that there is in such admission something repugnant to the right order of things, that when we see growing evidences of a different opinion among a minority perhaps, but a minority which already includes many of our most earnest thinkers of both sexes, and increases daily, it surely becomes a duty for all who do not, in the quaint language of Sharpe, "have their thinking, like their washing, done out," to test these statements by the above principles, and to see how far their truth is supported by evidence.

In the first place, let us take the testimony of Nature in the matter. If we go back to primeval times, and try to imagine the first sickness or the first injury suffered by humanity, does one instinctively feel that it must have been the *man's* business to seek means of healing, to try the virtues of various herbs, or to apply such rude remedies as might occur to one unused to the strange spectacle of human suffering? I think that few would maintain that such ministration would come most naturally to the man, and be instinctively avoided by the woman. I fancy that the presumption would be rather in the other direction. And what is such ministration but the germ of the future profession of medicine?

Again, imagine if you can that the world has reached its present standing-point, that society exists as now in every respect but this,—that the art of healing has never been conceived as a separate profession, that no persons have been set apart to receive special education for it, and that in fact empirical "domestic medicine," in the strictest sense, is the only thing of the kind existing. Suppose now that society suddenly awoke to the great want so long unnoticed, that it was recognised by all that a scientific knowledge of the human frame in health and in disease, and a study of the remedies of various kinds which might be employed as curative agents, would greatly lessen human suffering, and that it was therefore resolved at once to set apart some persons who should acquire such knowledge, and devote their lives to using it for the benefit of the rest of the race. In such case, would the natural idea be that members of each sex should be so set apart for the benefit of their own sex respectively,—that men should fit themselves to minister to the maladies of men, and women to those of women,—or that one sex only should undertake the care of the health of all, under all circumstances? For myself, I have no hesitation in saying that the former seems to me the *natural* course, and that to civilized society, if unaccustomed to the idea, the proposal that persons of one sex should in every case be consulted about every disease incident to those of the other, would be very repugnant; nay, that were every other condition of society the same as now, it would probably be held wholly inadmissible. I maintain that not only is there nothing strange or unnatural in the idea that women are the fit physicians for women, and men for men; but, on the contrary, that it is only custom and habit which blind society to the extreme strangeness and incongruity of any other notion.

I am indeed far from pretending, as some have done, that it is morally wrong for men to be the medical attendants of women, and that grave mischiefs are the frequent and natural results of their being placed in that position. I believe that these statements not only materially injure the cause they profess to serve, but that they are in themselves false. In my own experience as a medical student, I have had far too much reason to acknowledge the honour and delicacy of feeling habitually shown by the gentlemen of the medical profession, not to protest warmly against any such injurious imputation. I am very sure that in the vast majority of cases, the motives and conduct of medical men in this respect are altogether above question, and that every physician who is also a gentleman is thoroughly able, when consulted by a patient in any case whatever, to remember only the human suffering brought before him and the scientific bearing of its details; for as was said not very long ago by a most eminent London surgeon, "Whoever is not able in the course of practice to put the idea of sex out of his mind, is not fit for the medical profession at all." It will, however, occur to most people that the medical man is only one of the parties concerned, and that it is possible that a difficulty which may be of no importance from his scientific standpoint, may yet be very formidable indeed to the far more sensitive and delicately organized feelings of his patient, who has no such armour of proof as his own, and whose very condition of suffering may entail an even exaggerated condition of nervous susceptibility on such points. At any rate, when we hear so many assertions about natural instincts and social propriety, I cannot but assert that their evidence, such as it is, is wholly for, and not against, the cause of women as physicians for their own sex.

If we take next the ground of custom, I think the position of those who would oppose the medical education of women is far less tenable than is generally supposed; indeed, that a recent writer stated no more than the truth when he asserted that, "The obloquy which attends innovation belongs to the men who exclude women from a profession in which they once had a recognised place."[1] I believe that few people who have not carefully considered the question from an historical point of view have any idea of the amount of evidence that may be brought to support this view of the case.[2]

Referring to the earliest classical times, we find distinct mention in the Iliad of a woman skilled in the science of medicine,[3] and a similar reference occurs

[1] *Athenæum*, Sept. 28, 1867.

[2] In his "Essai sur les Femmes," Thomas points out that "Chez la plupart des sauvages . . la médecine et la magie sont entre les mains des femmes."

[3] The passage is thus rendered by Professor Blackie:—

"His eldest born, hight Agamede, with golden hair;
A leech was she, and well she knew all herbs on ground that grew."
Iliad, xi. 739.

In his Notes the translator remarks that "it seems undeniable that women have a natural vocation for exercising certain branches of the also in the Odyssey.[1] Euripides is no less valuable a witness on this point. He describes Queen Phædra[2] as disturbed in mind and out of health, and represents the nurse as thus addressing her: "If thy complaint be anything of the more secret kind, here are women at hand to compose the disease. But if thy distress is such as may be told to men, tell it, that it may be reported to the physicians;" thus indicating a prevailing public opinion that there were natural and rigid limits to the medical attendance of men on women, and that therefore some women were specially trained to do what the regular physicians must leave undone.

It is at least remarkable to find such evidence of general feeling on this matter in a state of society supposed to possess much less delicacy and refinement than our own.

We find records of several Grecian women who were renowned for their medical skill, among whom may be instanced Olympias of Thebes, whose medical learning is said to be mentioned by Pliny; and Aspasia, from whose writings on the diseases of women quotations are preserved in the works of Aëtius, a Mesopotamian physician.[3] On the authority of Hyginus

medical profession with dexterity and tact. . . . It is gratifying therefore to find that a field of activity which has been recently claimed for the sex . . . finds a precedent in the venerable pages of the Iliad. . . . In fact, nothing was more common in ancient times than medical skill possessed by females;" in proof of which assertion he mentions Œnone and others. (Professor Blackie's "Homer and the Iliad." Edmonston & Douglas.)

1 Odyssey, iv. 227.

2 Hippolytus, 293-7.

3 Finauer's "Allgemeines Verzeichniss gelehrten Frauenzimmer."

rests the history of Agnodice, the Athenian maiden whose skill and success in medicine was the cause of the legal opening of the medical profession to all the freeborn women of the State.[1]

In more modern times, when almost all learning was garnered into the religious houses, which were not only the libraries but the hospitals of the day, it seems evident that the care of the sick and wounded fell at least as often to the share of the Nunneries as of

[1] I subjoin as a curiosity the quaint version of this story that is given in a letter from Mrs. Celleor (a fashionable midwife of the reign of James II.), published in 1687, and now to be found in the British Museum. After saying that "Among the subtile Athenians a law at one time forbade women to study or practise medicine or physick on pain of death, which law continued some time, during which many women perished, both in child-bearing and by private diseases, their modesty not permitting them to admit of men either to deliver or cure them," she continues, "Till God stirred up the spirit of Agnodice, a noble maid, to pity the miserable condition of her own sex, and hazard her life to help them ; which to enable herself to do she apparelled her like a man, and became the scholar of Hierophilos, the most learned physician of the time ; and having learnt the art, she found out a woman that had long languished under private diseases, and made proffer of her service to cure her, which the sick person refused, thinking her to be a man ; but when Agnodice discovered that she was a maid, the woman committed herself into her hands, who cured her perfectly ; and after her many others, with the like skill and industry, so that in a short time she became the successful and beloved physician of the whole sex." When her sex became known to the public, "she was like to be condemned to death for transgressing the law . . . which coming to the ears of the noble women, they ran before the Areopagites, and the house being encompassed by most women of the city, the ladies entered before the judges, and told them they would no longer account them for husbands and friends but for cruel enemies that condemned her to death who restored to them their health, protesting they would all die with her if she were put to death. . . . This caused the magistrates to disannul the law and make another, which gave gentlewomen leave to study and practise all parts of physick to their own sex, giving large stipends to those that did it well and carefully. And there were many noble women who studied that practice, and taught it publicly in their schools as long as Athens flourished in learning."

the Monasteries, and probably medical skill, such as it was, found place among the sisters as often as among the brethren of the various religious Orders.

The old ballad of Sir Isumbras[1] gives one illustration out of many of the prevailing state of things, relating how the nuns received the wounded knight, and how

"Ilke a day they made salves new,
And laid them on his wounds,
They gafe hym metis and drynkes lythe,
And heled the knyghte wonder swythe."

In the fourteenth century, when the Medical School of Salerno enjoyed high reputation, we find record of a female physician named Abella, who lived there, and wrote in Latin various works on medicine.[2]

Early in the next century an Italian lady, Dorotea Bucca, was actually Professor of Medicine at the University of Bologna,[3] and among the traditions of the same University is preserved the name of Alessandra Gigliani, who, in even earlier times, was a learned student of anatomy.[4]

In the sixteenth century, at Alcarez in Spain, lived Olivia Sabuco de Nantes, who "had a large knowledge of science and medicine," and whose medical works were printed at Madrid in 1588.[5]

1 "Thornton Romances:" Camden Society.
2 "Nuovo Dizionario Istorico;" Bassano, 1796.
3 Fachini's "Prospetto Biografico delle Donne Italiane;" Venezia, 1824.
4 Medici's "Scuola Anatomica di Bologna."
5 Finauer.

It is clear that in England at this period women were commonly found among the irregular practitioners of medicine;[1] for, within a few years after the first incorporation of the Colleges of Physicians and Surgeons, an Act[2] was passed for the relief and protection of "Divers honest psones, *as well men as women*, whom God hathe endued with the knowledge of the nature, kind, and operaçon of certeyne herbes, rotes, and waters, and the using and ministering them to suche as be payned with customable diseases, for neighbourhode and Goddes sake, and of pitie and charytie," because the "Companie and Fellowship of Surgeons of London, mynding onlie their owne lucres and nothing the profit or ease of the diseased or patient, have sued, vexed, and troubled," the aforesaid "honest psones," who were henceforth to be allowed "to practyse, use, and mynistre in and to any outwarde sore, swelling, or disease, any herbes, oyntements, bathes, pultes or emplasters, according to their cooning experience and knowledge . . . . without sute, vexation, penaltie, or losse of their goods."

This provision clearly referred to general practice other than that of midwifery, which latter branch of the profession was then, as for centuries both before and after, almost exclusively in the hands of women. The very

[1] A quotation in a recent medical paper seems to prove that the practice can be traced much further back; for it relates that in the year 1421 a petition was presented to Henry V. praying that "no woman use the practyse of fisyk under payne of long emprisonment." (*New York Medical Gazette*, April 24, 1869.)

[2] 34 Henry VIII. c. 8.

word *midwife*, with its Latin synonym "*obstetrix*," is sufficiently significant on this point, for in neither language has it any masculine equivalent, and the clumsy term "Man-midwife" served, when first needed and used, to mark the general sense of what the writer in the *Athenæum* forcibly calls "masculine intrusion, into that which natural instinct assigns to woman as her proper field of labour;" and this same very suggestive title is the only one which at the present day in legal phraseology distinguishes the male practitioners of this branch of medical art.

From the time of Moses onwards this part of the profession has always been mainly in the hands of women, and in many countries of Europe no other usage has ever prevailed. The first regular French medical society, "La confrairie de St. Cosme and St. Damien," included within its organization the Company of Midwives,[1] and from that time down to the present it seems in France to have been the custom to give to these women a regular education, terminating in sufficient examinations, an example which England would have done well to follow.

In this country, however, midwives seem to have held a most respectable position some centuries ago; and a curious idea of their importance, their duties, and their credit, may be gathered from a MS. volume (without

1 The statutes of 1268 ordained that "les matrones ou sages femmes sont aussi de la dite confrairie, et subjects ausdits deux chirurgiens jurez du Roy au Chastelet, qui ont dressé certains statuts et ordonnances tant pour les droicts de la confrairie que pour leur estat de sage femme, qu'elles doivent observer et garder."—DU BREUL'S *Antiquités de Paris*, pub. 1639.

date) now preserved in the British Museum,[1] which was evidently written at a time when hardly any but women were employed in the "mysteries of the profession," and when it was a comparatively rare thing, that needed to be specially advised in certain cases, for them to "make use of (*i.e.* call in) a physitien." The writer remarks that "it is meet that the midwife be a woman well read and well experienced," and gives a caution that "drunkenness is a sordid sin in any who use it, but is a blemish worthy greater blame in ministers, magistrates, midwives, physitiens and chirurgeons."

Mrs. Celleor, in her letter previously referred to,[2] tells us that in 1642, "the physitiens and chirurgeons contending about it, midwifery was adjudged a chirurgical operation, and midwives were licensed at Chirurgeons' Hall, but not till they had passed three examinations before six skilful midwives, and as many chirurgeons;" but for some unaccountable reason, in 1662 the midwives were referred for their licence to Doctors' Commons, thus losing their official connexion with the medical world.

How it came that English midwives fell gradually from their high estate is partly explained by a very public-spirited book (with the appropriate motto "Non sibi sed aliis") written by a surgeon in 1736.[3] The

[1] "The Midwive's Deputie . . composed for the use of my Wife (a sworne Midwife), by Edward Poeton, Petworth, Licentiate in Physick and Chyrurgery."

[2] "Letter to Dr. ———," written by Elizabeth Celleor, "from my house in Arundel Street, Strand, Jan. 16, 1687-8."

[3] "A Short Account of the State of Midwifery in London. By John Douglas, Surgeon. Dedicated to the Right Hon. Lady Walpole."

writer adverts to the accusations of ignorance then brought against the midwives, and remarks that " the only method by which this fatal distemper can be cured, is to put it in the power of midwomen to qualify themselves thoroughly and at a moderate expense. . . . To which method of qualifying themselves I doubt not the midwomen will object, and say that they would readily be at any reasonable expense and fatigue to be so thoroughly instructed, but it is not in their power. The midwomen cannot, and the midmen will not, instruct them. The midmen will object and say that the midwomen want both capacity and strength (instruct them as ye please). To which I reply (ore rotundo, plenis buccis), that it is not want of capacity, docility, strength or activity . . . . which is evident to a demonstration from the successful practice of women in the Hôtel Dieu at Paris (the best school for midwifery now in Europe). . . . Would not any person then be deservedly laughed at who should assert that our women are not as capable of performing their office, had they the same instruction as the French women?" This chivalrous surgeon then proposes that regular provision should be made for proper instruction, and for examinations by two surgeons (who have lectured to the women), "and six or seven other persons appointed by His Majesty, because I don't think it reasonable that so many people's bread should depend on the humour or caprice of two men only;" adding, " If some such scheme was put in execution, I'm satisfied that in a very few years there would not be an ignorant midwife in

England, and consequently the great agonies most women suffer at the very sight of a man would be almost entirely prevented," and great expense and much life saved.

However, we must suppose that these noble words of protest fell upon deaf ears, and the midwives being left in their ignorance, their practice gradually passed into the hands of the medical men, who had every advantage of learning at their command.

It is well known, however, that Queen Charlotte was always attended by a woman,[1] and I believe that the late Duchess of Kent followed the same precedent.

Now that public attention is awaking to the subject, and educated women are once more desirous of undertaking this peculiarly womanly work, we may indeed anticipate, with the already quoted writer in the *Athenæum*, that a reactionary movement will soon make itself felt, and that the usage "which even up to the present time a large proportion of our English families, especially those of our northern towns and outlying country districts, have never adopted, will most likely be discontinued in all classes of English society before the end of the present century."

On the Continent of Europe, owing to their better education, the midwives retain much of the position that they have for a time lost in England; and we hear

[1] "Delicacy had in those days so far the ascendency, that the obstetrical art was principally practised by females, and on this occasion the Queen was delivered by Mrs. Stephen, Dr. Hunter being in attendance among the ladies of the bedchamber, in case of his professional assistance being required."—HUISH'S *Life of George IV.*

that in Russia "a medical man is very rarely called in; notwithstanding, fatal cases are of far less frequent occurrence in Russia than in England;" and the same authority tells us that ladies practising midwifery are admitted into society as doctors would be, and are well paid, both by the Government and by private fees.[1]

While thus briefly tracing out the history of midwifery in modern times, and the causes which led to its practice passing from the hands of women into those of men, I have not paused to mention, in due chronological order, those women who, in the last three centuries, have been distinguished for a knowledge of the other branches of Medicine and Surgery. Of these I will now enumerate a few, though my time and space are far too limited either to give a complete list, or to relate any but the most prominent particulars of each case mentioned; but I can promise that any one who will consult the authorities quoted will be abundantly repaid by the long and interesting details that I am forced to pass over in almost every instance.

In the seventeenth century, in England, one of the women most noted for medical skill was Lady Ann Halket,[2] born in 1622, daughter of the then Provost of Eton College. "Next to the study of Divinity she seems to have taken most delight in those of Physick and Surgery, in which she was no mean proficient; nay, some of the best physicians in the kingdom did not

[1] "Rites and Customs of the Greco-Russian Church," by Madame Romanoff. Rivingtons, 1868.

[2] Ballard's "Memoirs of several Ladies of Great Britain." Oxford, 1752.

think themselves slighted when persons of the greatest quality did consult her in their distempers, even when they attended them as their ordinary physicians. Many from England, Holland, and the remotest parts of the kingdom, have sent to her for things of her preparing; and many whose diseases have proved obstinate under all the methods of physicians have at length, by the physicians' own advice, been recommended and sent to her care, and have been recovered by her."

In 1644 was born Elizabeth Lawrence, afterwards wife of the Rev. Samuel Bury, of Bristol, who wrote her life,[1] and who bears witness that "it was not possible there should be a more observant, tender, indulgent and compassionate wife than she was; a more sympathising spirit is very rarely found." He records that "she took much pleasure in Anatomy and Medicine, being led and prompted to it partly by her own ill health, and partly with a desire of being useful." The difficulties that she encountered in her studies may be guessed, since "she would often regret that so many learned men should be so uncharitable to her sex, and be so loath to assist their feebler faculties when they were anywise disposed to an accurate search into things profitable and curious; especially as they would all so readily own that souls were not distinguished by sexes, and therefore she thought it would have been an honourable pity in them to have offered something in condescension to their capacities, rather than have propa-

[1] "An Account of the Life and Death of Mrs. Elizabeth Bury."—Bristol, 1721.

gated a despair of their information to future ages." Her husband, however, tells us that "she improved so much, that many of the great masters of the Faculty have often been startled by her stating the most nice and difficult cases in such proper terms;" and, remarking that "How much knowledge and skill soever she attained in the practice of Physick, by long observation, conversation, and experience, yet she was very distrustful of herself," he adds, that the "instances of her successes in the preservation of human lives were not easily numbered."

As a contemporary of these Englishwomen, we find in Germany Elizabeth Keillen, who published several medical works, and died in 1699. She is said by Finauer to have had "great knowledge of medicine and chemistry."

In comparatively recent times, Bologna was remarkable as ever for its liberal encouragement of learned women, and about the middle of the last century the Chair of Anatomy at that University was filled by Anna Morandi Mazzolini, whose exquisitely delicate anatomical models, executed in wax, became the pride of the Museum at Bologna. Medici, in his records of the Anatomical School of Bologna, speaks of this lady with profound respect, as distinguished alike by "rare powers, great erudition, gracious manners, and delicate and gentle temperament," and relates that her fame reached the ears of the Emperor Joseph II. who visited her in 1769, and "having seen her works and heard her conversation," loaded her with public honours. She died in 1774. Her example seems to have inspired others of her countrywomen to follow in the steps of one so honoured, alike in the stern duties of her profession and in the sanctities of household life; for in the course of the next half century several Italian women availed themselves of the thorough medical education which the Italian Universities never refused. In 1788 Maria Petraccini[1] took a degree in medicine at Florence, and we find her, a little later, lecturing on anatomy at Ferrara, in presence of the medical professors. She married Signor Feretti, and has left several works on the physical education of children.

Her daughter, Zaffini Feretti, seems to have inherited her mother's talents, for she studied Surgery in the University of Bologna, and there received a medical degree.[2]

Still more distinguished in the annals of Medicine was Maria delle Donne, who also studied in the University of Bologna, and "received the doctoral laurel" in 1806.[3] She "constantly practised both Medicine and Surgery," and was appointed by Napoleon Bonaparte to the Chair of Midwifery at Bologna. The "Raccoglitore Medico," in recording her death in 1842, speaks of her as "une des gloires scientifiques de Bologna."[4]

Nor was Italy alone noted as the birthplace of women skilled in Medicine. In Germany, early in this century, Frau von Siebold so greatly distinguished

1 Fachini. 2 Ibid. 3 Ibid.
4 *Gazette Médicale*, du 10 Janvier, 1846.

herself in the practice of midwifery that the degree of M.D. was conferred on her by the University of Giessen,[1] and her daughter Marianne, afterwards Frau von Heidenreich, studied in the Universities of both Göttingen and Giessen, and took her degree in the regular way in 1817. She is spoken of as "one of the most famed and eminent female scholars of Germany," and as being "universally honoured as one of the first living authorities in her special branch of science."[2] She died only in 1859.

In France, the name of Madame Lachapelle[3] was known and honoured as that of one of the ablest teachers of Midwifery during the latter part of the last century. She has left several valuable works on subjects connected with her specialty. Her pupil and successor, Madame Boivin,[4] was still more distinguished for her medical knowledge and skill, and for her contributions to anatomical science. In 1814 she was appointed co-director (with the Marquis de Belloy) of the General Hospital for Seine and Oise, and in 1815 was entrusted with the direction of a temporary Military Hospital, for her services in which latter capacity she received a public vote of thanks. She was honoured with the degree of M.D. from the University of Marbourg.

These numerous instances of the successful practice of Medicine by women seem to have been little known, or

[1] Klemm, "Die Frauen." [2] *Athenæum*, July 1859.

[3] Arnault's "Biographie nouvelle des Contemporains."

[4] Quérard's "Littérature Française."

else forgotten, to judge by the surprise expressed when, after surmounting many difficulties, an English lady named Elizabeth Blackwell succeeded in obtaining medical education and the degree of M.D. from a medical school in America in 1849. The novelty, in truth, was not in the granting of the medical degree to a woman, but in its being received by an Englishwoman, for it is hardly gratifying to one's national pride to find that England never has accorded such encouragement to female learning as was found in Italy, Germany, and France; and it is still more painful to realize that this country almost alone stands still aloof from the movement of liberal wisdom that has now in all these lands, as well as in Switzerland, and even in Russia, granted to women the advantage of University education and degrees. English women are not behind others in desiring knowledge, but as yet they are forced to seek it on foreign shores, for hitherto no British University has ever admitted women to its educational advantages, and a few years ago that of London, with all its professions of liberality, refused a woman's petition even for examination for the degree of M.D.!

So much for the historical evidence bearing on this question. I am indeed sorry to have paused so long on this part of the subject, but it seemed essential to a proper statement of the whole case.

If, then, nature does not instinctively forbid the practice of the healing art by women, and if it cannot be denied that some at least of its branches have long been in their hands, we must go further to seek on what grounds their admission to the medical profession should be opposed.

Probably the next argument will be that women do not require, and are not fitted to receive, the scientific education needful for a first-rate Physician, and that "for their own sakes" it is not desirable that they should pursue some of the studies indispensably necessary. To this the answer must be, that the wisest thinkers teach us to believe that each human being must be "a law unto himself," and must decide what is and what is not suitable for his needs, what will and what will not contribute to his own development, and fit him best to fulfil the life-work most congenial to his tastes. If women claim that they do need and can appreciate instruction in any or all sciences, I do not know who has the right to deny the assertion.

That this controversy is no new one may be proved by reference to a very curious black-letter volume now in the British Museum,[1] wherein the writer protests: "I mervayle gretely of the opynyon of some men that say they wolde not in no wyse that theyr doughters or wyves or kynneswomen sholde lerne scyences, and that it sholde apayre their cödycyons. This thing is not to say ne to sustayne. That the woman apayreth by connynge it is not well to beleve. As the proverbe saythe, 'that nature gyveth maye not be taken away.'"

If it be argued that the study of Natural Science may injure a woman's character, I would answer, in the words of one of the purest-minded women I know, that "if a

[1] "The Boke of the Cyte of Ladyes," by Christine Du Castel, 1521.

woman's womanliness is not deep enough in her nature to bear the brunt of any needful education, it is not worth guarding." It is, I think, inconceivable that any one who considers the study of natural science to be but another word for earnest and reverent inquiry into the works of God, and who believes that, in David's words, these are to be "sought out of all them that have pleasure therein," can imagine that any such study can be otherwise than elevating and helpful to the moral as well as to the mental nature of every student who pursues it in a right spirit. In the words of Scripture, "To the pure, all things are pure;" and in the phrase of chivalry, "Honi soit qui mal y pense."

It has always struck me as a curious inconsistency, that while almost everybody applauds and respects Miss Nightingale and her followers for their brave disregard of conventionalities on behalf of suffering humanity, and while hardly any one would pretend that there was any want of feminine delicacy in their going among the foulest sights and most painful scenes, to succour, not their own sex, but the other, many people yet profess to be shocked when other women desire to fit themselves to take the medical care of those of their sisters who would gladly welcome their aid. Where is the real difference? If a woman is to be applauded for facing the horrors of an army hospital when she believes that she can there do good work, why is she to be condemned as indelicate when she professes her willingness to go through an ordeal, certainly no greater, to obtain the education necessary for a medical practitioner? Surely work is in no way degraded by being made scientific; it cannot be commendable to obey instructions as a nurse when it would be unseemly to learn the reasons for them as a student, or to give them as a doctor; more especially as the nurse's duties may lead her, as they did in the Crimea, to attend on men with injuries and diseases of all kinds, whereas the woman who practises as a physician would confine her practice to women only. It is indeed hard to see any reason of delicacy, at least, which can be adduced in favour of women as nurses, and against them as physicians.

Their natural capacity for the one sphere or the other is, of course, a wholly different matter, and is, indeed, a thing not to be argued about, but to be tested. If women fail to pass the required examinations for the ordinary medical degree, or if, after their entrance into practice, they fail to succeed in it, the whole question is naturally and finally disposed of. But that is not the point now at issue.

That the most thorough and scientific medical education need do no injury to any woman might safely be prophesied, even if the experiment had never been tried; but we have, moreover, the absolute confirmation of experience on the point, as I, for one, will gladly testify from personal acquaintance in America with many women who have made Medicine their profession; having had myself the advantage of studying under one who was characterised, by a medical gentleman known throughout the professional world, as "one of the best physicians in Boston," and who, certainly, was more remarkable for thorough refinement of mind than most women I know,—Dr. Lucy Sewall.

Of course there may always be unfortunate exceptions, or rather there will always be those of both sexes who, whatever their profession may be, will be sure to disgrace it; but it is not of them that I speak, nor is it by such individual cases that the supporters of any great movement should be judged.

The next argument usually advanced against the practice of medicine by women is that there is no demand for it; that women, as a rule, have little confidence in their own sex, and had rather be attended by a man. That everybody had rather be attended by a competent physician is no doubt true; that women have hitherto had little experience of competent physicians of their own sex is equally true; nor can it be denied that the education bestowed on most women is not one likely to inspire much confidence. It is probably a fact, that until lately there has been "no demand" for women doctors, because it does not occur to most people to demand what does not exist; but that very many women have wished that they could be medically attended by those of their own sex I am very sure, and I know of more than one case where ladies have habitually gone through one confinement after another without proper attendance, because the idea of employing a man was so extremely repugnant to them. I have indeed repeatedly found that even doctors, not altogether favourable to the present movement, allow that they consider men rather out of place in midwifery practice; and an eminent American practitioner once remarked to me, that he never entered a lady's room to attend her in confinement without wishing to apologize for what he felt to be an intrusion, though a necessary and beneficent intrusion, in one of his sex.

I suppose that the real test of "demand" is not in the opinions expressed by those women who have never even seen a thoroughly educated female physician, but in the practice which flows in to any such physician when her qualifications are clearly satisfactory. In England there is at present but one woman legally qualified to practise Medicine, and I understand that already her time is much more fully occupied, and her receipts much greater, than is usually the case with a medical man who has been practising for so short a period. Her Dispensary for poor women is also largely attended, no less than 9,300 visits having been paid to it during the past year.

When we turn to America, we find that a considerable number of women have very extensive practice and large professional incomes (more indeed than in some cases seems warranted by their medical qualifications). The Report of a little hospital, managed entirely by women, in Boston, U.S., relates, that during 1867 the number of in-patients was 198; of persons visited at their homes, 281; and of those able to attend at the dispensary, 4,576; all these patients being women and children only. In fact, the attendance at the dispensary became so excessive in proportion to the resources of the charity, that in 1868 a rule was passed by the Committee requiring each patient to pay twenty-five cents (or about ninepence) for medicines, at each visit, except when she brought "a certificate of her poverty properly authenticated." This regulation brought out still more strongly the distinct *choice* of poor women in this matter; for though the General City Dispensary gave medicines gratuitously, the number of those who attended at the Women's Hospital was much less diminished than was expected, being still 3,236 in 1868. In New York also, where the dispensary managed by women doctors is but one of many, the crowd of patients is very great, the numbers being, in 1867, no less than 6,354, while 545 persons were attended at their homes either in confinement or during severe illness. Of course it will be understood that each patient thus entered on the books implies not one visit, but many, paid to the dispensary, or often repeated attendance at the patient's home.

Of the Boston Hospital for Women and Children I can speak from lengthened experience in it as a student. When standing in its dispensary, I have over and over again heard rough women of a very poor class say, when questioned why they had not had earlier treatment for certain diseases, "Oh, I *could not* go to a man with such a trouble, and I did not know till just now that ladies did this work;" and from others I have repeatedly heard different expressions of the feeling that "It's so nice, isn't it, to be able at last to ask ladies about such things?"

As I am alluding to my own experience in this

matter, I may perhaps be allowed to say how often in the same place I have been struck with the *contingent* advantages attendant on the medical care by women of women; how often I have seen cases connected with stories of shame or sorrow to which a woman's hand could far more fittingly minister, and where sisterly help and counsel could give far more appropriate succour than could be expected from the average young medical man, however good his intentions. Perhaps we shall find the solution of some of our saddest social problems when educated and pure-minded women are brought more constantly in contact with their sinning and suffering sisters, in other relations as well as those of missionary effort.

So far from there being no demand for women as physicians, I believe that there is at this moment a large amount of work actually awaiting them; that a large amount of suffering exists among women which never comes under the notice of medical men at all, and which will remain unmitigated till women are ready in sufficient numbers to attend medically to those of their own sex who need them, and this in all parts of the world. From India we hear urgent demands for "educating native women of good caste, so as to qualify them to treat female patients and children."[1] We are informed that "this is a work which can only be carried on by women, as the native women in many cases will rather die than be seen by a man in times of sickness," and arrangements are already being made for

[1] *Delhi Gazette*, 1866.

a systematic "Female Medical Mission," though perhaps the standard of medical knowledge required, can, under existing circumstances, hardly be fixed as high as is desirable. No doubt the value of this measure, among others, must depend in a great degree on the facilities for thorough medical study, and subsequent examinations, given or refused to women in England.

About eight or ten years ago, "several of the wild tribes of Russian Asia petitioned the Government to send them out properly qualified women to act as midwives. Their petition was granted, the Government undertaking all the expense of the education and maintenance of a certain number of women for this purpose. After a time one of these tribes, the Kirgesen, petitioned further, that the women thus sent to them should also be taught some branches of the art of Medicine. One of the women then being trained as a midwife, hearing of this petition, wrote to the Kirgesen, proposing that she should study Medicine thoroughly, and go out to them as a qualified doctor. She suggested at the same time that they should try to get permission for her to enter the Academy of St. Petersburg as a regular medical student. The Kirgesen welcomed the proposal, and, through an influential Russian general, obtained an official document, empowering their future doctor to attend the Academy as a student. They have regularly sent money for her education and maintenance, and from the first have taken the greatest interest in her progress and welfare, requiring, among other things, periodical bulletins of her health. Hearing last summer that she was not well, they sent money for her to go abroad for her holiday, and asked for an extra bulletin."[1]

I cite the above facts to show that the demand for female physicians is no artificial or imaginary one, and that it does not spring out of any fanciful whim of an over-refined social state; but lest it should be supposed on the other hand to be confined to half-barbarous nations, I may quote the opinions expressed on this subject two years ago in one of the most thoughtful of our English journals: "We heartily admit that the only way to discriminate clearly what practical careers women are, and are not, fitted for, is to let them try. In many cases, as in the medical profession, we do not feel any doubt that they will find a special kind of work for which they are specially fitted, which has never been adequately done by men at all, and which never would be done but by women. . . . We have heard the opinion of one of the most eminent of our living physicians, that one of the new lady physicians is doing, in the most admirable manner, a work which medical men would never even have had the chance of doing."[2]

There can be little doubt that an enormous amount of preventible suffering arises from the unwillingness of very many girls on the verge of womanhood, to consult a medical man on various points which are yet of vital importance, and to appeal to him in cases of apparently slight illness, which yet issue but too

[1] *Macmillan's Magazine*, September 1868.
[2] *Spectator*, April 13, 1867.

often in ultimately confirmed ill-health. I firmly believe that if a dozen competent women entered upon medical practice at this moment in different parts of England, they might, without withdrawing a single patient from her present medical attendant, find full and remunerative employment in attending simply to those cases which, in the present state of things, go without any adequate treatment whatever; for I believe that many suffering women would be willing to consult one of their own sex, if thoroughly qualified, when they refuse, except at some crisis of acute suffering, to call in a medical man. Probably Queen Isabella of Castile[1] was neither the first nor the last woman whose life was sacrificed to her modesty. Even if such extreme instances are rare, I think it cannot be denied that very much needless pain, "and pain of a kind that ought not to be inflicted," is caused, especially to young girls, by the necessity of consulting men on all occasions, and I believe that those who know most of the facts insist most strongly on this point.

I do not know how far the Medical Profession would acknowledge the truth of the above statement: it is probable that they are really less competent to judge about it than women are themselves, for, as an eminent divine remarked that it was considered a point of politeness not to express theological doubts before a clergyman, it may probably be thought still more

[1] "Concerning her death, it was magnanimous and answerable to the courage of heroes," &c.—*Gallerie of Heroick Women*, written in French by Pierre le Moyne, and translated by the Marquess of Winchester, 1652.

obligatory not to question the adequacy of the existing medical profession before one of its members. One can hardly imagine a lady sending for a doctor to tell him why she will not consult him; it is sufficient to know that many cases of disease among women go without treatment: it is surely open to us, at least, to suggest the above as one of the possible reasons.

And indeed, if no such special suffering were often involved in the idea of consulting a man on all points, it seems self-evident that a woman's most natural adviser would be one of her own sex, who must surely be most able to understand and sympathise with her in times of sickness as well as of health, and who can often far more fully appreciate her state, both of mind and body, than any medical man would be likely to do.

Of course, time will show whether my belief in this matter is well founded; but allowing even for considerable over-statement on my part, there may still remain subject for serious consideration. Even if I am wholly mistaken, and if all that needs doing *can* in England be effectually done by men, we have still, I think, no reason for the exclusion of women from the medical profession;—there is still no ground on which it can be right to refuse to every patient the power of election between a physician of her own sex and of the other, when women as well as men are desirous of qualifying themselves for their work, seeing that it will after all be always a matter of choice; for we cannot suppose that the time will ever come when women will be arbitrarily prevented from employing men, as they now are arbitrarily prevented from employing women, as their medical attendants.

The assertion that women *are* at present "arbitrarily prevented from employing women as their medical attendants" may sound startling, but it is at this moment practically true in England in the most literal sense. Since medical practice has been, for the protection of the public, made a matter of legislation, it has been absolutely illegal for any physician or surgeon to practise as such in this country, unless registered by the appointed Medical Board, and that Board is not obliged to register any one who has not a British medical degree. It is evident, then, that to deny all British medical degrees to women,—not only to refuse them instruction, but to refuse to examine them if they have acquired knowledge elsewhere,—*is* most arbitrarily to prohibit all women, whatever their qualification, from practising medicine in the United Kingdom, except under legal pains and penalties.

Of course no such arbitrary action was ever contemplated when the Act of 1858 was passed, and I think that when once the great practical injustice of the present state of things is fully understood by the public, a change is inevitable,—either British medical degrees will be thrown open to women, as is most desirable, or the legal conditions of practice will be modified to meet the case of those to whom such degrees are denied. It is perhaps hardly to be expected, though very much to be desired, that medical men as a body should themselves take the initiative in this matter, and throw open the doors to all women who desire worthily to join their fellowship, for it proverbially "needs *very* good men to give up their own monopoly;" but the action of the general public in the matter can hardly be doubtful except as a question of time;—no English court could be expected to condemn to legal penalties a succession of highly-educated ladies who may have seized, often with great effort, every opportunity open to them to fit themselves thoroughly for a work which they believe to be especially their own.

The recent action taken in the matter by the authorities at Apothecaries' Hall is exactly of the kind to outrage an Englishman's sense of fairness, and therefore is sure before long to bring its own redress. As the facts may not be thoroughly understood in the non-medical world, I will briefly recapitulate them. When Miss Garrett first began to study medicine in 1860, she tried to obtain admittance to one School and University after another, and finally found that Apothecaries' Hall was the only body which, from its charter (using, I believe, the word "homo" instead of "vir,"), had no power to refuse to examine any candidate complying with its conditions. She accordingly went through the required five years' apprenticeship, and obtained her diploma in 1865, having gone to very great additional expense in obtaining privately the required lectures by recognised Professors,—sometimes paying fifty guineas for a course when the usual fee, in the classes from which she was debarred, was but five. Not content, however, within directly imposing this enormous pecuniary tax on women, the authorities now bethought them to pass a rule forbidding students to receive any part of their medical education privately,—this course being publicly advised by one of the leading medical journals as a safe way of evading the obligations of the charter, and yet effectually shutting out the one chance left to the women!

Of course the efficacy of this measure ceases the moment that any regular medical school opens its doors to women; but till that day comes, it presents a formidable, if not insuperable, difficulty. Commenting on this proceeding, the *Daily News* remarks: "We recommend these facts to the good people who think that coercion, restriction, and the tyranny of combination are peculiar to any one class of society. It will be a great day in England when the right of every individual to make the most of the ability which God has given him, free from interested interference, is recognised, and to that goal we are surely advancing; but our progress is slow, and it is very clear that it is not only in the lower ranks of the community that the obstructive trades-union spirit is energetically operating."

While such is the state of affairs in England, other European nations have taken a very different position. We have already seen that the Italian Universities were in fact never closed to women, and that at Bologna no less than three women held Professors' chairs in the Medical Faculty.[1] We have several instances of degrees

[1] Besides these we have, at Bologna,—Maddalena Buonsignori, Professor of Laws, 1380; Laura Bassi, Professor of Philosophy, 1733; Maria Gaetana

granted to women in the Middle Ages by the Universities of Bologna, Padua, Milan, Pavia, and others; the earliest instance that I have found being that of Betisia Gozzadini,[1] who was made Doctor of Laws by the University of Bologna in 1209. In Germany also such instances have occurred. At the University of Paris no less than four degrees in Arts and Sciences have been granted to women within the last five years, and three women are now studying in its Medical School. In answer to inquiries, the Secretary to the Minister of Public Instruction made the following communication:—

"Je m'empresse de vous faire savoir que le Ministre est disposé à vous autoriser, aussi que les autres dames anglaises qui se destineraient à la médecine, à faire vos études à la faculté de Paris, et à y subir des examens."[2]

One woman received a degree in Arts from the University of Lyons in 1861, and another obtained the same at Montpellier in 1865. A Russian woman named Nadejda Suslowa took a degree in Medicine at the University of Zurich in 1867, and eight women are now studying in the Medical School there. Even the Medico-Chirurgical School of St. Petersburg granted the degree of M.D. to a woman but a few weeks ago (1869), and two ladies have recently been studying in the Medical School at Vienna.

The contrast here presented is not agreeable to English

Agnesi, Professor of Mathematics, 1750; Clothilde Tambroni, Professor of Greek, 1794; and also other instances at Milan and at Cordova.

[1] Ghirardacci, "Historia Bologna;" Bologna, 1605.

[2] *Spectator*, August 1868.

self-respect, and it is to be hoped that it will not be of long duration.

There seems to be practically no doubt now that women are and will be doctors. The only question really remaining is, how thoroughly they are to be educated and fitted to take their share of responsibility in the care of the life and health of the nation ; how far their difficulties are to be lightened or increased ; and whether the state of things shall continue by which they are driven into unwilling quackery on the one hand, or made to suffer real oppression from irresponsible authority on the other.

Men who, after an irregular education and incomplete training, claim the name of physicians, are justly stigmatized as quacks, and excluded from honourable fellowship, for they have refused the straight and direct path as too laborious, and have sought admittance by crooked ways. It is right enough to impose heavy penalties on them for practising without a diploma, which it needs only industry on their part to obtain ; but what shall we say when women are refused admission to every regular Medical School, and then, when they have perhaps painfully and laboriously gathered their own education, either in England or abroad, are excluded from the fellowship of the profession, for the sin of having been unjustly treated ! That some women have succeeded in acquiring most competent medical knowledge and skill can hardly be denied, except by those who really know nothing of the facts, or are wilfully blind to them ; but in almost every case they have done so at a cost of money, effort, and personal sacrifice, that can be expected only from the few. Imagine all medical students met by the difficulties which female students must encounter,—how many properly educated doctors should we have?

Many persons, however, who would gladly see women engage in the practice of Medicine, yet think it undesirable that they should obtain their education in the same schools as men; and here another practical point arises for consideration.

If it is indeed true that no one is fit for the profession of Medicine unless able to banish from its practice the personal idea of sex, it certainly seems as if all earnest students, seeking the same knowledge for the same ends, ought to be able to pursue their studies together. We are constantly told (and I think rightly) that no woman *need* object, when necessary, to consult a medical man on any point, because the physician will see in it simply an impersonal "case," and will, from his scientific standpoint, practically ignore all that would be embarrassing as between persons of opposite sexes. If this is and ought to be true, it does not seem too much to demand equal delicacy of feeling among those who will in a year or two be themselves physicians; and from personal experience when studying in large American hospitals with students of both sexes, I believe that no serious difficulty need ever occur, except in cases of really exceptional coarseness of character on one side or the other. That such joint study will be for the first few days novel and embarrassing is of course natural; but I believe that, as the first novelty wears off, the embarrassment too will disappear in the interest of a common study, and that no thoroughly pure-minded woman, with an ordinary amount of tact, need ever fear such association with students of whom the majority will always be gentlemen. It is of course a radically different thing to study any or all subjects with earnest scientific interest, and to discuss them lightly in common conversation.

Not only in America has the system of joint education been tried, but at Paris and at Zurich ladies are at the present moment studying in the regular Medical Schools, and friends at each place assure me of the complete success of the experiment, if such it is considered.

Miss Putnam (the first lady ever admitted to the Parisian Medical School) writes thus: "There is not the slightest restriction on my studies or my presence at the Classes. . . . I have never found the slightest difficulty in studying with the young men with whom I am associated, not only at lectures, but in the hospitals, reading-room, laboratory, &c. I have always been treated with a courtesy at once frank and respectful." Another lady, now studying at Zurich, reports, that "in the Medical School of Zurich, no advantage which is afforded to the male students is denied to the women. Every class is open to them, and they work side by side with the men. The students have invariably been to me most friendly, helpful, and courteous." In answer to an official letter of inquiry, the Dean of the Medical Faculty at Zurich writes: "Since 1867, ladies have been regularly admitted as matriculated students, and have been allowed all the privileges of *cives academici.* As far as our experience has gone, the new practice has not in any way been found to damage the interests of the University. The lady students we have hitherto had have all been found to behave with great good taste, and to be diligent students." Such evidence must surely carry more weight than the opinions of those who merely theorize about probabilities, especially when such theorists start, as is often the case, with a predisposition to find "lions in the way."

If the admission of women to the regular Medical Schools has been proved to bring no evil consequences, it needs strong arguments to justify their exclusion from advantages which they can hardly obtain elsewhere; for it has been well remarked, that nothing can be more false than to confound a "small injustice" with "injustice to a small number."

It is simply a mockery, and one calculated to mislead the public, when an influential medical journal[1] announces that "We would offer no obstacle to any steps which women may think would be conducive to their own benefit. But if it be indispensable that they should study Anatomy and Medicine, let them, in the interests of common decency, have an educational institution and licensing body of their own." And again, "If women are determined to become Medical Practitioners, they are at perfect liberty to do so; but it is only consistent with decency that they should have their own special Schools and examining bodies." Such writers know perfectly well that it is utterly impossible for two or three strug-

[1] *Medical Times and Gazette,* Feb. 23, 1867, and April 24, 1869.

gling women students to found "their own special Schools," (though, when a sufficient number of women are educated, they may gladly make such provision for those who will succeed them,) and that, if in truth women as well as men have a right to claim opportunities of education, the duty of providing separate instruction for them clearly falls on the existing Schools, if the authorities refuse to admit them to share in the general advantages offered.

For myself, I cannot see why difficulties that have in France and Switzerland been proved chimerical, should in England be supposed (without trial) to be insurmountable ; as I, for one, cannot believe that less good and gentlemanly feeling should be expected from English and Scotch students than is found among those of foreign Universities.

But this is a point which I do not greatly care to urge; although Medical Science can undoubtedly be most favourably studied under those conditions which only large institutions can command, and which could for many years be but imperfectly attained in a Medical College designed for women only. Still there is no doubt that women thoroughly in earnest, and with a certain amount of means at their command, can obtain adequate medical instruction without entering any of the existing Schools for men, and no doubt arrangements could be made to secure all that is necessary, with much less effort and expense than at present. We should be very thankful to have the Medical Schools thrown open to us, to be allowed some share in the noble provision made, chiefly with public money, for the instruction of medical students: but this is not absolutely indispensable; we may be refused this and yet gain our end, though with greater toil and at greater expense. As time goes on, and as the number of women attracted by the study of Medicine increases, it will probably, apart from all extrinsic considerations, be both natural and convenient that they should have a Medical School of their own, in which every means of study should be specially provided for, and adapted to, their needs. It is not however, I think, desirable that this should be done until the number of students is sufficient to guarantee funds for the liberal payment of first-rate teachers, and the ample provision of all needful facilities. If no women are to be made competent physicians till they have a school of their own, there never will be any at all; for those who broadly oppose the movement will always be able to say, "Women have never proved that they can use such advantages as will be thus furnished; do not establish a College for them till they have."

So the double argument would run thus: "Do not found a Female Medical School till we are sure that women can successfully study Medicine; do not let any woman study Medicine except in a Medical School of their own." Between such a Scylla and Charybdis, who can steer clear?

Supposing, however, that this dilemma were escaped, and that adequate means of instruction were provided (with men, or apart from them, I care not), it would still I think be essential, not only to the interests of women doctors, but to those of the public at large, that the standard for medical practitioners of both sexes should be identical; that women should be admitted to the examinations already established for men, and should receive their medical degree on exactly the same terms. I do not for a moment desire to see degrees granted to women by a College of their own, or to see a special examination instituted for them; for there would be extreme difficulty in measuring the exact value of any such diplomas, and danger would arise, on the one hand, of injustice being done to those thoroughly competent, but possessing "only a woman's degree," and on the other of the standard being really lowered, and the medical degree coming to possess an uncertain and inferior value.

Of this latter danger we have abundant warning in America, where every fresh College is allowed the right of "graduating" its own students on whatever terms it pleases, and where, indeed, one is confounded by the innumerable diplomas granted by all sorts of Colleges to all sorts of people, so that one has need to inquire whether the M.D. attached to a name represents a degree granted by some "Eclectic" or "Hygeio-therapeutic" College of mushroom growth, or by the Universities of Harvard and Yale.

We cannot wish for such a state of things in England. Let British degrees continue to be of perfectly definite value; make the conditions as stringent as you please, but let them be such as are attainable by all students, and are clearly understood by the general public; and then, for all that would worthily win and wear the desired honours, "a fair field and no favour."

Is there not one of the English, Scotch, or Irish Medical Schools or Universities that will win future laurels by now taking the lead generously, and announcing its willingness to cease, at least, its policy of arbitrary exclusion? Let the authorities, if they please, admit women to study in the ordinary Classes, with or without any special restrictions (and it is hard to believe that at least the greater part of the lectures could not be attended in common); or let them allow the women to matriculate, and then, if they think needful, bid them make their own arrangements, and gather their knowledge as they can; with this promise only, that, when acquired, such knowledge shall be duly tested, and, if found worthy, shall receive the Hall-mark of the regular Medical Degree.

Surely this is not too much to ask, and no more is absolutely essential. If indeed the assertions so often made about the incapacity of women are true, the result of such examinations (which may be both theoretical and practical, scientific and clinical) will triumphantly prove the point. If the examinations are left in the hands of competent men, we may be very sure that all unqualified women will be summarily rejected, as indeed we desire that they should be.

If, on the contrary, some women, however few, can under all existing disadvantages successfully pass the ordeal, and go forth with the full authority of the degree of Doctor of Medicine, surely all will be glad to welcome their perhaps unexpected success, and bid every such woman, as she sets forth on her mission of healing, a hearty God-speed!

V.

THE TEACHING OF SCIENCE.

BY JAMES STUART, M.A.

In this Essay there are three things that fall to be considered. The first is, What it is that we wish to teach when we say, let us teach Science to women; and the second is, How we are to teach it; and the third is, Why we are to teach it. I shall not consider these three things separately, because each involves the other. At the beginning too I should like to say, that when I speak of teaching Science, I speak of teaching it not to the few, who may extend its boundaries, but to the many, who may learn its lessons. To those few Nature, I dare say, is the best instructor, and her own philosophy will plead her own cause. But for the mass of people there is a great benefit to be gained from the study of Science. Science teaches us to look outside of ourselves, and to look at *things;* and it teaches us that the foundation of all true argument is experiment, whereby I mean a previous knowledge of the things about which we argue. And, besides teaching us to look outside of ourselves, it teaches us to think for ourselves. One of the true objects of all education is to teach people to think for themselves. And there is perhaps nothing more fitted for this end than Science, and especially that department of it which is called Natural Philosophy. For to think well we must think clearly. What Education has to do is to engender the habit of forming clear and distinct notions of things, and, above all, of clearly seeing the distinction between these things themselves and our notions of them. The process of acquiring clear and distinct notions is of as much importance as having them. And to reap the benefit of that process we each must go through it for ourselves. In getting into the habit of going through such a process for ourselves we may be helped in three ways. We may be taught by example what the holding of a clear and distinct notion is; we may learn to some extent the successive steps by which some such have been elicited out of confusion; and we may be furnished with some materials from which to elicit some clear and distinct notions for ourselves. All these three ends are well accomplished by the teaching of Natural Philosophy, or, as it is otherwise called, Physical Science; on account of which pre-eminent union of these three qualities there is nothing which can form a fitter introduction to a course of Education, nor anything therefore with which those, whose education like that of women has been somewhat backward, can better begin. The only objection which might be anticipated to such a subject is that it might be too difficult. But everything which is clear and distinct is easy; it is obscurity only that makes difficulty. Nor need any be afraid of the name Physical Science—Astronomy, Light, Heat, and the like. It is certain that these sciences, in so far as they have been scientifically treated, have been usually involved in the language of Mathematics. But there is no need for that. It is very fortunate that Science has had Mathematics for its handmaid, for therein is the best pioneer and the best registrar of its discoveries; but it is unfortunate for the general scientific education of the world that it has usually refused the services of all other ministers. It is no more necessary to express the great truths of these matters in mathematical language than in the French or in the Greek language; and when the whole is put in our own homely language, perhaps then better than at any other time are we enabled to see how grandly immutable are the facts we have to deal with as compared with the means by which we may happen to express them. For though mathematical language entails an accuracy of expression, it is by no means co-ordinate therewith. Certainly I believe, though there be notable instances to the contrary, that yet scientific eminence is seldom attained by those ignorant of the Mathematics; and while I therefore believe every teacher of Science ought to have that knowledge, yet that by no means implies such a knowledge in those taught. And the more acute the mathematical ability of the teacher, the less will he require to presuppose that ability in those whom he teaches. There are some of the processes of nature which are most generally represented in the language of differential equations, to translate which requires a very thorough comprehension of them; but yet it can be done, and that in many complicated cases. I mention this, for it behoves us to remember that in teaching Science to women we have to teach it to those who, in the present state of women's education, for the most part are quite ignorant of the usual preliminaries, and especially of the Mathematics. On which account it has been that, generally speaking, there have only been small portions of Science to which women have ever been admitted, and those rather of a vague and indeterminate kind; whereas one of the chief benefits of Science is in its freedom from vagueness. And on this same account it has been that most of the scientific teaching that has been given to women has consisted rather in the mere enumeration of simple unsuggestive facts, or of the detail of theories, that is, the results of processes, the processes themselves being altogether omitted.

And there can be little wonder that such study has never prospered among women, who thereby get a distaste, and exhibit a disqualification, not for Science, but for that which they are taught. But the true education which may be brought to us by the teaching of Physical Science consists not in the detailing of facts, nor in the detailing of results; nay, nor even in the detailing of a process, but in so presenting facts that the learner shall at each step be able to advance along the next step of the process for himself. For as we advance along our thought, we come at each succeeding step to many diverging roads; to throw a light across the whole landscape bewilders the young traveller, to carry whom blindfold to the end leaves him unstrengthened for the next attempt. But true teaching is so to hold the lantern that he may at each turn choose the right road for himself. Thus, if I were to conclude it in a word, I should say that the true process of scientific teaching is to lead the learner along a road of continual discovery. For that process of ourselves repeating a discovery is that whereby, far beyond all talk of it, we learn what suggestion means; and that whereby we learn, from the repetition of our own success, that which no argument could lead us to.

To teach a process suggestively we must of course adapt ourselves to that which will be suggestive to the person taught; so that teaching of this kind is somewhat of a sympathetic thing, for some need more prompting to a suggestion than others. And it is on this account that nothing can ever supersede the oral teaching of Science and the Mathematics, for in oral teaching alone is there that facility of adaptation.

What is exactly meant by suggestive teaching is, like all good things, best learned by that most practical of answers, the invitation to the practice of it; and within the limits of an Essay like the present it is hard to give an example. If some one were to ask me why the moon has phases; then, if I were to call his attention to the fact, and bid him look for several nights to see, that it was rounded towards the sun, and bid him watch how its bright part increased or diminished, and then were to show him a dusty ball illuminated by a candle, that would be a piece of suggestive teaching. To some the process would have to be carried a little farther ere their mind would anticipate the explanation. To others, their first observations would be sufficient : these are they to whom so far Nature is herself suggestive, which she is in a large way to those called discoverers, whose frame of mind it is that we aim at, and not the making of discoveries in the natural world. For let us steer clear of that error that the only reason that Science is to be taught to us is that we may extend its boundaries ; but that for which we learn it is this, that we may learn its habit of mind in all things, and that habit of mind is one in which we see what things have to do with one another. For it is a mistake into which men sometimes fall, to see in each piece of instruction nothing beyond its own specialty, wherefrom there arises that utilitarian argument that those things which are of immediate use are the rather to be taught.

A point of importance here occurs ; for it would seem that the full benefit of oral teaching was only to be gained when that teaching was individual. And there can be no doubt that to a certain extent this is true; but not so much as at first sight might be thought ; and especially in the case of the ignorant, who are generally pretty fairly in one stage of advancement. Nay, further, even to a very mixed audience much true Science may be thus suggestively taught ; for there are some paths which may be trod by all ; and there is nothing which is true, however simple, which is not instructive, so that from a rude and almost mechanical delineation of the deduction of gravity from Kepler's laws, I have seen fair mathematicians learn a clearer comprehension of that process.

To extend the benefit of the oral teaching of Science to a large class by means of lectures is a point which is very desirable. It is very desirable on this account, that there is a growing demand throughout the country for the teaching of Physical Science; a livelier interest is displayed in it, the questions which it involves are brought before people, and they desire to have some knowledge of these questions for themselves; and, further, the knowledge of the great excellence of scientific study as a discipline of the mind and a means of general education is becoming daily more and more recognised. From the nature of the subject and its growing interest, I believe this demand and that recognition will continue to increase. Now, there are not many competent to teach Science, so that it is apt to fall into hands unfit to teach it; and to obtain true scientific teaching is thus not very possible at present, except for large classes. Those who are competent from their knowledge to teach it are for the most part so much engaged in the pursuit of it themselves, that their services as oral teachers can only be available to a restricted section of the community; and Science falls into the danger of being taught by those who have what they teach entirely at second-hand, whereby it is too apt to become superficial.

They who are the true teachers of a thing are they who speak out of a mind very full of it; and the more simple a view we try to give of a complicated process, the more necessary is it that we should understand that process thoroughly in all the refinements of its details; for it is then, and then only, that words become full of suggestion and bear with them more than they say; so that the number of those at present both able and willing to undertake the oral and elementary teaching of Science is small. Under these circumstances, it seems to me that any experience as to the teaching of Science to large classes is a matter of considerable importance. And so, at the risk of being egotistical, I will give a short account of my own experience in that matter. It is a good thing for a man who is acquainted with some part of Science to give a lecture about it, and especially a good thing if he gives a course of lectures; but this can hardly be called teaching Science in an elementary way. It may rouse up in all a sort of desire of the subject; and to hear a man who knows a thing talk about it cannot fail to instruct us. Yet, in any attempt to make Science a means of imparting Education—to employ it, in fact, as a means of higher education—the class to whom it is taught must be carried on as a whole, and their understanding of the subject must be tested. In the autumn of 1867 I lectured on Physical Astronomy to four classes of ladies in Liverpool, Leeds, Manchester, and Sheffield, numbering respectively, 80, 100, 160, and 200. These ladies were unacquainted with Geometry or Algebra. In order that they might have some knowledge of the subject, and therefore be in a better position to reap benefit from what they might hear, I had recommended, several months beforehand, the reading of certain very elementary works about Natural Philosophy, taking care that any abridgment which I recommended had been made by some one who was well acquainted with the subject he abridged. Each lecture lasted for an hour. In some instances where it might be difficult to follow it, I had printed beforchand a syllabus to which I referred as I went on. After each lecture I either had distributed printed papers, or dictated a few questions upon the subject of the lecture, which were to be answered in writing at home by those who should choose to answer them. On an average about 300 of the whole number gave me written answers to these questions, which I looked over and corrected, and returned to the writers with occasional verbal comments. This occupied generally about half an hour after the conclusion of each lecture. I encouraged the asking of questions in these papers, which I answered either individually or to the whole class, according to their nature. The questions which were asked of me were in general very much to the point, and gave me the most valuable assistance, as showing me where the class was succeeding or not succeeding in appreciating what I said. The lectures occurred at weekly intervals; and I believe the chief part of the instruction which the pupils got was that which they gave themselves in the necessary consideration of the subject which the answering of these questions entailed. Of the papers which I received some were pre-eminently good, and the average of the papers showed a thorough appreciation of the subject. The point of a question was seldom missed. I generally before each lecture made some verbal comments on the answers which I had received to the questions proposed after the preceding lecture; and I found that a great benefit arose from beginning each lecture with a careful *resumé* of the one which went before.

In teaching such matters to women perhaps the chief difficulty lies in their general ignorance of Arithmetic, arising, as far as I have been able to observe, from the inefficient way in which for the most part it is taught to them. This ignorance of Arithmetic, and of any intelligent practice in the application of it, is a hindrance to women acquiring much from books which they might otherwise acquire, and occasions waste of time often in the explanation of things; and I mention this matter here, as I believe that undoubtedly the most practical contribution which can at present be made at women's schools to their scientific education, and which is needed to be made, is the improvement of the teaching of Arithmetic, including therein, as there ought always to be included, the very elementary parts of Algebra. Improved teaching in that respect can be got from those whose services may be obtained at women's schools; and if such, along with some of the most elementary considerations of Geometry, were substituted for all that which usually goes there by the name of Science, great good would be wrought for women's general education.

I have spoken in the first person; but the reader will kindly understand that I only do so for the sake of definiteness, and that others have pursued similar plans with similar results, and have formed similar opinions. And they have found, too, that the average appreciation shown by women for scientific subjects is undoubtedly high. Mr. Aldis, who has lectured to them on the history of Physical Science, says, "Some write admirable papers, good in matter, in style, and in writing; and I certainly have found a large number capable of taking a real enlightened interest in the subject brought before them. . . . . What pleased me the most were the questions asked after the lectures; I saw so clearly then what the difficulties were which they chiefly felt." If any one feels an intelligent difficulty, he is in a fair way to learn.

These testimonies from various hands are satisfactory, as showing that large classes may obtain individual benefit, and, to a great extent, the equivalent of individual instruction; and thus, that the teaching of a good man may be obtained where at present it otherwise could not be obtained.

If there be any lesson which is taught us by Science it is this,—that to be helped we must help ourselves; and that which is a meaningless accident to some, is the material of a discovery to those from whose eyes previous thought has removed the scales. Whence, not only before but during the lectures too, it is well to recommend some reading, and continual observations and rude experiments on points connected therewith; for one thing done is worth a thousand heard; and there is a great solver of many difficulties and a great guide to truth in something looked at and investigated for ourselves, something experimental, upon which to base our argument. For there is no success in Science—nay, and I would fancy there is no success in anything—which is not based upon such a procedure. And it is a method which the world stands vastly in need of learning just now; for, though we boast of ours being a very scientific age, the multitude therein are going under cover of the character of a few. But among the greater part of mankind there is a great evil, the evil of speculation unbridled by experiment; for experiment is the great tamer of wild theory. But hypothetical experiments may be bandied about easily, and hypothesis is grandly favourable to a preconception. Hence it is that many fair wits in the world, full of speculation and full of power and full of leisure, are all astray as to their knowledge of things, and tossed on the waves of their own theories, from the lack of that "fountain of the rivers of our arts," real experiment, the habit of which education is at present too little given to foster, and without which history tells us, and our own experience might show us, no question of Physical Science can be determined. I talk of Physical Science—I would go farther, and speak of moral things. It seems to me that the whole of our true knowledge of all things, material and of the Soul alike, is founded on experiment—various indeed in the two cases, but yet experiment;—that is, knowledge gained by ourselves, the immediate result of our own labour, free from preconception.

Much theory is founded on the imaginary results of hypothetical experiments; between which kind of theory and that which is founded on experiment actually made with our own hands, and seen with our own eyes, there is a difference so vast as to be comprehended in no argument, but to be learned only by the experience of that magic which there is in our recognition of the magnitude and reality of things as altogether apart from our views of them. For there are two kinds of theorists. There are those who make a great framework which is their theory, and into which they fit the facts; and there are those whose theory is like a map of the things, which are placed thereby more within the grasp of our immediate handling. For things are real and existing, and we wander among them and look; and the true spirit of Science recognises the greatness of things as compared with our views of them, which views are fleeting, and moulded variously according to our vantage-ground.

What shall we say then of those who, destitute of the spirit of true Science, would compel a whole prospect within the limits of their theory, to whose imagining the double-sided shield can only be the metal it presents? There is but one thing they want, which is Humility; whence it is that there rise about us such mazes of man's conceptions, buildings of sophistries, concealed assumptions, and procrustean beds.

And lest any think that in these remarks I have sprung to too great a generality but too faintly connected with the subject in hand, it is to be remembered that it is from the lack of that which I would call the true spirit of Science that Science is sometimes objected to for the education of women. To deny to women the study of Science is a procedure which begets its own argument; as, if I were to beat a child for future crimes, the future would most likely justify that punishment, which vicious circle of action is bended round a preconception. And our attempt to bend things to our preconceived notion of what they should be is the fundamental of many errors.

The absence of the true Scientific spirit in our day is nowhere more evident than in the popular judgment of this matter of the Education of women. There is scarcely any subject on which there is among men so much of dogmatic assertion based on the imaginary results of a hypothetical experiment, and sometimes having not even so much basis as this. It has been affirmed, and not in this age and country alone, that women do not *need* to be taught Science, an immediate and direct utility being all that has been kept in view, and the true end lost sight of.

By some it is maintained that women do not need to learn Science to make them better women or abler to help and bless the world, and that they also are incapable of being scientifically educated. Those who make this double assertion are consistent, so far as their theory goes; for if their theory be true, God has done wisely in so far that He has limited the capacity to the need, as in the case of the lower animals, to whom He has given neither the need nor the capacity for a scientific education. But experiment, so far as it has gone in the education of women, has thrown these unscientific persons into an inconsistency. For they either have to prove in the face of experiment, by some arguments not yet discovered, that their position is a consistent one, or they have to give up their position; the only other alternative being that they should accuse the Creator of women of a great folly. For when they confess (and now facts drive them to this confession) that women are very capable indeed of receiving a true scientific education, and while they at the same time declare that women do not need such scientific education, inasmuch as it will not, they say, make them better women, wives, and mothers, they traduce the wisdom of God, who gave to these women the capacity for Science, and who has adjusted every means to an end, as Science hath itself shown, and every gift to some good result to be wrought out by the use of it. And herein, they being not only theorizers on this head, but being the stronger, and therefore practically the awarders to women of such share in the means of knowledge and education as they think fit to grant to them, they are not only impugners of the loving wisdom of God, who adapted women's brains wisely to the end which He designed for their exercise, but they create a great moral evil, and a sorrow, and a loss, by this shutting up of powers, and by this denial to women of the means of using and improving the good gifts which they have got. Truly those who will not base their theories concerning such weighty things on true experiment are continually driven to accuse God of folly, as palpably as a zoologist would who should shut up an eagle within a narrow cage for its life, and then assert that it had never mounted into the air, could not do so, and did not need to do so, albeit he had found by examination that its pinions were so constructed as to lift it forward and upward with a great strength and swiftness.

Now, speaking from experience, I should readily say that there is as great an aptitude for the study of these things in the mind of a woman of average capacity as in the mind of a man of the same. For, of all things, that which is required to pursue the study of Science is that which that study doth itself generate,—a certain humility of mind, which I think I have observed, at least in these matters, to be greater among women than among men;—whereby they are led to hold their conclusions rather in suspense, which is the desirable state of mind for the pursuit of Science.

But there is one objection which I believe to lie near the heart of many people when it is proposed that Science should be taught to women, or at any rate when it is proposed that it should form an introduction to their education, and any large portion of it: that is, that it is a kind of study which unfits them for the duties which more particularly belong to them; it is, say they, a harsh, masculine sort of study; it is one opposed to woman's grace and woman's simplicity; to that noble character of a true woman, which is so fair a thing in the world. This is an objection to which, if it were valid, I would readily give place, very different from that unkindly one which would deny them the study of it because they do not clamour for it. Yet I do not fear but that Nature will ever vindicate herself, and the glorious character of true womanhood would rise from all the attacks of a false Science; for I have seen it rise hitherto above the lack of true Science. Nor am I so distrustful of the strength of woman's nature as to think it to be in such unstable equilibrium. Nay, but there is in woman's nature that peculiar union of humility and of conviction which all Science is, as I would take it, God-sent into the world to teach, whereby she is led to assimilate those lessons therein to which her own heart is tuned, as in music those strings that are tuned to a certain note do vibrate when that note is sounded.

There are many women who are now saying, after but a short period of instruction in Science, that they look upon these studies as little less than divine. Whereby they mean that they have brought to their minds and hearts a degree of that help and strength, light and health, which they are accustomed to recognise as a direct gift from God, whether He sends them by means of these messages of His which are hidden up and down everywhere in the natural world, or in answer to the prayer of the humble soul without these things. They say that these studies supply them with a constant store of great thoughts; and in this they are a true blessing to them; for inasmuch as the thoughts which usually press most on the minds of women are of too personal and subjective a kind, and are connected with the troubled and unrestful life of man on earth, and with the small details and anxious cares of daily living, the thoughts engendered by the study of the Mathematics and

Physical Science, in most of its branches at least, are above all these, in a calm region wherein we find inexhaustible matter for wonder, and joy, and worship, and praise. And we do the duties of earth better when our minds dwell among the harmonies of God, and not always among the discords of human society. Women have often said that they were able to return with a calm mind to the right performance of domestic work after going out to gaze for awhile upon the great multitude of stars on a cloudless night; and they now say that the calmness and strength so attained is far more permanent and real when to the mere sentiment of beauty, which however may be a powerful aid, is added some knowledge of the wondrous working, in the laws which regulate the universe, of the Supreme will and control of Him who made them all.

I cannot do better than quote here a letter written by Mrs. Somerville, a lady whose scientific and mathematical attainments have lately been publicly recognised, and who is behind no woman of her age in feminine virtue and refinement. And the readers of this Essay will excuse me if I quote her letter, even beyond the limits of its application to this one particular, because of its application to the whole tenor of this Essay, and because the writer was only hindered by her great age from contributing to this volume:—

Naples, May 10, 1869.

DEAR MRS. BUTLER,

Although I cannot grant your request to write an Essay for a volume on female education, of which you are to be the editor, I sincerely wish you success; for the low estimation in which our intellect has hitherto been held has been a grief and mortification to me from my earliest years. While the improvement of man's education has occupied so much attention in the present age, it is wonderful that one-half of the human race should have been comparatively so much neglected. Great duties have been demanded from us, and our minds have not been prepared by solid instruction to fulfil them. Much prejudice still exists against high intellectual education for our sex, from the mistaken idea that it would render a woman unfit for the duties of a wife and mother. A woman that would neglect her family for her studies would equally neglect them for frivolous pursuits and dissipation. A solid course of instruction gives a high tone to any mind, whether male or female; it would render a wife capable of understanding and appreciating the pursuits of her husband; at any rate she would be an intelligent and agreeable companion.

Hitherto usefulness and duty to men have been thought the only objects worth caring for with regard to women; it would, at least, be generous to take the individual happiness of the sex into consideration in the scheme of education. Thousands of women never marry, and even those that do, have many solitary hours. I can only say from experience, that the higher branches of mathematical science as well as natural history have been inestimable blessings to me throughout the whole course of my life, and more especially in extreme old age, when other resources fail. As a source of happiness as well as of intellectual strength, mathematical science and classical learning ought to be essential branches of study in the higher and middle classes of women. Were these women highly cultivated, they would be followed, to a certain degree, by the lower ranks, but the general standard of all would be raised. Every assistance should be afforded, more especially to the numerous class who have to gain their livelihood by teaching or other employments, of which there are many peculiarly suited to the female sex, if, by instruction, they were fitted to fill them.

It has been assumed that the constitution of girls would be weakened by a classical and scientific education, in addition to the indispensable branches of study; but that is by no means the case, if they be taken progressively. Children at a very early age learn to speak several languages at the same time with perfect facility; they never confuse them, and as soon as they learn to read and are supplied with amusing story-books, a great point is gained and much time saved before real education begins. Besides, the mind is not fatigued if the child be amused. The essential branches of geography and history may, to a certain degree, be combined; for, in describing the boundaries of a country and its geographical features, it would amuse a child to be told about its inhabitants, their manners and customs, something of their previous history, and also the animal and vegetable productions. It is thus in the power of a highly educated mother or governess to make study agreeable, and gradually prepare the mind for its higher branches, when at a later age a girl is capable of understanding them.

Do not suppose that I undervalue accomplishments; on the contrary, I am a zealous advocate for refinement; but surely the graces of life are not incompatible with solid endowments. Even when every opportunity of improvement is given, education will necessarily be subservient to the natural disposition of the child. There is no need to fear that all will be too learned, though all may be improved; but the important point is, that a girl should be perfectly taught any branch of science or literature for which she shows an inclination, that she may be really learned. This is particularly the case with regard to music and painting; for if there be genius, both afford the most refined enjoyment, and enable a woman to appreciate works of art and the higher compositions in music; but if there be no natural taste for the fine arts, it is a mere waste of time to cultivate them.

Needlework is useful and feminine, though less important now that it is done by machinery.

There are so many sects in Britain, that religion and morality must be taught at home. I have not mentioned them among the duties of women, though by far the highest, because I consider them equally imperative on men.

I have lived so long abroad that I am no judge of the plans that have been laid and institutions established for the education of women; but I am glad to hear that the London University is at last willing to grant diplomas to governesses, and I am grateful to the members of the illustrious University of Cambridge who have so generously espoused our cause.

Yours, dear Mrs. Butler,
With much esteem,
MARY SOMERVILLE.

But, as I take it, the origin of that feeling which many have against opening up scientific teaching to women, is to be found in that misapprehension which there is abroad about Science, that it is something which is opposed to Religion. Faith in spiritual things is to be desired. The wisdom of many men hinders them therefrom; and there is something in a woman's character which seems to be that which, as it were, retains trust and hope in the world. So that women herein, as it appears to me, suffer on both hands—from those that despise them, and from those that fear for them. Those that despise them are not scientific; and those that fear for them are too distrustful: first, of woman's nature, and secondly of the teaching of true Science, whose flattery hath for the most part usurped its place. And there is abroad among the vulgar a notion that men of Science are for the most part irreligious, which, if it were true, might argue that the teaching of Science led that way. But the irreligious men of Science are, as I take it, for the most part the vulgar extollers of it, those who would be irreligious in any event, and who, laying hold of certain crude notions, and being given to dogmatism, point to some instances wherein there is a great blindness to all that is not material, and loudly proclaim it, as if Science were against Revelation. These are the vulgar of Science, ever clamorous, concerning whom and their theories bended about their preconceptions, it may be said, "Woe unto them, for they have made the heart of the righteous sad whom God hath not made sad." But it is not just to say that Science makes men irreligious, which, I think, any will see if they look over its great names. And among men of Science, I think, more than among most men, there is a humble piety leading them to repeat those excellent words of Kepler, when he said :—

"If any one be too dull to comprehend the science of Astronomy, or too feeble-minded to believe in Copernicus without prejudice to his piety, my advice to such a one is that he should quit the Astronomical Schools; and condemning, if he has a mind, any or all of the theories of philosophers, should look to his own affairs, and leaving the struggle, should go home and plough his fields. And as often as he lifts up to this goodly heaven those eyes with which alone *he* is able to see, let him pour out his heart in praises and thanksgivings to God the Creator, and let him not fear but that he is offering a worship as acceptable to God as is his to whom God has granted to see yet more clearly with the eyes of the mind."[1]

The noble humility of which words might well be learned a little by those, who, on a smaller knowledge of Science, base their despising of all, save "intellectual appreciation."

But indeed, I would fear many evil consequences if that which I contemplate being taught were that which is usually understood by the term Popular Science, such as popular lectures too often set forth, wherein the gaps of an inconsequent reasoning are too often supplied by an inconsequent experiment; whereby there are disseminated too often concerning Science itself, the very evils at the root of which Science would strike, dogmatic assertion and inconsequent deduction. Now, in bringing matters of Science even before the most ignorant in the most elementary way, we must never

[1] The words of this translation are quoted from an article by Professor Kelland.

lose sight of the constant necessity of rigid and accurate thought. But there is a great difference between that which usually goes by the name of Popular Science and that rude but yet accurate delineation of a scientific process which may be made to those ignorant of it. A rude method is not by any means necessarily an inaccurate one; and I should like to say a few words about the way of bringing a true mathematical investigation before those ignorant of mathematics.

As a general rule, anything geometrical may be easily reduced to a form in which it may be apprehended readily, and with a sufficient distinctness; I mean, distinctly apprehended so far as it *is* apprehended. Such a fact, for instance, as Kepler's law about the "Equable description of Areas." Again, a process which can be geometrically exhibited is generally readily apprehended; as for instance, the deduction of the law of gravity for a particular planet from Kepler's first and second laws; for the lengths of various subtenses may be actually measured. I have seen a mechanic apprehend this so well in the case of the ellipse as to be able to apply the same process to the determination of the force to the pole necessary to make a body move in an equiangular spiral. And to those well acquainted with the nature of such curves it is never a hard matter to fall upon some way of rudely describing them graphically, which may be easily apprehended by the class of people with whom we are dealing. Geometrical ideas seem to be implanted in men's minds, and apparently, if we consider of any geometrical fact, it is axiomatic; at any rate, there is no geometrical fact which is not rudely to be apprehended upon its own merits.

It is not so with Algebra; and it is considerably more difficult to bring before the ignorant those parts of the processes of Science which are more naturally expressed in algebraic form. For instance, Kepler's third law I have found to be always much harder of apprehension to most people, and so of the process by which it is deduced from it that the force of gravity is the same for all planets. Many such processes are capable, with a little pains, of expression in a geometrical form; yet the attempt to impart such a process, even in an algebraical form, is often attended with the most beneficial results, and a deal of algebra may be taught in that way, which may come to be very useful afterwards; for people are much readier to learn a technicality when they see its application. And indeed, it is sometimes a matter of wonder to me that at schools, and at the University, what is called Pure Mathematics is not approached more from the side of its direct application to special and important Physical Problems.

I have hitherto spoken of the Mathematics as if they were something to be avoided rather than aimed at; I should not like to leave the reader with that impression. I only would avoid their technicalities in the teaching of the ignorant when their technicality is not the point in question. But regarded in themselves, the Mathematics afford a means of education scarcely if at all inferior to that which is afforded by the facts of Physical Science;

and those arguments which apply to the true study and teaching of Science do apply also to that of Mathematics. Nay, there is to be got from an intelligent study of Mathematics a benefit which is of a most peculiar kind. For where there is anything in Mathematics that is in error, it can be allowed for, as an instrumental error or an approximation, and the limits of its effect can be definitely assigned; whereby there is engendered in us a clearer conception of what we may require to know before we say our knowledge is complete. And the reason of this in Mathematics is, that we thoroughly know that which we do know; whereas in the world about us there is so much about which we know a good deal, but yet wherein there is part unknown, which may mount into such an importance as to overturn all the approximations of our reasoning. For in the world of ordinary life we do not know the magnitude of that which we neglect. Whence I believe that there are none who would so readily confess the insufficiency of the apparent results of the mere processes of reason as those most skilled in their purest application.

The method of exhibiting a refined mathematical process in a rude form, yet one which shall be accurate so far as it goes, is, if the reader will consider it aright, a sort of amplification of Newton's first Lemma, wherein the statement of such a method is contained in its first and completest form. And the accuracy of a rude proof does, as is therein stated, depend entirely on that in which the rudeness consists. For the principle is this, that I am given something to prove, wherein I could not quite delineate or mentally follow the process, and I prove something which is not quite that which I was asked to prove by a process which I can grasp, but which has an error of rudeness in it; but if I have chosen it so that the error grows the less as the thing that I have proved thereby grows nearer to that which I was asked to prove, then my proof is an adequate one. It will be easily seen, then, from this, what is meant by a rude yet accurate process; and it will be as easily seen wherein it is that the difficulty of inventing such a process consists. To teach Physical Science so as to be a fit branch of education some such attempt must be made, and it calls for those to make it who are well versed in such methods; and any attempt to diffuse through the world some sort of true conception of the nature of such accurate reasoning, and to assist the ignorant into the habit of it, does always meet with the greatest return. It is well-spent time, and it is a great benefit which many may confer. Nor let any think that by doing so they are wholly sacrificing themselves, nor that by stopping to teach they are wholly in danger of being left behind. The exercise of making an intricate process free from its technicalities is most beneficial to ourselves, and in nowhere so much as in the Mathematics, wherein the greatest danger and the commonest error is that we should not comprehend the significance of the processes which we ourselves employ. And that such is as I say I have good authority, for Mr. Airy says, speaking of an elementary work on gravitation, "The simple considerations which have been forced upon me in the composition of this treatise, have in several instances contributed much to clear up my view of points which were before obscure and almost doubtful." And I think that those who impart to women the teaching which Science can give, do a good deed for the world; for women are the teachers of the world, and especially in moral matters, and our mothers are the real teachers of us all. And I would argue for the teaching of Science upon the very ground on which many object to it; for I think that, of all the means of higher education, there is none which does so greatly engender in us a right way of looking at moral questions; and the possession even of an intellectual conscience alone seems to incline towards Charity.

There are other things in the world besides bodily things; there is a world of matter and a world of mind, and human beings have ever been seeking to know the interdependence of things in the one case as in the other. I am set in a world full of trouble, where my hopes are disappointed and my wishes are in vain; I see people oppressed, and weary, and troubled; I see the defenceless ill-used, the voiceless neglected; I see anxious virtue struggling to be free, oppressed by satisfied ignorance; one by one my friends leave me, and I am left alone. I want to see what all these things have to do with one another; what life and death, and suffering and hope, have to do with one another. I want to have a Science of these things, as much as a Science of Astronomy. And I see that men have tried to feel their way through these things ever since the world began; and for the most part they miss it—on the one hand despising or despairing, as though all things were of the materialistic kind; and on the other hand substituting the dogmas of theology for the experimental teaching of the spirit of Charity; each forgetting one of those great lessons that Science might teach. For anything personally undertaken, in thought or in deed, is the one dispeller of a thousand mists of the reason; and the true spirit of Science is that which is humble enough to believe that there is nothing too humble to be great, nor aught despised but it might be the clue to guide us through our labyrinth. Whereby the practicalness of the study of Science is vindicated, altogether apart from the material benefits which its applications bring. For there is a very great and clear lesson to be learned from history, wherein we see the revenge which Nature takes upon the pride of the unscientific man for passing by the insignificant, as he calls it; the Nemesis which falls sooner or later on men for their presumptive cataloguing of importances, their pre-arrangements for the guiding of nature. For that small person, that small want, that small desire, which is to be passed by, may not be able perhaps to make a noise; nay, nor can even self-consciously proclaim itself; but through its very silence and repression it signifies much. Nor is there anything real that is trivial, though our views of it may be so. And then at last such small neglected wishes and troubles accumulate, till society bursts, or else rots away, and rulers wonder, and devise punishments, and prisons, and penitentiaries, and wish that things that cannot be cured were at the bottom of the sea, and curse those who have grown to be a curse to them, being slow to learn that they but transmit the sin of their fathers, whose punishment has descended upon them, untaught by the teaching of Science and the teaching of Christianity, that Opinion is not the criterion of the importance of Things. But that lesson which Science has learned, and found it so hard to learn, it is its reward and its office that it should teach to other things. For in active life surely the result of the unscientific way of thinking is more disastrous than it is in Science; for if a man bent on a discovery be foolish enough to put down mental gunpowder upon mental sparks, because they should not be there, the worst I fancy is the blowing to pieces of his own theory and the delaying of real scientific discovery, and also the failure, in his own case, to reach nearer to God, because of the failure to arrive at some truth,—because, in one word, of Pride. But in the world made up of men and women, and bodies and souls, the consequences are more grave, inflicting too often deep suffering and destruction. Wherefore I cannot believe those politicians who would hold that for the sake of the many any are to be despised. "It is not the will of your heavenly Father that one of these little ones should perish." "Take heed that ye despise not one of these little ones," is a lesson read from every corner.

Moreover, in concluding this subject, let us not fail to remember that there is an old proverb that "Knowledge is Power." But knowledge is power in more than one way, and what is better, knowledge is freedom, that is, if it be the knowledge of that which is true; for it has been said, "Ye shall know the truth, and the truth shall make you free." That which is sometimes called Knowledge includes all that is called the scientific spirit, both the scientific way of looking at things and the things at which Science looks. A better word might be Wisdom, or Understanding. And as we get into a better way of looking at things we become better men and women, better fitted for our position in the world. But the acquirement of knowledge brings another benefit. For somehow or other it brings us a peculiar delight. It is that fabled paradise in the desert, that castle free from care. Nor is it unpractical to praise it that it is so fair a place, the source of so much pleasure. There are few minds strong enough to endure the absence of what is called enjoyment: hence it is that not a few sins are to be laid to the account of the want of innocent intellectual pleasures; which pleasures Science doth always supply us with, antidotes to that enforced levity wherewith women are peculiarly oppressed. And ever as we dive deeper into the observation of nature, it doth engender in us a more humble admiration, and the recognition in creation of some handiwork like our own, wherein the problems of nature are solved with a variousness of adaptation as though they were done by some one who loved his work, over which he hath delayed with that fond but various repetition whereto Genius ever doth recur. Wherefore, fearlessly to study Science doth seem a fair and most religious advice, and a following of the Bible, wherein God is ever previously presented as the God of nature. For ofttimes men are ennobled by their surroundings, and there have been many meaner motives sublimed by the very elevation of that in which we engage; nor is there any such large address in the world as the language of the stars and created things, to the commonness of which language God doth Himself testify through the Psalms, wherein He saith, that there is no language but that their tongue is heard therein, whose words have gone to the end of the world, whereby the heavens, without respect of person, declaring the glory of God, do somewhat ease men's minds wrapped in the folds of that misbelief that introspection works, and do relieve them wearied by those woes that oppression doth deliver in entail.

VI.

ON SOME HISTORICAL ASPECTS OF FAMILY LIFE.

BY CHARLES H. PEARSON, M.A.

In the opposition which several members of Parliament offered to the Married Women's Property Bill, there was, as is not unusual in such cases, a great variety of arguments, but in the main a common conservative sentiment. Mr. Lopes objected to the Bill, "because if it became law it would go far to impair the confidence that ought to exist between husband and wife, and which was the mainspring of domestic happiness." Mr. Beresford-Hope said, that "if the principle of *separation des biens* were to be made a rule of law instead of an exception, our whole social relations would be changed. Old-fashioned people like himself could not help recollecting that it was written in Scripture, that the husband was head of his household, which if this Bill passed, would no longer be. . . . . The present system was one in which confidence and caution were firmly blended, whereas the proposed change would bring into existence a system in which mistrust would alternate with spasmodic improvidence." Mr. Henley remarked, that "no one had ventured to get up and say that the relations of married life in other countries, where other systems prevailed, were better than in this."[1] It would not, I think, be unfair to sum up these arguments briefly as the expression of a belief that the wife's dependence upon the husband is closely connected with English domesticity, and that where there is a divided control of property quarrels and separations are not unlikely to ensue.

No supporter of Mr. Russell Gurney's measure will wish that these arguments against it should not be estimated at their full force. That a certain institution should have lasted down more or less through man's history, working on the whole well and wisely, is no reason for keeping it up when its operations have become hurtful; but is the greatest of all reasons for considering whether it should be changed, and in what way. It may be questionable, indeed, whether society would have any right to purchase the greater happiness of a portion of its members at the cost of laws that were hard and unfair to the minority. But the purity and peace of domestic life are blessings of such vast significance, and it is of such importance to the State, that we should not diminish filial reverence by impairing conjugal relations, that I think most Reformers would be content with piecemeal legislation, and with the protection of women by marriage-contracts or magistrates' orders, if they were assured that the husband's control over his wife's property was an absolute condition of domesticity. Our belief on these points is, however, the exact opposite

[1] *The Times*, April 15, 1869.

of that held by Mr. Lopes, Mr. Beresford-Hope, and Mr. Henley. We think the legal relations of husband and wife are a relic of primitive times, when society required to be held together by stronger bonds than at present, when the family was an artificial compound, when delicacy in the man and self-respect in the woman were qualities which legislation did not need to take into account. We think that as higher moral ideals, or even higher material civilization, have come into the world, it has been found impossible to preserve the old system in its entirety. It has partly been abrogated by laws; in part been tempered by manners and right feeling; and wherever these correctives have been wanting or insufficient, there has been some deplorable result, shattering for a time the whole fabric of household life. We think that many influences have conspired to build up English domesticity—the affections common to all mankind, Christianity, chivalry, and tradition, but that these were in part prior to our marriage-laws, have derived nothing from them, and will work the more freely for their abolition. We even believe that English domesticity has few worse enemies than the law which vests the husband with the control of his wife's property and earnings.

It is impossible in treating this question to abstain from going back to the first beginnings of society. Whatever English domesticity may be, the laws that determine the control of husbands over their wives' property are a fragment of an old system, which every civilized nation has at one time or another adopted more or less completely. Nor is it a difficult point of archæology. Savigny, Maine, Coulanges, and many others, have explained, in their various ways, that the family is the unit of early societies, and that the family is an artificial compound. For us society consists of individuals, many of whom, it is true, are unable to act for themselves, but over all of whom the State watches. If a man ill-treats his wife, or neglects to bring up his children, he is liable with us to be called to account by the law. On the other hand, there are cases every day in which a father applies to the magistrate for support in the exercise of his parental authority. Our system is not yet free from all anomalies, and perhaps will never be so, but its tendency is to emancipate wives and children from control, rather than to bring them under it. Now the father of a family in old States, notably in Judæa, Greece, Rome, and among the Germanic nations, was invested with rights like those of absolute sovereignty. The family was a unit, because it had only one legal representative. It was in some respects artificial, because its perpetuity would be endangered if it might not at times supply deficiencies from without. In some forms of development it even counted among its members, not only the wife and the adopted son, but the freedman and the slave.

These differences will not seem remarkable if we take the first needs and instincts of primitive societies into account. The need of a simple organization is among the earliest, and nothing is on the whole easier than to deal only with heads of families, to make them accountable for the police of their households, and of course to entrust them with corresponding powers. Among the first instincts is that which connects the well-being of the dead with the pious care lavished on them by the living. Plato couples relationship with the fellowship in the gods of the race;[1] and it meant this very actually to every citizen of Athens and Rome in their first centuries. There were certain gods of the family to whom only its members could offer sacrifices, and certain religious dues which must be rendered, if the dead were to rest happy in their graves. Hence it became necessary, and is so to this day in the East, that children should be adopted into families which were without natural issue. But again, as the tutelary deities of each family were peculiar to it, the bride must become, as it were, the adopted child of her husband; and his gods, in the literal language of Orpah, must be her gods. The strong feeling against divorce, which existed in the early days of Rome, probably arose from the extreme hardship to the woman, who was thrown outcast upon the world without natural protectors or a household religion; and the first Roman who (in the sixth century of the Commonwealth) put away his wife for sterility, though he only exercised a legal right, was condemned by public opinion.[2] Even the slave was affiliated to the family; initiated into the sacred rites, allowed to take part in the

[1] Plato's Laws, p. 729.

[2] This was Spurius Carvilius Ruga (Valerius Maximus, lib. i. c. 2). Dionysius observes that the old and binding marriage forced women to conform to their husband's manners, as they had no refuge elsewhere (Dion, "Halic." lib. ii. c. 25).

offices, and finally consigned to the family tomb. If he became freedman or client, he still belonged by this invisible link to his old master's household. It is true that no number of such men were sufficient by themselves to maintain the worship of the race. But in the eye of the law, and to public opinion, they were members of the family, while the chief's uterine brother or his sister's son were aliens. The patron might bear witness against a "cognatus;" he could not do it against a client.[1]

Hitherto we have not found many traces of English domesticity; and further inquiry will only show that every law concerning family life had for its first object the perpetuity of the race. If this could be ensured, as it often could be, by making marriage indissoluble, divorce was prohibited; but where the motive failed, the law was relaxed. Opinion in Rome pronounced against the divorce of a barren wife, because children could be supplied by adoption. But if the husband was taken prisoner and enslaved, the wife might dissolve the marriage-tie, because she could no longer be of use to perpetuate the race.[2] Adultery in the wife married by the most binding religious ceremonies, or even by weaker but corresponding forms, might be punished with

[1] Cato laid down this rule very explicitly. "Adversus cognatos pro cliente testatur; testimonium adversus clientes nemo dicit" (Aulus Gellius, v. 19, xx. 1).

[2] Digests, lib. xlix. tit. xv. c. 8. This is the original (the Canon Law being the connecting link) of a wife's liberty at common law to marry again without incurring the penalties of bigamy, if she has not heard of her husband for seven years; but by English practice the husband may reclaim the wife.

death down to a late period, because the introduction of spurious issue into a family was a profanation of the household religion, and virtually the extinction of the family. But the marriage of mere cohabitation, suspended once a year for a short interval, though inferior in religious sanctity, was valid, and socially recognised, and in later times constantly practised. Again, nothing to our notions is more closely connected with the duties of family life than the care of children; but where the perpetuity of the race was secured, the Greek, Roman, and German father exposed them without scruple; and naturally was least careful of daughters, who were certain at some time to become aliens to his race. The foundling is a constant incident in classical novels and plays.

A few instances of Roman domesticity, such as this system made it in the better days of the Commonwealth, will speak more forcibly to its workings than any statement of the laws. Pliny tells us [1] that women at Rome were not allowed to drink wine: "We find among instances, that the wife of Egnatius Mecennius was scourged to death by her husband, because she had drunk wine out of a cask, and that he was acquitted of having murdered her by Romulus. Fabius Pictor has written in his Annals that Matrona was starved to death by her family, because she had put a new seal on the chest containing the keys of the wine-cellar. Cato says, that relations kissed the women of their families to see if they smelled of wine." Valerius Maximus records

[1] Pliny, "Hist. Nat." lib. xiv. c. 13.

two instances in which daughters who had been seduced were put to death by their fathers.[1] Cassius, a patrician, scourged and put to death his son for carrying out agrarian law in the exercise of his duties as tribune: and Aulus Fulvius, with more justice, killed a son who had joined Catiline.[2] It is perfectly true, that with the growth of civilization the authority of fathers and husbands was mitigated, and assumed a judicial character. But it is true also that the mitigation was felt by statesmen to strike at the root of the whole family system, and was only conceded in deference to public opinion. When Erixo scourged his son to death, the Emperor interposed to save the father from the just wrath of the multitude.[3] Domitian is an excellent instance of a man personally impure and worthless, but who was reactionary by insight, policy, and conviction, and who accordingly startled society by the contrast of an immoral life with a strict enforcement of the almost obsolete laws on which Roman domesticity had been based. Yet Domitian rarely swayed from his own standard of virtue. His was the old ideal of a commonwealth in which an absolute reserve of manners should be maintained by an unswerving discipline among all who were subject to the head of the house, while the head himself was responsible for none but flagrant excesses to none but the State.[4] But this ideal, whether

[1] Val. Max. lib. vi. c. 1. [2] Ibid. c. 8.

[3] Seneca, de Clementia, i. 14. Erixo was mobbed and all but killed in the Forum.

[4] Merivale's "Romans under the Empire," vol. vii. chap. 62.

good or bad, was as much among the things of the past as Roman liberty.

It is not, I think, a forced view to assume that the stringency of the old laws concerning property had something to do with the changes introduced into the constitution of the family. By the early theory, the whole property of the family, or at least the realty, which was its more valuable part, was a trust vested in the father for the use of the race. Strictly speaking, he was bound not to alienate it; and the Jewish law of the year of jubilee, the prohibitions against removing a neighbour's landmark, and the curses against those who add field to field, are familiar instances of the intense popular religion that consecrated the inheritance of every race.[1] The land where the household gods had settled down, and where the ancestors were buried, ought never to pass away into the hands of strangers. Naturally enough, therefore, whatever dowry the wife brought was thrown into the common stock of her new family, and was administered by its head for the time being. But that institutions should remain in force presupposes a stationary condition, or at least a very gradual growth of society; and in proportion as a state became powerful, inequalities of

[1] Compare the following passages:—"And Naboth said to Ahab, The Lord forbid it me, that I should give the inheritance of my fathers unto thee" (1 Kings xxi. 3). "Let this be the first law . . . . that no one move the boundaries of land" (Plato's "Laws," p. 842). "Nor do thou (O God Terminus) grant anything to thy neighbour asking, lest thou seem to prefer man to Jupiter" (Ovid's "Fasti," ii. 676, 606). An old German law directed that a man moving a terminal stone should be buried up to the head on the spot, and his neck ploughed through (Grimm's "Deutsche Rechts-Alterthümer," s. 547).

wealth arose within it, reversing the old limitations under which alliances had been contracted, or an alien population grew up, to which the family system was only the symbol of patrician exclusiveness. To the contemporaries of Cincinnatus the wife's dowry was probably nothing more than a yoke of oxen or a few sesterces: in the days of Cæsar, trade, successions, and the spoils of provinces had enriched many families and created a class of heiresses. The Roman lady had acquired something of Greek culture, and was indisposed to be given away into servitude. It was equally the interest of her family that she should retain the control of her property, which might under certain circumstances revert to them. Prescription and the interest of a large number in the upper classes were opposed, and, as is commonly the case, interest triumphed.

But precisely the converse to what English conservatives fear actually happened. It was not the *separation des biens* that was introduced and brought divorce in its train, but the old binding forms of marriage were discarded, to secure the wife in possession of her property. The wife by habit or cohabitation remained a member of her own family, and the husband had no power over her property that was not given him by contract. Indeed, the ingenuity of Roman lawyers was exhausted in finding reasons why gifts between married people should be forbidden; and Ulpian condemned them as likely to lead to extravagance; Paulus as tending to withdraw funds that should go to the support of the children; and Sextus Cæcilius because domestic peace would be disturbed, if presents which it was possible to make were withheld.[1] Divorce was now in every woman's power, and might follow a moment's wrath: it was but to break the tablets of the marriage-contract, to give notice, or even to marry another man without notice to the bereaved husband.[2] The consequences may easily be imagined. Juvenal speaks of the woman with eight husbands; Seneca of her who computes her life by the number of marriages: and Martial jested upon the lady who had ten husbands in a month.[3] Divorces, however, were not the worst evil of the new system. Many permanent unions were now those in which family dishonour was condoned for considerations of interest; and the husband was only married to his wife's income.

Such had been the working, and such was the failure of marriage-laws resembling our own, in the Roman Commonwealth. The system by which women were kept under tutelage had been maintained in theory long after it had become inapplicable in daily life; and the practical issue had been, first, that women marrying had preferred to remain in the tutelage of their own families, and next, that even this partial control had been reduced

[1] "Digest," lib. xxiv. tit. i. ss. 1, 2.

[2] Juvenal, "Satires," ix. l. 75. Tacit. "Annales," xi. 30.

[3] See the instances collected by Gibbon ("Decline and Fall," vol. v. p. 297; ed. Smith), among which, however, the case quoted from St. Jerome (Epist. ad Ageruchiam), of the woman who had been married to twenty-two husbands and was carried to the grave by the survivor of twenty previous wives, perhaps points rather to marriages for inheritance than to divorces. Epictetus's testimony to the depravation of moral feeling among the Roman women is as strong as anything I know ("Fragments," 53).

by degrees almost to a nullity.[1] The wife was no longer wife, and the daughter was emancipated. Meanwhile a new religion was growing up, which was destined to be the solvent of the old society. The Apostles and first professors of Christianity were not men so minded as to look with indifference on the general dissolution of all morality. The counsel of Epictetus,[2] to be moderate in carnal indulgences, is separated by impassable limits from the severe asceticism of teachers who just tolerated marriage, were distinctly opposed to more marriages than one, and regarded the state of celibacy as the highest. Still more wonderful perhaps is the contrast between the Christian and the Pagan view of the family. Christianity, be it remembered, was not the religion of the best-educated or most intelligent men; it recruited its teachers from the lower classes, and found its largest congregations in those parts of the Empire that were least Roman. It could not rise to the level of the highest Roman jurisprudence; and as it became more and more leavened with the feelings and thoughts of Gothic and Vandalic invaders, it relapsed more and more into the patriarchal conception of the husband as supreme in his family: irresponsible guardian of his wife, and, in a less degree, of his children. St. Paul, whose whole writings exhibit the jurisconsult in the garb of the theologian, had prepared the way for this result, by the often-quoted passage in which

1 Maine's "Ancient Law," pp. 155, 156. I may here refer my readers to this, and to "La Cité Antique," by Coulanges, for any further illustration of this subject they may desire.

2 Epictetus, "Enchiridion," 33.

he compares the union of wife and husband to the mystic and intimate union of the Church with Christ.[1] I do not wish to deny or to evade the significance of this passage. Whether it be inspired or not, in the sense commonly given to that word by theologians, it announces a theory of the conjugal bond which most highly-toned men, whether nominally Christian or not, will regard as among the greatest treasures ever added to the world's thought. And if St. Paul's ideal could be lived up to, and every married union be one in which the husband was all wisdom and tenderness, these questions of legislation to secure the wife's property in her labour would either never arise or would be numbered among the grave trifles of a debating society. But until that time arrive, until the legislators who quote St. Paul as authority for depriving a milliner of her earnings shall be prepared to carry out the whole teaching of the Sermon on the Mount, and to govern the world on the principle that we shall take no thought for the morrow, we must surely stoop to the necessity of making laws for men as they are, rather than as they should be.[2] Explain away the literal words of the Bible, interpret its teaching by the needs of modern times, and you may arrive at many different

[1] Ephesians vi. 22, &c.

[2] "Christian society was meant to take in, as avowedly 'legitimate,' other forms of life than those insisted on and recognised at first. It was *not* always to have all things common; it was *not* always to decline the sword; it was *not* always to hold itself bound by the command, 'Sell all that thou hast.'" (Church, "Sermons preached before the University of Oxford," p. 57.) We may surely add, it was *not* always to limit its conceptions of family life by the institutions of primitive times.

results. Take it without reserve or equivocation; and let any candid man say whether the classes who send members to Parliament or a few continental Socialists be the more literal representatives of Gospel teaching.

Meanwhile, it is important to observe that the Church, following, as I believe, the higher inspiration of Him who taught that the Kingdom of God was to be preferred to parents or brethren, wife or children, qualified its acceptance of St. Paul's theory with reservations which gradually destroyed its meaning. The necessities of a militant faith are beyond compromise; and while in matters of property, for which in its better days it cared little, it allowed a barbarous principle to triumph again, the Christian Church has successively attacked and demolished the patriarchal system in every matter where personal rights were concerned. St. Paul taught that the wife was not to leave her husband, even where he was an unbeliever; but the Church canonized St. Lucia, who being betrothed professed virginity, and St. Margaret, who professed it on the night of her marriage.[1] St. Paul made no exceptions for the obedience of children; but the Church has repeatedly canonized those who turned Christians in defiance of a parent or guardian,—like St. Peter Martyr, who renounced the faith of his family when only seven years old; or St. Pancras, who saw the errors of his uncle at the maturer age of fourteen.[2] The institution of sponsors, whose duty it was to watch over the child's religion, was in fact a protest

[1] "Legenda Aurea," pp. 29, 676. [2] Ibid. pp. 277, 340.

against the father's authority, and the substitution of a Christian for the natural family. Nor was this creation, what it has now become among Protestants, a mere formal or sentimental bond, for the godchild and his sponsors were united by a spiritual affinity like that of the Roman father and an adopted child, and could not intermarry. Naturally, the right of exposing children was prohibited from the first. More gradually, the right of selling them into slavery came to be forbidden, as it was found that they were often sold into countries not in the jurisdiction of the Church. Even in cases where there was no question of faith, but only of a higher practice, the authority of the parent was by degrees abrogated, and a boy of fifteen had the right to make himself a monk.[1] Considering the extent and importance of all these modifications upon the old family system, it is not too much to say that Christianity has completed its demolition. Vestiges of it remain still, but in no country where Christianity has triumphed could any reaction have restored the patriarchal theory in its entirety.

I have said that the old Germanic conception of the family was the same as the old Roman and Greek, and exercised an injurious influence over the position of married women with regard to property. Several circumstances, however, conspired to give the Germanic wife, as we know her in historical times, a better

[1] "Penitential of Theodore," xix. 26. Two copies add that a girl of thirteen may make herself a nun. It followed naturally (27), that after she was seventeen, her parents were not to marry her against her will.

position than the wife enjoys in the oldest legislation of Greece and Rome. Courage, and strong will, and pure morals, characteristics for which the women of the Teutonic races were noted at an early period, asserted their natural influence in family life; and as Christianity raised the status of the single woman and the widow by limiting the jurisdiction of the natural family, it could not but exercise a reflex influence for good on the position of the wife. Accordingly, though the wife's property passed under her husband's control in Germany and England, as in Rome, it did not rest in him absolutely, but as a trust for which he might always be held accountable. In case of divorce, he was called upon to restore it. In case of his death, the widow received dower out of the estate, and administered it for herself, with power to leave it away from the natural heir. Nay, the *morgen-gifu*, or post-nuptial settlement, which was distinct from the price paid for the wife before marriage, was in the wife's control during coverture, and could be disposed of as she thought fit. "That," says the "Nibelungen Lied," "was Kriemhilda's property, for it was her *morgen-gabe*."[1] In that wonderful story of "Burnt Njal," which gives so vivid a picture of Icelandic life, Hallgerda, a rich heiress, appears throughout in independent control of her property, and Unna, divorced from her husband, receives back her dower.[2] "In several (Anglo-Saxon) wills," says Mr. Kemble, "the husband

[1] Grimm's "Deutsche Rechts-Alterthümer," s. 441.
[2] Dasent's "Story of Burnt Njal," vol. i. pp. cxx., 35, 36, 65—77, &c.

carefully points out the lands to which his wife has this claim; and in several cases women appeal to it as their title to lands which they are desirous of alienating."[1] It is probable, too, that in Saxon times the wife might acquire property by bequest. Ælfgiva, a cousin of Queen Edith, bequeathed her the Manor of Lewknor; and the Queen, with her husband's consent, gave it to the monks of Abingdon.[2]

How then, it may be asked, was this courtesy of the English law exchanged for the harsher practice of later times? One answer, I think, is, that as the extent of the *morgen-gifu* came more and more to be matter of previous contract, it got to be confounded with the dower, which was originally part of the consideration for which the husband's purchase-money had been paid. If a man gave value of 100*l.* and received in return a wife and 50*l.*, he would naturally regard the dower brought as acquired with his own money, and belonging to himself. But the main cause lies in that passionate study of canon law which distinguished the twelfth, thirteenth, and fourteenth centuries. Legists, who had so much to work upon in the substructure of barbaric codes, found no difficulty in adapting slight inconsistencies to the requirements of Roman jurisprudence; and the classes who had the largest interest in protecting the property of their married daughters were able to do it then, as now, by contract. Yet the encroachments on old liberty were not at first admitted without reserve.

[1] Kemble's "Codex Diplomaticus Anglo-Saxonicus," i. p. cx.

[2] "Chron. Mon. de Abingdon," i. pp. 460, 461.

If a husband alienated lands which had been in his possession at the time of his marriage, his widow could recover her customary third from his heirs, and a sale to the prejudice of her customary dower was invalid if her consent had been refused.[1] Modern legislation has seriously impaired this courtesy of England. It is now possible to insert a clause in the conveyance of land declaring that the widow shall not be entitled to dower; and the husband can sell land without any restriction. He may also bar the dower by a declaration in his will. The only offset to these provisions is that the wife is now entitled to dower out of equitable as well as legal estates.[2] But this new privilege only corrects an obvious injustice, created by subtle technicalities; and a wife unprotected by settlement would now have no legal remedy against her husband's profusion or injustice. As commonly happens, modern conservatism finds itself as much at variance with the old institutions of the country as with the first principles of natural right.

Fortunately for mankind, its moral well-being is determined by many various influences, of which the laws are only a part, and not always the most important. M. Guizot has shown, in a striking passage,[3] how the traditions of the mediæval castle have told on our modern ideas of domesticity. The dignified seclusion of those populous homes which were outside city life

[1] Bracton, f. 94, a; Glanville, vi. c. 3.

[2] These changes were introduced by the 3d & 4th Wm. IV cap. 105.

[3] Guizot, "Cours d'Histoire Moderne," Leçon 4; Mill's "Dissertations and Discussions," ii. p. 262.

and complete in themselves; the exact subordination of ranks, furnishing topics for endless books of courtesy; the grave responsibility thrown on the women who were constantly called upon to advise, to govern, or even to superintend a defence; the substitution of household cares, leechcraft, books or gardening, for the life of courts: these, and other such influences, have been in their time among the noblest of educations for the upper classes of a people. "The example of manners," said an old poet, "proceeds from their houses,"[1] and he said it with no disposition to praise the nobles of his time. Doubtless every generation had its own shortcomings; but surely the popular instinct is not far wrong when it associates the idea of a brilliant Court with memories of a Francis I. or a Charles II., and looks for pure lives among quiet homes. English domesticity owes much, I think, to those periods when the nobles were not great enough to defy the law, and too great to sit down contentedly within the shadow of a king's walls.

Neither must it be forgotten, that the very centuries in which lawyers were circumscribing the proprietary rights of wives were also those which witnessed the growth of chivalry. Never, perhaps, was the corrective of high, even overstrained sentiment, more needed for social relations which were eminently prosaic where they were not brutal. To the Church, woman was the source of original sin, cursed by God with child-bearing, and influenced by frailties of temperament that only

[1] Poems of Walter Mapes, p. 232.

the most rigid discipline could subdue; capable of good, it was true, and in some sense honourable, for the Virgin had been a woman; but most honourable when most withdrawn from the world.[1] To the lawyer, the wife was the child under her husband's rod.[2] To the writer of *fabliaux* and moralities, women were the sirens of old story—enchantresses, who thronged every haunt of life, who were always deceitful and impure, but to whom much might be forgiven if they loved much. Take the whole Arthurian cycle, and Sir Cradock's wife is the one chaste woman of its records. What is perhaps more marvellous is, that down to the time of the Reformation, the knights of romance as a rule are purer than their mistresses. Yet if the sanctity of the domestic hearth could have been preserved by any powers with which a husband may be armed, there ought to have been no laxity of morals in the fourteenth and fifteenth centuries. The book which the Knight of La Tour Landry compiled for his daughter's use tells us, with approbation, of one wife who was set to feed with swine to correct her peevishness; of two who were beaten for declining instant obedience to absurd orders; and of a third who had her legs broken for going out against her husband's will.[3] These and

[1] Compare Wright's "Anecdota Literaria," pp. 96—100; the Poems of Walter Mapes, pp. 77—84; and Chaucer's "Wife of Bath," and "Miller of Trumpington."

[2] Bracton, f. 7 a; Fleta, lib. i. c. 9.

[3] "Book of the Knight of La Tour Landry," pp. 27, 81, 95. Le Grand d'Aussy gives a story of a young wife who was counselled by her mother to make good trial of her husband's patience before she ventured on an intrigue.

[After

many such stories are, it is true, of French origin, and I think are not equally applicable to English society; but they enter largely even into our own literature. Chivalry was a perpetual protest against all the conventional feeling that they express. The respect for weakness in itself, the idealization of honour and constancy, and the faith that refuses to believe evil, took form, as it were, in a new religion, making men generous and women trustworthy. Nevertheless, there is always some danger in trusting to mere sentimental impulse as a corrective of social wrongs. It became natural in France and Italy to regard the lover as a sort of equitable corrective to the inordinate legal powers possessed, and often abused, by the husband. The sympathies of the romance-writer are with Lancelot rather than with Arthur. That this unfortunate fashion has never really taken root in England is, I think, partly due to the happy absence from our laws of anything like the Roman doctrine of parental authority. In France, to this day, a man forty years old cannot contract a legal marriage without his father's permission; and as the age when girls marry is rather earlier in Southern than in Northern countries, the *mariage de convenance*, or, to speak more truly, the marriage settled by parents, has for centuries been the only union recognised by Italian and French custom. On the other hand, English law and English custom have alike

After the third offence he caused her to be bled so severely that she kept her bed for weeks afterwards. (Le Grand d'Aussy, "Fabliaux ou Contes," vol. ii. pp. 311—321.)

recognised from all time the right by which a woman, when she is of age, can dispose of herself as she will. It can hardly be overstrained to assume that public opinion will be more likely to condemn the woman who is untrue to her own choice, than the woman who violates vows which she did not willingly take, and most Englishmen appear to think that our own system works well on the whole for family happiness. The one case, then, in which the chivalrous sentiment for women has failed to work for good, is where it has been perverted by contact with the oldest juridical theory of domestic life. And as the husband's control over his wife's property is historically derived from the parental power transferred to him by the marriage contract, we must either, to be consistent, remodel English society by adopting the laws that subject children to their parents, or we must extend the rights of the single woman to the married. Now, the first of these alternatives I take to be beyond our power. The family life of ancient Rome, Greece, and Germany, is as much a thing of the past as the Roman Empire or the mediæval Papacy.

Practically, of course, English conservatives have no desire to reconstruct, and a very great though a vague hatred of consistency. Not the unimpaired past as it was, but the fragmentary past that has not yet been detached from our laws and institutions, and that represents prerogative, caste, or monopoly against the equality of classes, sects, and persons, is the past that sensible men defend, when their interests or temperaments are opposed to change. Wholesale retrogression would not be possible; and there has been no state of society hitherto in which the interests of the rich have been on the whole so well cared for as at present. Even Glanville and Bracton held larger views of the wife's powers and rights than our courts accept. The general drift of conservative argument, when it does not go back to St. Paul, is therefore to prove that our present laws work on the whole well, and that where any change in them has been made, it has been productive of evil. This last argument, if it could be established, ought of course to be decisive. But there is a difficulty, which candid thinkers of both sides will deplore, in procuring any precedents that are absolutely decisive as to the point at issue. Either the changes made have not been the same, or they have been made under perfectly different circumstances.

Take, for instance, the case of France. Prior to the Revolution the law of France forbade divorce absolutely, as it is forbidden by Catholicism. The laws concerning the property of married women differed in the different provinces, but even in the less favoured parts the wife was entitled to dower out of her husband's property, which neither he nor his creditors could touch; and the *séparation des biens* was recognised as a possible form of marriage contract by the laws.[1] When the Revolution broke out, the prevalent impulse was to extend personal rights, and almost unlimited liberty of divorce was conceded. The results were found prejudicial to public

[1] Maine's "Ancient Law," p. 158; "Ordonnances de Louis XIV.," iii. Art. 36.

morality; and, after some partial but unsuccessful modifications, divorce was again forbidden as before, while the liberal practice of the southern provinces, which recognised the *séparation des biens*, was extended to all France.[1] Practically, therefore, the recognition of the wife's right to property has coincided with a stricter rule than our own as to the indissolubility of the conjugal bond. It may be said that this rigidity of the laws is tempered by a certain licence of manners, and that peace and purity in domestic life are more frequently found in England than in France. I am prepared to admit this assertion, for the sake of argument, and as partially true, though I believe its value has been enormously overstated. The question remains, whether there is any reason for ascribing French deficiencies to the wife's control of her property. The provinces where this right prevailed were not distinguished in old times by greater laxity of manners than those which observed something like the English custom, and were certainly purer than the capital. In fact, the early rise

[1] Marriage was declared a civil contract, dissoluble at pleasure, in 1793. In 1803 certain slight limitations were imposed, chiefly restraining the wife's power to separate from her husband. Divorces, however, were still very frequent; and Napoleon was of opinion that the number of foundlings had increased tenfold since the Revolution. Accordingly, in 1816, M. de Bonald brought forward a law for the entire abolition of divorce; and the proposition to introduce it passed unanimously. In 1848 M. Crémieux made a proposal to re-establish the liberty of divorce; but it was rejected. (Alison's "Europe" (1789—1815), ii. p. 613, iv. p. 762; Ibid. (1815—1852), i. p. 287, viii. p. 326.) Sir A. Alison gives extracts from the *Moniteur*, showing that the divorces at Paris were as one in four to the marriages for part of 1793-94, and the average for two years is stated at from 500 to 600 in Dumont's "Bentham," i. p. 357.

and abiding influence of an austere Calvinism in the South are, perhaps, as good evidence as can be got to the higher moral tone of the Mediterranean provinces. Probably, therefore, we must seek the cause elsewhere, and I should myself look for it in the prevalent systems of education, and in those relics of parental authority which survive so curiously in the French code. A girl brought up in a convent, religiously and purely, if you will, but with no wide or deep culture of the mind, married before she is twenty-two, at latest, to a man whom her parents have chosen for her and of whom she often knows nothing, comparatively emancipated from tutelage, and exposed to all the temptations of a new life, is, I think, less favourably circumstanced than most young wives among ourselves. Anyhow, these reasons may be fairly set off against the mere assumption that the *séparation des biens* is the real cause of the social shortcomings depicted in a portion of French literature. And what is true of France may be said also of other Catholic countries that have accepted or copied the Code Napoleon.

America will be found a truer parallel to England, and the lesson it teaches will be all the more instructive, because the experiments at change, though guided more or less by a common principle, have been almost as numerous as the States of the Union. As the Federal Judiciary decided long ago that every State had a right to legislate on this matter for itself, the confusion that sometimes arises is no argument against the system; and when it is said that in one State a man may be a married man, in another a bachelor, and in a third a bigamist, the case alluded to is of some one who has moved from one State to another to acquire fresh rights by fresh domiciles, and is still subject in some relations to the laws of his first home. A native of South Carolina where divorce was till quite recently forbidden would have been a bigamist to the South Carolina courts if he married again after a year's residence in Indiana: and the woman who married him would, I presume, have been a single woman before the law in Charleston. These unhappy discrepancies result, however, from the constitution of the Union, and are no more an argument against the laws of any particular State than European diversities of practice against English law. The position of an Englishman who acquired domicile in Germany, divorced his wife and married her sister, would appear scandalous to many people; and, unless he had acted under legal advice, might lead to curious complications, but proves nothing on either side of the marriage question. On the other hand, the position of the lady whom the Irish courts declared to be wife by a Scotch marriage, who it was thought by the Scotch judges might have been married in Ireland, and whom the House of Lords declared to have been married nowhere, is one instance of the perplexities that may occur even in our own country Nor can we much wonder if, in America, where a single State may be larger than France, each community claims the right to legislate for itself about the marriage-bond, when, after more than 150 years' union with Scotland, we have found it impossible to assimilate the marriage-laws of the two countries.

Dismissing this argument, then, we may examine the more formidable objection which connects the *séparation des biens,* either as cause or consequence, with what Mr. Beresford-Hope terms "free trade in divorce." The first supposition may be very briefly disposed of. In America, as in most new countries, a large part of the property of the first settlers was in land, and this has always followed the old English law, by which the husband only enjoys the usufruct of his wife's possessions at marriage. Consequently, the cases of grievance from the wife's inability to own property have been few, and do not seem, till quite recently, to have been the subject of legislative enactment. On the other hand, there has long been a strong feeling for personal liberty. Connecticut led the way with a law of divorce as early as 1702; but the chief legislation on the subject seems to have been between 1809 and 1840, during which period eleven States framed or extended laws for dissolving the marriage-bond.[1] On the other hand, the legislation for securing their property to married women began about 1847, and eight States adopted measures more or less liberal within five years.[2] There is no exact corre-

[1] Kent's "Commentaries," vol. ii. pp. 76—80. The States in question are Connecticut, Maine, Vermont, New Hampshire, New Jersey, Kentucky, Indiana, Ohio, Missouri, Tennessee, and North Carolina. This list, however, is very inadequate; and Kent, in fact, says (edition of 1856) that in most States (New York and South Carolina being then exceptions) ill-usage, desertion, absence, or habitual drunkenness, would be considered ground for a divorce more or less complete.

[2] Vermont, Connecticut, Texas, Alabama, New York, New Jersey, Maine,

spondence between the two movements. Georgia, where divorces have been very frequent, passed a reactionary law in 1845, extending the husband's power over his wife's personalty to realty. Kentucky, which ranks with Indiana as the State where the marriage-bond is most easily severed, retains the English law as to the property of married women. On the other hand, the State of New York, where divorces are only allowed in case of adultery, has given the wife the position of a single woman as regards property since 1848. It would be interesting to know whether there has been any sensible change for the worse in the household life of citizens of New York since the experiment of 1848 has been tried. But, after all, the proof of deterioration would establish little; for not only must we take into account the demoralization that results, in every society, from civil war and a sudden increase of wealth, but we must allow for the undoubted influence of the lax marriage-laws of other States upon a neighbouring community. If English people could be divorced as easily as married by acquiring domiciles in Scotland, the rigour of our present divorce system would lose much of its efficiency.

Practically, then, we are reduced to pure theory when we come to argue the second alternative, whether separation of properties would tend to break up or sow dissension in families; for the countries where this is an old institution are mostly those where the conjugal

and Wisconsin (Kent's "Commentaries," vol. ii. pp. 108, 109, 126). This list has been very much extended since the date referred to.

bond is indissoluble, and the countries where it is newly adopted are already familiarized by long practice with divorce. It is true, conservatives appeal to the successful working amongst ourselves of our present system. But they habitually mean by this, not that working women are content with their husbands' control over their earnings, but only that in the upper classes, where wives as a rule earn nothing and have a competence settled on them at marriage, the legal theory of the husband's rights does not visibly impair domestic happiness. All things considered, it would be very wonderful if it did. The great mass of educated people are pretty well under the restraint of public opinion; and the gross cases of wrong which occur from time to time, and which it is well not to forget, are doubtless to be regarded as, on the whole, exceptional. Still, it must be borne in mind that domestic grievances are among those on which it is most difficult to procure satisfactory evidence, and that most people are at length schooled by life to endure a system, however bad, which they see no chance of remedying by any act of their own. The supposed acquiescence of married women in our laws would be more satisfactorily demonstrated if any political action, beyond petitioning, were open to them. I cannot, however, regard the position of women in the upper classes, secured by marriage contracts and the laws of society, fenced in by the numberless little safeguards of traditional culture and neighbourly surveillance, and commonly with an easy redress at law through the aid of relatives in cases of palpable wrong, as at all analogous to the status of wives in any condition below the professional classes, for whom every one of these securities is wanting. Mr. Russell Gurney mentioned, in the House of Commons, that the women of Jamaica were opposed to marriage, because of the law which transferred the wife's earnings to the husband. That it has not yet come to this pitch among ourselves is due, no doubt, to the long tradition of marriage and to religious feeling. But is it wise to bring some of the strongest sentiments in our nature into constant opposition? Even the love of money for itself is a motive power which we cannot easily disregard; but when money means self-respect in the wife, food for her children, and the means of education, is it well to put all these at the mercy of a husband, and to give the concubine an independence which is denied to the married woman? I cannot myself conceive anything more likely to break up families than that all the woman's earnings should be disposed of by the man. But what I regard with more apprehension than any domestic unhappiness, is the chance that, if the natural remedy be denied, a laxer system of divorce will be demanded and obtained. In fact, the thin end of the wedge has already been introduced through the vices of our present system. Desertion is now a reason for a protection-order, which emancipates the wife from her husband's control, and assumes a separation *a mensâ et thoro.* No one can wish that this security should be withheld in the actual state of the law; but it is difficult to suppose that a measure so insufficient for all its purposes will be left in its present incompleteness. If the property and earnings of married women be not secured to them by a general enactment, the system of protection-orders will be extended to cases in which the husband is cruel or wasteful. Given a few hundred marriages in which the husband's control is suspended by order of a magistrate, and a strong case will be made out for the ready dissolution of the conjugal bond.

Neither must it be forgotten that the progress of democratic opinion rather tends, for a time at least, to facilitate the movement for divorce. The right of either party to rescind a contract which no longer secures the objects for which it was formed, or to frame contracts in such a manner that they may one day be rescinded, appears consistent with the first notions of equity. That the experiment has been tried in France and failed signally, is now generally forgotten. The examples of North Germany and America are more recent and better known; and in both, despite some extreme instances, the law of divorce is believed to work well, or at least is maintained by public opinion. Perhaps the time has not yet arrived when the system can be estimated at its full value. But the arguments which Bentham adduced[1] for regarding the marriage bond as indissoluble seem to me to have lost none of their force; and while I believe that our present system was rendered necessary by the abuse of private Acts of Parliament, giving the rich a privilege which was withheld from the poor, I

[1] Dumont's "Bentham," vol. i. pp. 346—348. It is right to add, that Bentham summed up against these reasons, and in favour of divorce.

prefer the rigour of the French law, which assumes that the marriage union can only end with life. A man of forty may part from his wife and form a fresh connexion without sensible difficulty, perhaps even with manifest gain, if he has been professionally successful. A woman of forty and mother of a large family is in a very different position, and generally is likely to remain widowed. Moreover, easy divorces are only another form of polygamy; and in all polygamous countries the poor are comparatively at a disadvantage. Practically, too, the certainty of easy divorce would, I think, increase the number alike of injudicious marriages and of hasty separations. Nor is it easy to understand how the sanctity of filial relations would be preserved if the children of one father are scattered under the several roofs of his discarded consorts. For all these reasons, as well as for others which I need not discuss, as they rather belong to ethics than to politics, I look forward with the greatest dread to any further relaxation of the marriage-tie. The only class who will gain permanently by it will be wealthy voluptuaries, with a taste like Henry VIII. for forming temporary unions under the double sanction of the Church and the Law.

Yet to this we shall come, if any makeshift like protection-orders be adopted, not only because that system is itself a dangerous approximation to divorce, but because it strengthens the assumption that a married woman has no right of property. At this moment a woman may live with her son, her brother, or her lover, and dispose of every farthing she possesses or earns as she will. Tradesmen find not the smallest difficulty in dealing with such households, and would practically be better off if the law for all persons were the same, than now, when the lady whom they trusted as a single woman may suddenly shelter herself under the marriage-laws.[1] It is only when a woman assumes the most solemn responsibilities of her life that the law begins to treat her as irresponsible. It is only after the husband has sworn to endow her with all his worldly goods that the law regards her as incapable of possessing property. Even the compensation which she once possessed in the right of dower has been seriously impaired by recent legislation. At the same time, women are becoming not less, but more, tenacious of their rights; not less, but better, able to assert and use independence. The family system of Greece and Rome is broken up; the rigour of traditional discipline is a thing of the past; and the "moderate correction," allowed by our old laws and recommended by high authority, would now entitle a woman to separation for cruelty. In nothing does the husband retain the prerogative of old times, except in the power to confiscate his wife's property or earnings. Unless all analogy be deceptive, it is impossible that these anomalies should continue to co-exist much longer. But, practically, there are only two remedies which

[1] This is not an hypothetical case. It is only the other day that a woman who was summoned for rates, obtained an adjournment, and appeared at the next time of hearing protected by a certificate of her marriage to a vagrant hawker, whose domicile could not be ascertained. No doubt the case is an extreme one; but instances in which a married couple would deliberately combine to defraud tradesmen are also, I should hope, not numerous.

would be really final. One is, that divorces should be granted wherever the husband is cruel, wasteful, or unwise ; the other, that the wife should be put in the position of a *feme sole* as regards her property, rights, and liabilities. The former would be an extreme expedient, which we surely ought to defer till we have tried the more temperate measure.

VII.

THE PROPERTY DISABILITIES OF A MARRIED WOMAN, AND OTHER LEGAL EFFECTS OF MARRIAGE.

BY HERBERT N. MOZLEY, ESQ.

THE rights and disabilities arising from marriage are founded upon the maxim of the Common Law, that "husband and wife are as one person in law." In order to convey to our readers a clear notion of the legal relations of husband and wife, it will be necessary to show the import of this apparently paradoxical statement, and the extent of its application.

The principal illustration of this maxim is to be found in the property disabilities of a married woman. These disabilities, we are told,[1] are created by policy of law, for two reasons: first, to prevent, so far as can be by human precaution, the regard which the wife is supposed to entertain for her husband, and his influence over her, from stripping her of all her property during the marriage; and secondly, to exempt the husband from her acts and engagements to which he was not privy and consenting.

[1] Roper, "Husband and Wife," vol. ii. p. 95.

These disabilities operate generally, according to the Common Law, to restrain the wife from doing any act with reference to property without her husband's concurrence. The very being or legal existence of the woman is by the Common Law suspended during the marriage; or at least, it is incorporated and consolidated into that of the husband, under whose wing, protection, and cover she performs everything. The rule is subject to certain exceptions, which we shall presently notice.

The immediate effect of marriage is to place her personal property at once absolutely in the power of her husband, and to give him a certain qualified interest in her real property. It would be beyond our present purpose to enter at any length into the distinction between "real" and "personal" property; but for the present purpose it may be stated, without material inaccuracy, that "real property" comprehends all permanent interests in land, and that "personal property" comprehends all interests in land for fixed terms of years, as well as all property which is not property in land. In the ordinary case of a woman entitled to "real" property, marriage would confer upon the husband a right to receive the rents and profits for the joint lives of husband and wife.[1] And if there be issue of the marriage born alive capable of inheriting, the husband will be further entitled, "by the curtesy of England," to a further interest in his wife's property for his life, should he survive her. But with regard to personal property, marriage is an absolute gift to

[1] Roper, "Husband and Wife," vol. i. p. 3.

the husband of all the goods, personal chattels, and estate, which the wife was actually and beneficially possessed of at that time in her own right, and of such other goods and personal chattels as come to her during the marriage.[1] A distinction is drawn between things in the actual possession of the wife, and things not in her immediate possession; as, for instance, money at the bank. With regard to the latter, the husband may reduce them into possession if he pleases, and they will then be completely in his power; but if he die without having done so in the lifetime of his wife, she, and not the husband's representatives, will be entitled by survivorship.

Having regard, therefore, to the interest which the law gives the husband in his wife's property, it follows that a wife cannot do any act affecting her property without affecting her husband's rights. The disabilities of a wife in relation to property are, therefore, a necessary consequence of the rights of the husband.

But where a married woman has an *authority* over property distinct from any *interest* in it, she may exercise such authority without any concurrence on the part of her husband.[2] For in this case she cannot, by exercising the authority, injuriously affect her husband's interests; and, moreover, whatever she does in the exercise of such authority is deemed to be not her own act, but the act of her principal. An authority to make a conveyance of another's estate, for instance, may be exercised by her without her husband's concurrence.

[1] Roper, "Husband and Wife," vol. i. p. 169. [2] Ibid. vol. ii. p. 97.

And in cases where the husband has been banished for life or transported, or been prevented from coming into England by reason of his being an alien enemy, the wife may sue and be sued as if she were unmarried.[1] But the principle of these cases applies only when the husband's absence is involuntary, and enforced by law; if the husband's absence be voluntary, the mere fact of his being domiciled in a foreign country does not release his wife from the disabilities of the married state.

Again, a married woman may carry on a trade as a single woman within the City of London, by the custom of the city.[2] But this case can hardly be treated as an exception to the general rule of disability, seeing that it is in the power of the husband to put an end to his wife's trading in future if he think fit to do so, though he cannot do so in retrospect, nor do any act to injure creditors who have claims upon the wife's property so acquired.

Again, in certain cases a wife may bind her husband by her contracts. Where a married woman, living with her husband, orders articles for the use of the house and family, she will be presumed to have done so as her husband's agent. But this is only a presumption, and may be rebutted by evidence that the wife did not, in fact, act as her husband's agent. But if the articles ordered were *necessaries*, then the husband will not be allowed to show that the contract was made without his authority, or even against his wishes; for it is a husband's duty to provide his wife with necessaries.[3]

1 Roper, "Husband and Wife," vol. ii. p. 120. 2 Ibid. p. 124.

3 See, however, *Jolly* v. *Rees*, Scott's "Common Bench Reports, New Series," vol. xv. p. 628; *Weekly Reporter*, vol. xii. p. 473; *post*, pp. 216—219.

So, if a husband turns his wife out of doors, or by his own conduct renders it impossible for her to live with him, he will still be liable for contracts for supplying her with necessaries.

Necessaries have been defined to be such articles as comport with the wife's situation in life and her husband's fortune, and which are usually worn or possessed by persons in similar conditions of life. We shall, however, consider this point more fully in a subsequent part of this Essay.[1]

We have been hitherto confining our observations to the cases where a wife acts, or affects to act, independently of her husband. There remains a further question, how far a wife may bind her property by acts done with her husband's concurrence. Now, this question cannot generally arise in the case of personal property; for, as we have seen, marriage is an absolute gift to the husband of all a wife's personal property *in possession;* and with regard to her personal property not in possession, the husband may at any time make it his own by reducing it into possession. A wife's *real property* may be disposed of by the husband and wife acting jointly in any manner they may think fit; though for this purpose it was necessary, before the year 1834, that they should go through a fiction called "levying a fine," and now a married woman cannot dispose of any interest in real property without being "separately examined"[2] as to whether she freely consents to such a disposition. It is to be hoped

[1] See *post*, pp. 215—219.

[2] Stat. 3 & 4 Wm. IV. c. 74, s. 79.

that this farce of a "separate examination" will before long be abolished.

If a husband dies without making a will, his widow is entitled to one-third of his personal property if he leave children, and to one-half if he leave none.[1] She is not, however, entitled to any share in his real property, except in so far as she may be entitled to "dower." "Dower" is a life-interest in one-third of the husband's real estate; but, for reasons which it is not necessary to mention here, this right of "dower" very seldom attaches.[2]

A husband, surviving his wife, becomes entitled for his own use to the whole of her personal property, to the exclusion of her children or other relatives.[3] In her real estate he takes, as we have seen, a life interest, provided there has been issue born alive *capable of inheriting*,[4] for otherwise he gets nothing. And it must be borne in mind that a married woman cannot, under the Common Law, make a will, except by the licence of her husband.

Such is a brief and necessarily very imperfect sketch of the legal effects of marriage as regards property, according to the doctrines of the Common Law. We proceed to consider how far the law in this respect has been affected by the doctrines which obtain in Courts of Equity.[5]

[1] Statute of Distributions, 22 & 23 Car. II. c. 10.

[2] "Williams on Real Property," part i. ch. 11; Stat. 3 & 4 Wm. IV. c. 105.

[3] Statute of Frauds, 29 Car. II. c. 3, s. 24.

[4] If issue be born *incapable of inheriting*,—as, for instance, if an estate be limited to a married woman and the heirs *female* of her body, and a *son* be born,—this will not give the husband a title to curtesy. (Roper, "Husband and Wife," vol. i. p. 32.)

[5] See Haynes' "Outlines of Equity," Lecture VII. These lectures were

The manner in which the severities of the Common Law are evaded is, usually, by settlement or will giving property to the trustees for the separate use of the wife. The property then becomes, in law, vested in the trustees; but the Court of Chancery compels the trustees to use their legal rights in such manner as to carry out the directions of the settlement or will under which they act. If property be given or left to a wife's separate use, without the intervention of trustees, the Court of Chancery will consider the husband as a trustee of the property for his wife, and direct him to deal with it as she may appoint.

The doctrine of the separate use appears for the first time in the reign of Queen Elizabeth;[1] but it cannot be said to have grown into a system until the last century. The principal doctrines connected with it have not been settled until within the last few years, if indeed they can be said to be fully settled now.

The first question suggested by "the separate use" clause is, Would it afford a real protection to the wife? or, Would not a husband be easily able to induce his wife by undue influence to dispose of her separate estate according to his wishes? In order to avoid this result, a device called the "restraint on anticipation" was invented by Courts of Equity. Where a clause inserted

delivered in the year 1857, when the subject was much canvassed. Bills were brought into Parliament by Lord Brougham and Sir Erskine Perry for the amendment of the law in this respect. Mr. Haynes (p. 201) distinctly anticipates the passing of such a measure as Mr. Russell Gurney's, which differs but little from that of Sir Erskine Perry. See also Smith's "Manual of Equity," Title V. ch. iii.

[1] Haynes, pp. 203, 204.

in a settlement or will forbade a married woman to anticipate the income of property settled or bequeathed to her separate use, such clause was allowed its full effect, so as to give to a married woman the enjoyment of property without suffering her to encumber it in any way.

Now, in order to explain this point fully, it is necessary to observe, that, in ordinary cases, it is impossible to make a gift by deed, will, or other instrument to A. B. simply, and then to affix a restriction upon the use of the gift; as, for instance, in the case of a gift of money, a donor could not prescribe how much should be spent every year, or do anything which should interfere with the absolute enjoyment of the gift. Nor can this result be avoided even by the intervention of a trustee. If money be given to a person in trust for A, who is of full age, to be accumulated until A attains the age of fifty years, A may nevertheless claim the sum from the trustee at once. The only way of avoiding this result is by what is called a "gift over;" in other words, by a condition that if A attempts to part with the money, or do anything inconsistent with the donor's intentions, the money should go "over" to somebody else.

It will be readily understood that if A be under age, no trustee would be justified in handing him over the trust-money until he attains his full age. Now, a married woman may, by means of the "restraint on anticipation," be put on the same footing as a minor in this respect;[1] so that, where this "restraint on antici-

[1] Haynes, p. 211. See *Tullett* v. *Armstrong*, 1 Beavan, 1.

pation" exists, it is possible for a married woman to induce a trustee to part with the money held upon trust, and afterwards to take proceedings against him for doing so. Where no such restraint exists, a married woman's separate estate is her property to all intents and purposes; and she may bind it by her contracts, or encumber it in any way she may think proper.[1] And any contract, by which a married woman possessed of a separate estate without any restraint on anticipation attempts to bind herself, is held to bind her separate estate. As to the precise import of such a contract, and the manner in which it ought to be held to operate, several technical questions have been raised, into which it is not necessary to enter here.

It will, of course, be borne in mind that the privileges, of which we have been speaking as conceded to married women by Courts of Equity, do not, in general, arise by the mere operation of circumstances. In other words, some definite act on the part of the married woman, or some one acting in her interest, is necessary to bring them into existence. In order that a married woman may enjoy property to her separate use, with or without power of anticipation, it is necessary that this enjoyment should have been secured to her by a marriage-settlement, or by the express terms of the instrument (whether deed, will, or otherwise) by which she becomes entitled to the property in question.

But there are some cases where the Court of Chancery

[1] *Hulme* v. *Tenant*, Brown's "Cases in Chancery," vol. i. p. 16; White and Tudor's "Leading Cases," vol. i.

will itself order a settlement of a married woman's property. As, for instance, when a ward of Court marries, whether with or without the sanction of the Court; in these cases the Court will insist on a proper settlement, even though the lady be willing to waive her right to a settlement.[1] And cases have been known, where, on a runaway match with a lady who is a minor, her friends have taken immediate proceedings to make her a ward of Chancery before the marriage takes place, in order to secure her a proper settlement.

There is also a right called an "equity to a settlement," which in certain cases attaches to a married woman, without any forethought on the part of her or her friends. Among other arbitrary distinctions with which the English law abounds, there is one which we trust will soon be abolished, but which for our present purpose it is necessary briefly to explain. We allude to the distinction between *legal* and *equitable* rights. Speaking roughly, we may say that the former are those which can, the latter are those which cannot, be enforced without a suit in Chancery. Now, where a woman has a *legal* right to property, this right on marriage passes to her husband; and he may sue for it, and the Court of Law has no right to withhold it from him. But if a wife has an equitable right to property, or, as it is technically called, an equitable *chose in action*, and the husband sues for it in the Court of Chancery, the Court, acting on the maxim that he who seeks equity must do equity, will not in general give it up to him without requiring

[1] Smith's "Manual of Equity," 7th Ed. p. 442.

him to make a reasonable settlement of it on his wife and family.[1] The usual rule is to give half to the husband, and settle the other half on the wife and children; but the practice varies according to circumstances. And the wife may, if she pleases, waive her equity to a settlement; in which case the fund will be paid over to the husband.

Hitherto we have been speaking of the Court of Chancery as the *protector* of married women; but we cannot leave this part of the subject without alluding to a class of cases in which that Court appears in a very different character.

It is a doctrine which obtains in the Court of Chancery, that settlements of her property made by a woman before marriage, in fraud of the rights of her intended husband, are void as against him, and may at his instance be set aside.[2] Now, the scope of this doctrine is far wider than might at first sight appear. A "fraud on marital rights" will in general be deemed to have been committed if the lady, during the engagement, makes any disposition of her property without the knowledge of her intended husband. The following statement of the rule, and reasons for it, given in Roper's "Treatise on Husband and Wife," vol. i. p. 163, illustrate the notions prevalent at the commencement of the present century with reference to the subject:—

[1] Roper, "Husband and Wife," vol. i. p. 256. *Lady Elibank* v. *Montolieu*, White and Tudor's "Leading Cases," vol. i.

[2] See *Lady Strathmore* v. *Bowes*, and Notes on that case, in White and Tudor's "Leading Cases," vol. i.

"Deception will be inferred, if, after the commencement of the treaty for marriage, the wife should attempt to make any disposition of her property without her intended husband's knowledge or concurrence. The injury he would sustain, if such a transaction were to be sanctioned, is obvious; for *since the wife's apparent fortune in addition to his own may be a weighty consideration and inducement for entering into the contract*, the happiness of both might be endangered, if, after *the treaty began under such calculations and persuasions*, the wife should be enabled, prior to the marriage, to disappoint them by disposing of or abridging her interest in the property that belonged to her. It is presumed, therefore, that, without the consent of the intended husband, the law will not permit any disposition of the wife's fortune to be made before the marriage then in contemplation; and that under no circumstances, after a treaty for marriage has commenced, will any such voluntary disposition of her property be binding upon her subsequent husband."

And it does not follow that the intended husband should have been aware of the existence of the property settled; for, in *Goddard* v. *Snow* (1 Russell, 485), a woman, ten months before her marriage, made a settlement of property, of which the future husband did not know her to be possessed. Here there could be no fraud in holding out to the husband the prospect of a fortune which it was intended to disappoint. That the parties were on terms of intimacy and friendship before the date of the settlement was fully admitted. The date of the settlement was the 28th of August, 1812, and the engagement took place in that year, but whether before or after the settlement did not clearly appear from the evidence. The wife died ten years after the marriage, and after her death the husband took proceedings to impeach the settlement. The settlement was set aside by the then Master of the Rolls, and the husband declared entitled to the money which had been so settled, on the ground that "it was intended to be in fraud of the marriage which she was about to contract."

The whole doctrine of the Courts of Equity on this subject has never, perhaps, been more fully stated than by Vice-Chancellor Sir James Wigram, in the case of *Taylor* v. *Pugh* (1 Hare, 608). In giving judgment, the Vice-Chancellor observed (p. 613) :—

"It was urged for the defendants who resist this claim, that the plaintiff (the husband) was ignorant, until after the marriage, that the wife was possessed of the property in question; and I was referred to cases in which the Court had apparently laid some stress on that circumstance, as a ground for refusing relief to the husband. In *De Manneville* v. *Crompton*,[1] Lord Eldon made the important observation that, in the absence of any representation having been made as to specific property, no implied contract is raised on the part of the lady, during the treaty of marriage, that her property, as it existed at the commencement of the treaty, shall be *in no way diminished.* This undoubtedly shows Lord Eldon's opinion to be, that it is not every alienation of the wife's property during the treaty which can be regarded as fraudulent, only because the husband was not a party to it. But I should have great difficulty in applying the proposition so laid down by Lord Eldon, to a case in which every farthing of the wife's property was, without the knowledge of the husband, wholly withdrawn from his control, and settled on herself, her children, or her appointees, to the total exclusion of the husband. A very special case must be made out before the Court would carry the proposition so far. I think that Lord Eldon meant only to decide that there being no implied contract on the part of the lady that her property should not be in any way diminished, it is for the Court to determine whether, having regard to the condition in life of the parties, and the other circumstances of the case, a transaction complained of by the husband should be treated as fraudulent or not.

---

[1] 1 Vesey and Beames, 354.

"I think another argument on behalf of the defendants was also carried beyond its just limits, in contending that actual fraud or deception on the husband must be proved. Notwithstanding there are some dicta which may at first be considered as implying the contrary (but which may, I think, be explained), I take the rule of the Court to be correctly stated in Mr. Roper's Treatise:—'Deception will be inferred if, after the commencement of the treaty for marriage, the wife should attempt to make any disposition of her property without her intended husband's knowledge or concurrence.' This way of stating the law does not exclude inquiry into the circumstances by which the apparent deception may be explained."

We would not leave the consideration of this doctrine without referring to the case of the *Countess of Strathmore* v. *Bowes,* which is a leading case on this point, and shows that at all events the doctrine in question has its limits. On the 10th of January, 1777, Lady Strathmore, being engaged to a Mr. Grey, made a settlement of her property with his concurrence; but a few days afterwards (the 16th), hearing that a Mr. Bowes had fought a duel on her account with an editor who had traduced her character, she resolved to marry Mr. Bowes, and she married him accordingly the next day.[1] Mr. Bowes

[1] The facts of the case appear to be these:—Bowes (whose name at the time of the engagement of Lady Strathmore with Mr. Grey was Andrew Robinson Stoney, but who on his marriage with Lady Strathmore assumed the name of Bowes, being Lady Strathmore's maiden name) recommended himself to Lady Strathmore's notice by various devices. He aspersed her character in a newspaper, and afterwards pretended to vindicate her from such aspersions, by engaging in a pretended duel. On the 16th of January, 1777, Lady Strathmore, hearing of the duel, and that Bowes was mortally wounded, was prevailed upon that evening to visit him at his lodgings in St. James' Street. He spoke in a low tone of voice, and pretended to be very ill, but expressed pleasure at her visiting him. He did not expect, he said, to survive twenty-four hours, but he hoped to marry her before he died. If she would only consent to be married to him, he would die happy. She believed the truth of his story, and, from motives of gratitude and com-

finding her property settled, in May 1777 by threats and violence compelled her to execute a deed revoking the settlement of January 1777. Having separated from him in 1785, she took proceedings in Chancery to set aside the latter deed, and to establish the settlement of January 1777. He, in his turn, in 1786 took counter-proceedings to impeach the settlement of January 1777, as a fraud upon his marital rights. It appeared from the evidence that the duel which he had fought was a sham duel, got up for the purpose of securing Lady Strathmore's affections. The following positions are maintained in the argument on behalf of Mr. Bowes (March 2, 1789):—

"A wife by the marriage contract becomes extinct, from the nature of it, for several civil purposes, with regard to which she merges in

---

passion, consented to marry him. The marriage was solemnized next morning, Bowes being carried to church on a litter. From the time of the marriage he cut off her intercourse with her friends, and treated her with the greatest cruelty, and, by blows and menaces, compelled her to sign any deeds he wanted her to sign; among others, the deed of revocation of the settlement of the 10th of January, 1777. She experienced the most cruel treatment from him for several years; and at last, in February 1785, she succeeded in effecting her escape.

After that she lived separate from him, except that in November 1786 she was seized and forcibly carried away to Streatlam Castle in the county of Durham, by armed men hired by Bowes for the purpose. She was deprived of her liberty, and was treated with great cruelty; but at the end of ten days she regained her liberty. She then took proceedings in the King's Bench for compelling him to keep the peace towards her. She also took proceedings in the Consistory Court of the Bishop of London for a judicial separation, which was granted. Bowes appealed successively to the Arches Court and the Court of Delegates, but without success. His appeal was dismissed with costs, amounting to 1,742*l.* 14*s.* 2*d.*; and failing to pay the costs, he was excommunicated by the judges delegates. (Brown's "Cases in Parliament," *Settlements*, vol. vi. pp. 429 *et seq.*)

the husband. He becomes liable to all her debts, and answerable for all her acts that do not amount to felony; and even for that, if committed in his presence, because her mind is supposed to be under his coercion. In order to enable him to answer this, he has by law all her property. Marriage by the law of England gives the husband the whole dominion over the property, and also over the person of his wife, except as to murder; for by the old law he could not be punished for cruelty to her. The civil existence of the wife merged in that of the husband; he is the head of the family; to make another would be against the policy of the law. If the wife can by her own act, against the consent of the husband, make herself independent of him, it will destroy that subordination so necessary in families, which is analogous to that in the State, and tends to support it; for if Lady Strathmore is right in this, the husband is become a cipher in his own house; for he cannot educate his children, or do any other act which by law he has a right to do."[1]

We have seldom seen the positions of the extreme defenders of marital rights put so forcibly as in the passage just quoted, and it is on this account that we have given the above extract. The argument, however, does not seem to have made much impression upon Lord Chancellor Thurlow, who stated in his judgment,—

"I never had a doubt about this case. . . . Marriage in general seems to have been Lady Strathmore's object; she was disposed to marry anybody, but not to part with her fortune. This settlement is to be considered as the effect of a lucid interval, and if there can be reason in madness, by doing this she discovered a spark of understanding. The question which arises upon all the cases is, whether the evidence is sufficient to raise fraud. Even if there had been a fraud upon Grey, I would not have permitted Bowes to come here and complain of it. But there was no fraud even upon Grey, for it was with his consent. It is impossible for a man marrying in the manner Bowes did to come into equity and talk of fraud."[2]

---

[1] 1 Vesey junior, 23; White and Tudor's "Leading Cases," vol. i. pp. 365, 366.

[2] 1 Vesey junior, 28; White and Tudor, vol. i. pp. 371, 372.

Mr. Bowes appealed to the House of Lords. Four reasons were alleged by his counsel for the reversal of the decrees appealed from :—

1. That the deeds were a fraud upon the marriage, being made without the appellant's knowledge.

2. That the deeds would have been fraudulent against creditors, or purchasers for valuable consideration, and therefore would be void as against Bowes, who by the marriage gave Lady Strathmore a legal title to dower in his own estate (worth at that time, as he said, about 1,000*l.* a year), and became responsible for the obligations of a husband, and particularly for debts contracted, or to be contracted, by her.

3. That all the cases on the subject agreed in regarding such a disposition as void.

4. That if the decrees complained of should be established, a precedent would exist destructive of confidence in every matrimonial engagement.

After what we have already stated, we need not discuss the first, third, and fourth of these reasons. It is the second to which we would call the special attention of our readers, as throwing some light upon the reason of the "equitable" doctrine of which we are speaking.

By a statute of Queen Elizabeth (27 Eliz. c. 4), a prior voluntary conveyance is void as against a subsequent purchaser for value; so that if A makes a gift of property to B, and A subsequently conveys the same to C for valuable consideration (which would generally be for a sum of money), C may take the property as against B.

Now in the cases we are considering, the "consideration" consists in the rights acquired by the lady under the marriage. It was argued therefore by Mr. Bowes' counsel, that on the *principle* of the statute just referred to, the conveyance in the anticipation of the marriage with Mr. Grey ought to be set aside. And there was a good deal of plausibility in the argument.

With regard to the allusion to creditors, it may be remarked that creditors are protected in a similar way by another Act of Queen Elizabeth (13 Eliz. c. 5).

However, having regard to the circumstances of the case, the House of Lords ordered that Mr. Bowes' appeal be dismissed, with 150*l.* costs.[1]

In the class of cases we have been considering, Courts of Equity, so far from protecting the wife, hand her over to the tender mercies of the Common Law, though the Common Law itself could not touch her. It might perhaps be said, that where a woman attempts to commit a fraud on her intended husband she ought not to be allowed to reap any advantage thereby. But the rule, as in many other branches of equity jurisprudence, goes far beyond cases of attempt to defraud. As we have seen, a disposition of property by a woman before marriage may be set aside even in cases where the husband was wholly ignorant of the existence of the property of which the disposition was made. Again, perhaps it might be said that a woman's settlement of her property might be unreasonable, and that a Court of Equity would probably consult the best

[1] Brown's "Cases in Parliament," vol. vi. pp. 435, 436.

interests of both parties by setting it aside. This is a point which is involved in the question of the general merits of the present law relating to married women's property, on which we propose to speak more fully in the course of this Essay. For the present, we would remark, that the obvious remedy is, not to hand over the money to the husband, but to settle the property in such manner as may be most for the interest of everybody concerned; as is done in the case where a ward of Chancery marries, or a wife has an "equity to a settlement," under the circumstances we have already explained. But it is considered that a married woman who has committed fraud is not entitled to the protection of the Court. No one would consider it to be reasonable that a woman should be allowed to take advantage of her own wrong; although it might be a question whether a law which tempts women occasionally to act in this manner is worthy of approbation. But the scope of the doctrine, as administered in Courts of Equity, embraces many cases besides those of intentional fraud.

The bill, of which Mr. Russell Gurney has charge, has for its object the entire change of the law with regard to the property and status of married women. This bill we believe in the main to be a good measure, though we are not concerned to defend every clause, nor would we deprecate the most searching investigation into its details. In discussing the desirability of any proposed change, however, the first thing to be considered is, whether any change is desirable at all. Let us consider what the operation of the existing law really is. In the absence of a settlement, a husband by marriage acquires, not only the entire property of his wife, but a right to sweep away everything which she may afterwards earn for herself. Her existence, so far as the right to personal property goes, is entirely merged in that of her husband. It is not that she has to contribute a certain proportion of her property to the expenses of the family; it is not that she gives her property to her husband as trustee for their common welfare. This no doubt he is, morally, and a conscientious husband would recognise the moral obligation. But so long as persons recognise their duties to their neighbours, and are able to perform them, there is no scope for the operation of the law on one side or the other. It is only in the case of the dishonest and unconscientious, or the unfortunate, that the question can ever arise. Now, on what grounds can such a state of things be justified? Is it on the ground of the inferiority of the woman? If so, we ought not to confine the property disabilities to *married* women. We ought to revert to the Perpetual Tutelage of all women as practised in the old Roman Law. The reason alleged for such a system, *propter levitatem animi*, was, at any rate, consistent enough. But the term "inferiority" is not an absolute term, but must have reference to something in respect of which the inferiority exists. Now, a woman may be inferior to a man in physical strength, and yet be quite as competent to take a part in public duties; or, again, she may be unfitted to take a part in public duties, and yet be fitted to vote for a member of Parliament; or, again, she may be unfitted to vote for a member of Parliament, and yet be perfectly competent to manage a private estate. There are confessedly many things which women are quite as competent to do as men; and to assert that the management of property is not one of them is at least to beg a very important question. But the fact is, no mere inferiority as regards capacity could justify the existing state of the law with respect to married women's property. Let us consider some of the cases of this kind of inferiority. The most obvious is that of the relation of Guardian and Ward. The Guardian has certain duties to perform towards his Ward—to superintend his maintenance and education, and for the money so expended he would be entitled to be indemnified; but no one has ever imagined that because a Guardian has certain duties to perform towards his Ward, therefore a Guardian should be at liberty to pocket the whole of his Ward's fortune. The feudal right, by which a lord was entitled to the entire income of an infant tenant's property without accounting for it, was considered so great a grievance that it was put an end to, along with other feudal abuses, in the year 1660 (12 Car. II. c. 24). And so with regard to other persons who are placed in positions of trust. According to the like analogy, a husband ought, after applying such a proportion of his wife's property as might be held a reasonable contribution to the necessary expenses of the family, be a trustee for her as regards the rest of her property. We are anxious to insist upon this point, for the usual defence of the existing law is, that the law conveys the marital rights to the husband because it charges him with all the burdens, which are the consideration he pays for them.[1] This reason, however, suggests two considerations; first, Why should the marital rights of the husband be more than co-extensive with the marital burdens? secondly, Why should the marital burdens involve the entire burden of the wife's debts and liabilities?

In addition to the illustration above given, we may adduce the case of an executor dealing with his testator's goods. The executor, as regards the world at large, for the purposes of suing and being sued, stands generally in the place of his testator, and is clothed with the rights and liabilities of his testator. But these rights and liabilities are not personal, but representative. For every shilling that comes to him through his testator he has to account, not only to the testator's creditors, but to the persons entitled under the testator's will. If the testator's estate when properly administered is unable to pay his debts, the executor is not liable to the creditors beyond the amount received. In fact, the transfer on marriage of the entire personal property of the wife to a husband, is the only instance known to the English Law of *universal succession* in the fullest sense: that is, of the entire assumption by one person of the rights and liabilities of another. Such cases of *universal succession* were not unknown to the Roman law. When a wife entered the family of her husband by a marriage "*in*

[1] Lord Thurlow, in *Strathmore* v. *Bowes*, 1 Ves. jun. 28.

manum" (as it was called), her legal existence became entirely merged in her husband. So, if a citizen *sui juris* entered into a family by "arrogation" (a species of adoption), his legal existence would become merged in that of his adoptive father. Again, the heir succeeded to the entire rights and liabilities of his testator. These rules, in course of time, became very much modified; and in the later periods of Roman jurisprudence a marriage "in manum" was quite unknown.

The complaint, then, with regard to the law as it at present exists in England, is, that on the one hand, by enabling the husband to possess himself of the *whole* of his wife's property, without any liability at all corresponding to the property so gained, it holds out peculiar temptations to scheming and unprincipled men to secure the affections of ladies with large fortunes; that by subjecting all the earnings of a wife to a husband's rapacity, it enables idle and dissolute husbands to plunder their wives at pleasure; that, on the other hand, it is iniquitous to make a husband liable for all his wife's debts contracted before marriage, or for wrongs committed by her, whether before or after marriage. The law, in fact, operates with excessive caprice, though in practice the injustice is most usually on the side of the husband against the wife.

Before we consider the specific objections to Mr. Russell Gurney's measure, there is one point on which it is necessary to insist in connexion with the present law, and that is, that the property of which a woman is possessed before marriage, becoming on marriage the property of the husband, becomes also subject to his debts; so that, unless the wife's money be protected by settlement, it is not safe against her husband's misfortunes. Many of our readers have no doubt heard of cases in which a banker has on marriage settled all the money in the bank upon his wife, with the intention of defrauding the customers of the bank, and has done so most effectually. For money deposited in a bank becomes at once the property of the bank, and the right of the customer is a right *in personam* against the banker to recover so much money It constitutes, in fact, a personal debt from the banker to the customer. Hence, if a banker on marriage settle so much money on his wife and his family, it is his own money which he is settling; and therefore, unless the wife be an accomplice in the fraud, it would be impossible to set aside the settlement; as it is made, on the part of the wife, *bonâ fide*, and for a valuable consideration, that of marriage.

Of course such a transaction is simply dishonest. We have merely alluded to it as an illustration of the efficacy of marriage settlements. But, on the other hand, it is most reasonable and proper that a man on marriage should wish to have his wife's property, and so much of his own property as may be necessary for the maintenance of his family, protected from future contingent liabilities. It is for the interest of both husband and wife that it should be so; nor can such an arrangement give the slightest ground of complaint to the husband's creditors.

We trust, therefore, that it will be borne in mind that

it is not merely against the rapacity, but also against the misfortunes of their husbands, that the proposed measure is intended to protect married women.

The objections to Mr. Russell Gurney's measure may be divided into two classes—positive and negative. On the one hand, it will introduce, it is said, certain definite evils; on the other hand, it will *not* remove the evils against which it is ostensibly directed.

There is no doubt that the changes contemplated by it are grave and important; and we should deeply regret to see a measure of this kind pushed through Parliament in a partisan spirit, without allowing the fullest consideration to the objections which may be urged against it. We do not think any of these objections conclusive; still they are for the most part sufficiently plausible to deserve the candid consideration of the Legislature.

We have, first of all, the general objection that the changes proposed are revolutionary. Waiving other replies to this objection, we may remark that it is not in its nature conclusive. It is quite right to proceed with caution before introducing a sweeping change; but where there are distinct evils to be remedied, it is idle to assert that the change by which you propose to effect the remedy is revolutionary, unless you can show—

1. That the remedy is worse than the disease; or

2. That the disease does not require so violent a remedy.

To consider the first of these two points would be anticipating. With regard to the second, the usual suggestion made by the opponents of any change is to extend the system of protection-orders. The system of protection-orders was introduced by the twenty-first section of the Divorce Act of 1857 (20 & 21 Vict. c. 85). We may here remark, though this probably would be admitted, that the provisions of that section are miserably inadequate. First, a wife cannot claim a protection-order except in case of desertion: and yet it is perfectly clear that desertion is not the only case in which it would be improper to allow a husband control over his wife's earnings. Secondly, the section which provides for the granting of protection-orders also provides that they may be discharged at the discretion of the magistrate. The latter is a most monstrous provision; for it is difficult to conceive a case in which it would be proper to discharge a protection-order which had been once properly granted. On what ground can a husband who, by deserting his wife, has forfeited his legal right to her earnings, ever afterwards come to a court of justice and ask to have that legal right restored to him? The result is, that a wife who has gained a protection-order holds her property subject to the caprice of a bench of magistrates.

But we will go further, and ask whether *any* system of protection-orders is likely to be efficient? On this point we cannot do better than quote from the Special Report[1] of the Select Committee of the House of Commons appointed last year on the Married Women's Property Bill (p. iv.):

[1] Ordered by the House of Commons to be printed, 17th July, 1868. See *post*, p. 222.

"It has been stated that the extension of such protection-orders to the case of women whose husbands are intemperate, reckless, idle, or cruel, would be a very insufficient remedy, inasmuch as few women, while continuing to live with their husbands, would come forward to claim in public a protection which would involve giving publicity to their domestic grievances, and an application adverse to their husbands. In many cases also the protection-order would be too late, as it often is in the case of desertion. The small fund which the wife has saved before or after marriage is swept off before the application can be made."

But it is objected that the proposed measure will produce discord in families. Those who urge this objection very seldom give reasons for it; and a reason is certainly required. Seeing that under the present law every woman of property (unless she be singularly destitute of good advisers) has her fortune settled when she marries; seeing that the change proposed to be made for England and Ireland has already been made throughout the greater number of the American States and in Canada;[1] and seeing it is not uncommon for members of the same family in other relations—as, for instance, brother and sister, or two or more sisters, though not "one person" in law—to keep house together; the objectors would have had plenty of opportunity of stating facts, if there were facts to state, in support of their objection. At the same time we must remark that it is not sufficient to urge isolated instances, or vague generalities, in support of this or any other objection. Before the Select Committee in July, last year, witness after witness gave accounts of the evil effects of the present law, from an extensive experience

[1] Special Report, p. v.

among the poorer classes, where settlements are impracticable. It is not too much to expect that, if it be the fact that the possession of separate property by a married woman be productive of mischief, there should be witnesses forthcoming to demonstrate its evil effects among the wealthier classes, or in countries which have adopted the proposed change. Not only was this not the case, but the witnesses from the United States and Canada were able to state that the change in the law in those countries had worked extremely well.

Again, it is objected that the proposed change will operate unfairly against the husband, as he will still be liable to support his wife, and will not have her property to help him in doing so. We have already considered the *principle* of this objection. With regard to the bill before Parliament, we may remark that it proposes to remove a husband's liability for his wife's debts before marriage, and for all wrongs committed by his wife, whether before or after marriage.[1] But perhaps it might be urged that in these cases the husband would be held morally bound to pay his wife's debts to prevent her being sent to prison. But it is clear that we cannot enter into the question, "What would be expected of a husband?" under such circumstances, further than to say, that husband and wife would in this respect be in

[1] This is clearly the case with regard to the Original Bill; but the language of the Amended Bill is not clear on this point. (See *post*, p. 228.) The language of Sir Erskine Perry's bill of 1857 was clearer and more emphatic than either: "A husband shall not be liable for the debts of his wife contracted before marriage, nor for any pecuniary damage caused by her wrong, whether before or after the marriage."

the same relative position as brother and sister. Indeed, the analogy of brother and sister keeping house together is, for most purposes, so complete, that we wonder that it has hardly ever been grappled with by the opponents of the proposed measure. Except so far as regards liability for the maintenance and education of children, and the liability of husband upon his wife's contracts for "necessaries," there is no objection to the proposed change in the law which would not apply with equal effect in every case of relatives keeping house together.

Now we come to one of the most plausible objections which can be urged against the proposed measure. It is urged that the proposed law still leaves a husband liable for his wife's debts contracted after marriage. On this point the bill is silent, and therefore we must refer to the existing law for a solution of the question. The question being, In what cases will a wife's post-nuptial contracts bind her husband? we may answer, generally—

1. Where the wife has acted as her husband's agent.

2. Where the contract is for necessaries which the husband has neglected to provide for her.

The first class of these cases presents no difficulty. The question of agency is a question of fact rather than of law, and is of course not peculiar to the relation of husband and wife. So far as it is a question of law, it must be solved by the aid of the general principles of the law applicable to cases of agency. It must, however, be observed, that the fact of husband and wife living together begets a presumption of the husband's assent to debts incurred by the wife for articles suitable to his position in life. But this, like other presumptions, may be rebutted by evidence to the contrary.

We proceed to consider the second class of cases, which involve the question really important for our present purposes: "To what extent may a wife, by her contracts, bind her husband *against his consent*, expressed or implied?" The answer to be given to this question depends on the meaning of the term "necessaries."

The first case to which we shall refer is that of *Montague* v. *Benedict*, 3 Barn. & Cress. 631; Smith's "Leading Cases," vol. ii. (ed. 1867), p. 429. The facts were these:—

In an action by a jeweller against a husband for goods sold to the wife, it appeared that the plaintiff, in two months, delivered jewellery to the amount of 83*l.* to the wife of the defendant. The defendant lived in a ready-furnished house, of which the annual rent was 200*l* His wife's fortune upon her marriage was less than 4,000*l.*, and she had, at the time of her marriage, jewellery suitable to her condition. She had never worn, in her husband's presence, any articles furnished by the plaintiff. The plaintiff, when he went to the defendant's house, always inquired for the wife, and not for the husband. It was held that the goods furnished were not necessaries, and that, as there was no evidence of any assent of the husband to the debt incurred by his wife, the action could not be maintained.

The case, however, which, more than any other, illustrates the doctrine of our law upon the subject, is that of *Jolly* v. *Rees,* decided in 1864.[1] The facts were these :—

The plaintiffs, Messrs. Jolly, were hosiers and linen-drapers at Bath. The defendant, Mr. Rees, was a gentleman of small fortune, residing near Llanelly, in Carmarthenshire. The goods in respect of which the action was brought were supplied by Messrs. Jolly upon the orders of Mrs. Rees during the years 1860 and 1861. The prices were fair and reasonable.

The defence set up was, that the wife had a sufficient allowance to enable her to obtain articles of the description of those in question without pledging her husband's credit for them: and that he had expressly forbidden her to do so.

The jury found, (1) that the articles supplied were necessaries in the sense of being suitable to the estate and degree of the defendant's wife and daughters; (2) that the wife's authority was revoked by her husband in 1851.

It was agreed that the parties should abide the judgment of the Court of Common Pleas on the question of law.

In the argument on behalf of the defendant, Mr. Rees, the following dicta of Justice Wyndham, in a similar case in the year 1660, were cited :—

"If the husband shall be bound by this contract, many inconveniences must ensue. 1. The husband will be accounted the common enemy; and the mercer and the gallant will unite with the wife, and they will combine their strength against the husband. . . . 3. Wives will be their own carvers, and, like hawks, will fly abroad and find

[1] 15 C. B. N. S. 628; 12 W. R. p. 673; *ante*, p. 189.

their own prey. . . . 4. *It shall be left to the pleasure of a London jury to dress my wife in such apparel as they think proper.*"

The judgment of the majority of the Court in *Jolly* v. *Rees* was delivered by Chief Justice Erle, Justices Williams and Willes concurring, Justice Byles dissenting. We give the principal portions of it; and we would call the attention of our readers to the fact that the plaintiffs, when they supplied the goods, had no notice that the defendant had forbidden his wife to pledge his credit:—

ERLE, C. J.:—"The action was for goods sold. Upon the trial the plaintiffs raised a presumption of the defendant's liability by showing that the goods were ordered by his the defendant's wife, while living with him, for the use of herself and children. The defendant rebutted this presumption by showing that he had forbidden his wife to take up goods on his credit, and had told her that if she wanted money to buy goods, she was to apply to him for it; and there was no evidence that she had so applied and been refused. The plaintiffs proved, in reply, that the goods were necessaries suitable to the estate and degree of the defendant; that the wife had 65*l.* per annum to her separate use; and that the defendant had promised to allow her 50*l.* per annum in addition, but had not paid it regularly, and had not supplied her with such necessaries or with money sufficient for the purchase thereof. The plaintiffs also showed that they had received no notice of the defendant's prohibition to his wife against taking up goods on his credit.

"These facts are in effect found by the jury: and the question is raised whether the wife had authority to make a contract binding on the husband for necessaries suitable to his estate and degree, against his will and contrary to his order to her, although without notice of such order to the tradesman.

"Our answer is in the negative. We consider that the wife cannot make a contract binding on her husband, unless he gives her authority as his agent so to do. We lay down this as the general rule, premising that the facts do not raise the question what might have been the rights of the wife, either if she were living separate without any default on her part towards her husband, or if she had been left destitute by him. . . . .

"In supporting this conclusion, our decision does not militate against the rule that the husband, as well as every principal, is concluded from denying that the agent had such authority as he was held out by his principal to have, in such a manner as to raise a belief in such authority, acted on in making the contract sought to be enforced. Such liability is not founded on any rights peculiar to the conjugal relation, but on a much wider ground. . . . .

"It is not our province here to inquire whether it is advisable to give to the wife greater rights. But taking the law to be that the power of the wife to charge her husband is in the capacity of his agent, it is a solecism in reasoning to say that she derives her authority *from his will,* and at the same time to say that the relation of wife creates the authority *against his will,* by a *presumptio juris et de jure*[1] from marriage: and if it be expedient that the wife should have greater rights, it is certainly inexpedient that she should have to exercise them by a process tending to disunion at home, and pecuniary distress from without. The husband sustains the liability for all debts: he should therefore have the power to regulate the expenditure for which he is to be responsible, by his own discretion, and according to his own means. But, if the wife taking up goods from a tradesman can make her husband's liability depend on the estimate by a jury of his estate and degree, the law would practically compel him to regulate his expenses by a standard to be set up by that jury,—a standard depending on appearances, perhaps assumed for a temporary purpose, with intention of change.

"Moreover, if the law was clear that the husband was protected from the debts incurred by the wife without his authority, not only in the ranks where wealth abounds would speculations upon the imprudence of a thoughtless wife be less frequent because less profitable, but also in the ranks where the support of the household is from the labour of the man, and where the home must be habitually left in the care of the wife during his absence at his work, more painful evils from debt which the husband never intended to contract would be checked.

[1] That is, a presumption which the law holds to be absolutely conclusive, and does not allow to be called into question by any evidence, however strong. See Best on Presumptions, p. 20.

"As we collect from the report of the learned judge that the verdict is for necessaries suitable to the estate and degree of the husband, obtained from the plaintiffs by the wife of the defendant without his authority and contrary to his order, according to our view of the law this verdict cannot be supported."

It may be remarked that Mr. Justice Byles, the dissentient judge, rested his opinion of the husband's liability, not on any universal marital obligation, but on the general law of principal and agent. He observed, that "the wife's power to bind her husband may repose, not merely on her actual authority, but on the *apparent authority with which the husband invests her by cohabitation*." No merely private revocation of authority, or private agreement between husband and wife, could (according to Mr. Justice Byles) affect the tradesman's right to rely on the apparent authority of the wife.

According to this view, a husband might, if he pleased, repudiate his wife's agency, though, if he were living with his wife, the repudiation would be attended with great practical difficulties. All that Mr. Justice Byles seems to have contended for is, that the facts of this particular case were not sufficient to rebut the presumption of agency.

It would seem to follow from the judgment in the above case, that a husband's legal obligation to support his wife means merely that he is to keep her out of the workhouse. And if this be so, it is surely a most inadequate objection to the proposed change in the law, that because a man is bound to provide his wife with the bare necessaries of subsistence, therefore he should be entitled to the whole of her property.

We would here briefly allude to the extent of the liability of a father to support his children. In the case of *Shelton* v. *Springett*,[1] decided in 1851, it was the unanimous opinion of the Court of Common Pleas, that the moral obligation on a parent to maintain a child affords no legal inference of a promise to pay a debt contracted by him, even for necessaries. Mr. Justice Maule, in that case, expressed the opinion that a son did *not*, in this respect, stand upon the same footing as a wife. Hence it must be inferred that Mr. Justice Maule held the doctrine with regard to a husband's liability which was afterwards overruled in the case of *Jolly* v. *Rees*.

If, however, the proposed change in the law were to bear much more hardly on the husband than in fact it would, still, as the bill does not do away with marriage settlements, it would be competent for any intending husband, by proper provisions in his marriage settlenent, to escape its operation, at least as between himself and his intended wife; just as at the present day women with large fortunes who marry would certainly have their fortunes settled, if they are properly advised. It is in cases where women are not properly advised, or cannot afford the expense of marriage settlements, that the power with which the law arms an unprincipled husband is most severely felt.

The last objection to the proposed measure which we shall notice is a negative one. It is said that women cannot be prevented from giving their money to their

[1] *Shelton* v. *Springett*, 11 Common Bench Reports, 452.

husbands if they like. This of course is quite true, and it is not intended to prevent them doing so. Still, under the proposed measure, money may be tied up in settlement, with a remainder to the children after the deaths of husband and wife. This would prevent a wife dealing freely with the property settled, though it would not prevent her entering into bonds and covenants with her husband's creditors, in cases where the "restraint on anticipation" does not exist. Still, women who give their money to their husbands, or execute bonds or covenants on their husbands' behalf, at least know what they are about: whereas under the existing law a woman may marry without realizing the fact that marriage is a gift to her husband of all her personal property. If a young man who has just attained his majority makes an improvident surrender of his rights in favour of a parent, the Court of Chancery will examine narrowly into the transaction, and will set it aside if it appear that there was any pressure exerted by the parent, or that the son had not independent legal advice. It appears to us that a similar reason ought to apply against holding marriage to be a gift of a woman's personal chattels to her husband, at least unless it can be shown that she had good advice, and was aware of what she was doing.

We cannot leave the consideration of the Law of Husband and Wife, so far as it is proposed to be amended by Mr. Russell Gurney's measure, without earnestly recommending to the attention of our readers the Special Report of the Select Committee of the House of Commons appointed last year to consider the subject.[1] The Report is much too long to quote here, but the following is the result arrived at by the Select Committee (pp. vi. vii) :—

"Looking to the result of experience, and to the general tendency of the provisions of equity, your Committee is of opinion that a change in the law of this country, with reference both to the property and earnings of married women, is necessary.

"It does not appear to be necessary to make any alteration in the liability of a husband to maintain his wife in consequence of a change in the law with regard to the property of married women. A married woman living apart from her husband can only bind him for what is necessary, and her possession of property of her own *pro tanto* negatives the authority arising from necessity. A married woman living with her husband has an authority which, in spite of some fluctuation and uncertainty of judicial decisions, seems to be regulated by the general principles of the law of agency. Agency is a mixed question of law and fact, and the Courts will give due weight to such fact as the possession of property by a married woman, without any express statutable direction."

Hitherto we have been dealing with the general principles of the proposed measure. We now proceed to consider in detail the provisions of the bill as amended in Committee, and to compare them with those of the original bill. Both bills will be found in the Appendices, pp. 238–245.

Section 1 gives a married woman full power over her property, and imposes upon her the capacity of suing and being sued, as if she were a single woman. This section is clogged with a proviso that it is not to empower a married woman to dispose, otherwise than by

[1] Special Report from the Select Committee on the Married Women's Property Bill; together with the Proceedings of the Committee and Minutes of Evidence, Appendix, and Index. Ordered by the House of Commons to be printed, 17th July, 1868 (441).

will, of real estate, or reversionary interests in personal estate, but the power of disposition now vested in married women in such property is to remain the same as if the Act had not passed.

By "the power of disposition" is meant, apparently, "the power of disposition *inter vivos;*" otherwise the last clause is inconsistent with the earlier part of the section, which by implication (very properly) enables a married woman to dispose of real and reversionary interests *by will.* But it is difficult to see why, if a power of disposition *inter vivos* is meant, a power of disposition *inter vivos* should not be expressed.

It must be strictly borne in mind that this section must be read subject to Section 18 of the Amended Bill, which reserves the husband's "tenancy by the curtesy." The propriety of this reservation we shall consider in the discussion of Section 18: but for the present we would say that this tenancy by the curtesy constitutes a right on the part of a husband to his wife's real estate after his wife's death.[1] This right is paramount to any disposition she may make, and extends to all real estate to which she may become entitled during the continuance of the marriage. The right, as we have already stated (p. 191), attaches only in the event of issue of the marriage being born alive, *capable of inheriting.*

So that if an estate be limited to heirs *male*, the birth of a female child will not entitle a husband to curtesy; and *vice versâ.*

Let us suppose that two persons marry young, a year

[1] See *ante*, p. 187.

afterwards a child is born of the marriage, and (let us say) lives only an hour. The mother dies also. The husband survives his wife half a century. For all that time the husband will keep the wife's relatives out of the inheritance to her property, though he may marry and have families by subsequent wives. This may or may not be right, but we may remark that it certainly ought not to depend on the accident of a child being born alive; and moreover, if the principle be sound, it ought to apply to widows as well as widowers. Yet a widow's right to "dower," under the Dower Act, is postponed to any disposition which her husband may have made.

The husband's right to curtesy would interfere with the wife's power of alienation, during her lifetime, as well as by will. This would of course very materially interfere with the operation of the bill as it originally stood. But the Amended Bill does not profess to give any power of disposition of real estate, except by will; and the express reservation of curtesy is confined to such real estate as the wife was entitled to at her death. There was, of course, no occasion for such an express reservation in other cases.

The second section provides that a married woman shall not be "taken in execution" upon a judgment founded upon acts done during marriage, nor is such judgment or execution to affect any property, except such personal for which she may be entitled for a *present* interest.

It would be well to consider the import of the proviso of the first section and the whole of the second section together.

Assuming the provisions of the first two sections to be proper, we cannot applaud their arrangement. It will be seen that the first part of the first section of the Amended Bill enunciates the *principle* of the bill. The permanent exceptions to that principle are contained, not in a wholly separate section, but partly in a proviso of the first section, and partly in the second section.

The exceptions are these :—

1. A married woman is not to be subject to arrest for debts contracted during marriage.

2. The real property and reversionary property of a married woman is not to be taken in execution for any such debts.

3. The real property and reversionary property of a married woman is not to be subject to alienation *inter vivos,* except in such manner as is permitted by the present law.

The question then arises, What are the powers of married women over real or reversionary property according to the present law?

With regard to real property: a woman cannot dispose of interests in real property without her husband's concurrence, nor without being "separately examined" in the manner we have before alluded to, p. 190.

With regard to reversionary interests in personal property: a married woman's power of dealing with these is regulated by an Act passed in the year 1857 (20 & 21 Vict. c. 57). This Act provides that a married woman may dispose of reversionary interests in personal property, subject to the following qualifications and exceptions :—

1. No married woman is to dispose of reversionary interests in personalty without the concurrence of her husband (section 1), and with such formalities as are required in a disposition by a married woman of real estate (section 2).

2. A married woman cannot dispose of reversionary interests in personalty (1) which may have been settled on her by marriage (section 4); or (2) as to which she may have been restrained from disposing of it by the terms of the gift or settlement by which she became entitled to it (section 1).

It appears, then, that under the proposed law, a married woman's power of disposition over real property and reversionary personalty will not be much greater than it is at present: the only difference consisting in the power of disposition by will.

It is difficult to understand the object of these exceptions, which have been introduced by amendments, and run counter to the general principle of the proposed measure. At the same time, it must be remarked that the bill, even with these amendments, will get rid of the worst scandals of the existing law. A person may think the existing state of the law most objectionable, and yet not approve the principle of Mr. Russell Gurney's bill: and in this case he would have no objection to these amendments we are considering. But one who approves the principle of the bill, as declared in its first section, cannot approve the amendments.

Before leaving this subject, we must remark that a reversionary interest in personalty is transmissible to representatives in the same manner as a present interest. The following may perhaps afford a convenient illustration of what we have been stating:—

A father, on his daughter's marriage, settles a fund in trust for his daughter for life, and after her death to the husband, and, after the death of the survivor, to the children of the marriage.

To take the simplest case, let us suppose there are three children, A, B, and C. A is born alive, but lives only an hour; B, a daughter, lives to be married, but dies without children in the lifetime of her father and of her husband; C survives his parents. What will become of the fund on the death of the parents?

It might be answered, at first sight, that C, the only surviving child, ought to take the fund. This, however, would not be so.

The fund would be divided in three equal shares, one of which would go to the representative of A, another to B's husband or his representatives, the third to C.

Now, a father is entitled by law to the personal estate of a deceased child who has not made a will. So that A's share would be subject to his father's absolute disposition, and, if the father died insolvent, would be distributed among his creditors. Or if the father chose to leave his property away from C, it would go to the person to whom C's father might leave it, subject to the life-interest of C's mother, in case she should survive her husband. For A's right becomes vested (as it is called) at his birth (unless otherwise provided in the deed of settlement), and therefore, although it is only in reversion, would go to his father as his representative. The same consequence would follow if A died at any time before attaining twenty-one; for until A attains twenty-one, he cannot make a will. Of course, if A attains twenty-one, the right of A's father then becomes dependent on any will A may leave.

Similarly, B's share would go to her husband or his representatives, creditors or legatees, as the case might be.

Sections 3, 4, and 5 are clauses for carrying out the principle of the bill under different circumstances.

Section 6 provides that a husband shall not be liable for debts of his wife contracted before marriage.

Section 7 provides that no husband shall by reason of his marriage be liable for any wrong committed by his wife during the coverture.

The juxtaposition of these two last provisions might seem to render it doubtful whether a husband is still to be liable for a wrong committed by his wife *before* the marriage, although "debts" in section 6 would no doubt include liabilities of all sorts, whether arising from contracts or from wrongs. By the present law, it is impossible to bring an action against the wife without joining the husband; and a man would be without remedy if he could not sue the husband.[1] Will this liability of the husband, so far as regards wrongs com-

[1] Lord Chief Justice Tyndal in *Head* v. *Briscoe*, 5 Carrington & Payne, 486.

mitted by the wife before marriage, continue under the proposed law? It is to be regretted that the structure of the sentences in the Amended Bill is such as to obscure the meaning. The whole difficulty would be avoided by striking out those most needless words, "during the coverture," at the end of the seventh section, which are not found in the Original Bill.

The phraseology of the Original Bill was very much better. Section 5 of the Original Bill provided that "a husband shall not be liable for the debts of his wife contracted before marriage, and shall not be liable for any wrong committed by her."

Section 8 provides that no husband or wife shall be entitled to sue the other for a tort (that is, for a wrong), except in respect of property. So that for personal assaults and acts of cruelty the remedy of the parties will lie in the Divorce Court.

Section 9 provides that husband and wife may be sued together when either contracts as agent for the other.

Section 10 provides for the settlement of disputes between husband and wife as to the title to or possession of property.

Section 11 provides, that where a husband has received the rents and profits of his wife's estate with her permission, he shall not be bound afterwards to account for the same.

Sections 12 and 13 provide that a wife having property is to be liable for the maintenance of her husband and children in case they become chargeable to the parish.

These last-mentioned provisions are not in themselves open to objection; but it is worthy of consideration whether, if a wife's liability to support her husband and children is to be made co-extensive with a corresponding liability on the part of her husband, her control over the children should not be co-extensive with his.

Section 14 provides, in effect, that nothing in the Act contained shall affect any settlement, present or future. At the same time, a settlement made by a married woman of her property during the marriage is to have no greater validity against her creditors than a settlement made by a man would have. Hence a woman will not be able by post-nuptial settlement to restrain herself from anticipating the income of her property. But this will not prevent a married woman receiving, during the marriage, a gift of property subject to a restraint on anticipation.

Section 15 provides that property, whether real or personal, settled to the separate use of a married woman, without restraint against anticipation, shall be liable in Equity to the same liabilities as her personal property in possession not so settled would be subject at Law under the provisions of this Act.

This section should be read together with the proviso in section 1 and section 2. By these provisions, it will be remembered, a married woman's real property and reversionary personalty were excepted from the operation of the Act, so as not to be subject to her sole control, or to her debts. The present section provides that the exception is not to apply to property settled to the separate use of a married woman without restraint on anticipation, although it be realty or reversionary personalty, but that such property is to be subject to the general operation of the Act.

Section 16 provides that any woman during minority may make a valid marriage settlement with the consent of her parent or guardian and of her intended husband.

This provision requires a few words of explanation. Before the passing of an Act, to which we shall presently refer, it was settled law that a minor was (among other disabilities) incapable of making a binding marriage settlement. To such an extent was this doctrine carried, that the sanction of the Court of Chancery itself could not make the settlement of a minor valid. Thus, in *Savill* v. *Savill, Young* v. *Savill* (reported 2 Collyer, 721), a Mr. James Parker married a minor, a Ward of the Court of Chancery. Marriage articles, comprising real and personal property, were framed and approved by the Court. The wife died within a month of the marriage, and her heiress-at-law insisted on withdrawing the real estate comprised in the articles from the operation of the articles; and the Court decided that the heiress-at-law had a right so to do. The only way of effecting a binding marriage settlement was by a private Act of Parliament, if the parties were rich enough to procure one.

A distinction, however, must be made between real and personal property. A husband, by virtue of the marriage, became entitled to his wife's personal property; so that if a man on marrying a wife under age agreed to a settlement of her personal property, the agreement would bind *him*, and her consent would be unnecessary.[1]

By the statute 18 and 19 Vict. c. 43, persons under age may make valid marriage settlements with the sanction of the Court of Chancery. But the Act is not to apply in the case where the intended husband is under twenty or the intended wife under seventeen years of age.

It will thus be seen that the section we are considering alters the law very considerably in this respect, in cases where the intended *wife* is under age. The proposed measure does not affect cases where the husband is under age, if the wife be of full age.

Section 17 provides for the devolution of the personal property of a married woman intestate. The personal property of a married woman intestate is to be distributed in a manner analogous to that of a married man who dies intestate. When a married man dies intestate, leaving children, one-third of his personalty goes to his widow, and the rest equally among his children; but if he leave no children, the widow takes one-half, and the rest goes to his next of kin. So, according to section 17 of the Amended Bill, one-third of the personal property of a wife, dying intestate, will go to her husband if she leave children, and one-third if she leave no children.

[1] *In re Daniel's Trust*, 18 Beavan, 309: "Peachy on Settlements," 537.

Section 18 maintains the right of a husband to hold, as tenant by the curtesy, any real estate to which his wife shall be entitled at her death.

It is clear that this provision may interfere very materially with the will-making power granted by implication in the proviso of section 1, as a married woman's power to make a Will will be subject to the husband's rights as tenant by the curtesy, that is, to a life estate, where there has been issue of the marriage born alive capable of inheriting. The restriction in the Original Bill was, considering the general principle of the Original Bill, even more serious ; for section 7 of the Original Bill provided that " Nothing contained in this Act shall affect the right of any husband to hold his wife's real estate as tenant by the curtesy." The result would probably have been the invention of a form of "uses to bar curtesy" analogous to the "uses to bar dower," with which conveyancers are familiar. The right of the husband, " by the curtesy of England," to the rents and profits of his wife's freehold estates during his life, is paramount to any disposition which his wife may make, by deed or will. It is clear that this would be a most serious clog on the free power of disposition over real property which the first section of the Original Bill professed to give. It might have been avoided by substituting these words : — " Nothing in this Act contained shall affect the right of any husband to hold as tenant by the curtesy any real estate to which his wife shall be entitled at her death, and with respect to which she may have died intestate."

In any case, the right of curtesy ought to be made dependent on the intestacy of the wife.

Sections 19, 20, and 21 are merely formal. Section 19 provides that the Act is to come into operation on the 1st January, 1870; section 20, that the Act shall not extend to Scotland; section 21 gives the title of the Act as the "Married Women's Property Act, 1869."

We cannot leave the consideration of this measure without alluding to another measure, which has been brought forward by Mr. Locke King; the bill for assimilating the devolution of real property to that of personal property in cases of intestacy. This is a change of which the advocates of married women's property rights ought to be particularly suspicious, seeing that by the existing law a man is entitled to a life-interest only in the real property of his deceased wife (and that only under certain circumstances), whereas he is entitled to the *whole* of her personalty. If Mr. Locke King's bill passes, the immediate effect will be to give a husband the entire real estate of a deceased wife. Nor could the wife prevent this, as she cannot dispose of real property without the consent of her husband. So that the effect of the passing of Mr. Locke King's bill would be to give a husband the whole of his wife's real property in the event of his surviving her, unless her rights were secured by settlement.

Let us suppose that Mr. Locke King's bill has become law; in such a contingency, let us consider the operation of Mr. Russell Gurney's measure. And first, what interpretation to put upon the reservation of "curtesy" in Mr. Russell Gurney's bill. It will be remembered that "curtesy" is not a right arising out of an intestacy, but from the fact of issue having been born alive capable of inheriting. In the Original Bill, curtesy is reserved in its entirety, and would therefore apply to any real estate to which the wife might have been solely entitled during the marriage. In the Amended Bill, the reservation of curtesy is confined to the real estate to which the wife may be entitled *at her death*. The wife could not defeat this right, but, subject to it, she might dispose of her property as she pleased, by will or deed according to the Original Bill, and by will alone according to the Amended Bill. But if she died intestate, this singular result would ensue: The husband would be entitled to the whole of his wife's realty, according to the present law of personalty, which, by our supposition, would then be the law of realty: whereas he would be entitled to only one-half or one-third of her personalty under Mr. Russell Gurney's bill.

If Mr. Russell Gurney's bill were to pass first, and afterwards Mr. Locke King's bill, this would not affect the question of curtesy; but a husband's rights in his wife's real property under an intestacy, would be the same as in her personal property—one-third if she left children, one-half if she left none. Whether, as regards the realty, he would be compelled to elect between his rights by the curtesy and his rights under the intestacy, is a question which would have to be decided whenever the case might arise.

While on this subject, it may not be amiss to remark on the inequality of the law of intestacy as affecting the sexes. As our readers are probably aware, a son would succeed as heir to a father's real property before any of the daughters. The father and the most distant relative on the father's side will succeed as heir to the real estate of a deceased person before his mother. Where a person dies intestate without children, his father, if living, succeeds to his personalty; but if the father be not living, the personalty will be divided between the mother, brothers, and sisters, in equal shares.

There is one legal result of the unity between husband and wife to which we have not hitherto alluded: we mean the disability of a wife, in certain cases, to give evidence for or against her husband.[1] The general rule of the old law was, that husband and wife were not competent witnesses for or against each other. To this rule, however, there were several exceptions, even at Common Law; as, for instance, in the not infrequent case of a charge of personal violence brought by one against the other, and in cases of abduction. The exceptions created by statute are, moreover, extremely numerous; and the present law on this subject may be briefly stated as follows:

1. In Civil proceedings, the general rule is, that husband and wife are competent and compellable witnesses for or against each other; the only practical exception being the case of proceedings instituted in consequence of adultery.

[1] See "Best on Evidence," ed. 1866, pp. 245—256.

2. In Criminal proceedings the general rule is, that husband and wife are *not* competent or compellable witnesses for or against each other; the principal exceptions being cases of personal violence committed by one against the other, and cases of abduction.

There is at present a bill before the House of Commons, introduced by Mr. Denman, which proposes, among other things, to enable the parties to any proceeding instituted in consequence of adultery, and the husbands and wives of such parties, to be competent and compellable witnesses in such proceedings.

APPENDIX A.

MARRIED WOMEN'S PROPERTY BILL, 1869.

The Original Bill. (32 Vict., Bill 20.)

WHEREAS the law of property and contract with respect to married women is unjust in principle, and presses with peculiar severity upon the poorer classes of the community, and ought therefore to be altered :

Be it enacted by the Queen's most excellent Majesty, by and with the advice and consent of the Lords Spiritual and Temporal, and Commons, in this present Parliament assembled, and by the authority of the same, as follows :

1. A married woman shall be capable of holding, acquiring, alienating, devising, and bequeathing real and personal estate, of contracting, and of suing and being sued, as if she were a feme sole.

2. Every woman who marries after this Act has come into operation shall, notwithstanding her coverture, have and hold all real and personal property, whether belonging to her before marriage or acquired by her in any way after marriage, free from the debts and obligations of her husband, and from his control or disposition, in all respects as if she had continued unmarried.

3. Every woman married before this Act has come into operation shall, notwithstanding her coverture, have and hold all the real and personal estate, her title to which shall accrue after this Act shall have come into operation, free from the debts and obligations of her husband, and from his control or disposition, in all respects as if she had continued unmarried; but nothing herein contained shall exempt any such property from the operation of any settlement or covenant to which it would have been subject if this Act had not passed, or shall prejudice any vested rights or interest to which her husband may be entitled at the date at which this Act comes into operation.

4. The earnings of a married woman in any trade or other occupation carried on by her separately from the trade or other occupation of her husband shall be deemed to be her personal estate.

5. A husband shall not be liable for the debts of his wife contracted before marriage, and shall not be liable in damages for any wrong committed by her.

6. Upon the death of a wife intestate her husband shall take the same distributive share in her personal estate as a wife would take in the personal estate of her husband if he died intestate, and, subject thereto, her personal estate shall go as it would have gone if her husband had predeceased her.

7. Nothing contained in this Act shall affect the right of any husband to hold his wife's real estate as tenant by curtesy.

8. In any question between husband and wife as to the title to or possession of personal property, either party may apply by petition in a summary way to any judge of the High Court of Chancery, or (at the option of the petitioner irrespectively of the value of the property in dispute) to the judge of the county court of the district in which either party resides, and the judge of the High Court of Chancery or of the county court (as the case may be) may make such order with respect to the property in dispute, and as to the costs of and consequent on the application, as he thinks fit, or may direct such petition to stand over from time to time, and any inquiry touching the matters in question to be made in such manner as he shall think fit: Provided always, that any order of a judge of the High Court of Chancery to be made under the provisions of this section shall be subject to appeal in the same way as an order made by the same judge in a suit pending in the said court would be, and any order of a county court judge under the provisions of this section shall be subject to appeal in the same way as an order made by the same judge on an equitable plaint would be; provided also, that the judge of the High Court of Chancery or of the county court shall, if either party so require, be bound to hear such application in his private room.

9. When a wife having real or personal estate has allowed her husband to receive the rents and profits, or to use and dispose of the personalty, the husband shall not be held liable to account for such rents, profits, or personalty for any period during which he has so received and disposed of them.

10. Nothing in this Act contained shall prevent any settlement being made, whether before or after marriage, respecting the property of any married woman, or shall interfere with or render inoperative any restriction against anticipation at present attached or to be hereafter attached to the enjoyment of any property or income by a wife under any settlement, agreement for a settlement, will, or other instrument; but no settlement or agreement for a settlement of a wife's own property to be made or entered into by herself, and no restriction against anticipation contained in any such settlement or agreement for a settlement, shall (unless such settlement or agreement for a settlement have been made before marriage) have any greater force or validity against creditors of such wife than a like settlement or agreement for a settlement made or entered into by a man would have against his creditors.

11. Any woman during her minority may, with the consent of her parent or guardian and of her intended husband, make or enter into any settlement or agreement for a settlement in contemplation of marriage, and the settlement or agreement for a settlement so made or entered into shall be as binding upon her, and those claiming under her, as if she had been of full age at the date thereof; and where in any settlement or agreement for a settlement made in consideration of marriage before the first day of January one thousand eight hundred and sixty-nine,[1] the wife or intended wife being at the date thereof a minor, the husband or intended husband may have covenanted or agreed to settle the after-acquired property of such wife or intended wife, such covenant or agreement shall, after the first day of January one thousand eight hundred and sixty-nine,[1] be binding on and shall be enforceable during the marriage against the wife, and those claiming under her, as if she had herself entered into it under the powers by this Act conferred.

12. This Act shall come into operation on the first day of January one thousand eight hundred and seventy.

13. This Act shall not extend to Scotland.

14. This Act may be cited as the "Married Women's Property Act, 1869."

---

[1] The date 1869, in the eleventh section, is of course a mistake for 1870. The bill is the same as that of Mr. Shaw Lefevre's of 1868, and the printer neglected to make the necessary alteration in this section, though he has made it in the twelfth.

APPENDIX B.

MARRIED WOMEN'S PROPERTY BILL, 1869.

The Bill as amended in Committee. (32 Vict., Bill 122.)

WHEREAS it is desirable to amend the law of property and contract with respect to married women:

Be it enacted by the Queen's most excellent Majesty, by and with the advice and consent of the Lords Spiritual and Temporal, and Commons, in this present Parliament assembled, and by the authority of the same, as follows:

1. A married woman shall be capable of holding, acquiring, alienating, devising, and bequeathing real and personal estate, of contracting, and of suing and being sued, as if she were a feme sole.

Provided, that nothing herein contained shall empower a married woman to dispose otherwise than by will of any freehold or copyhold hereditaments, or any money subject to be invested in the purchase of freehold or copyhold hereditaments, or any future or reversionary interest, whether vested or contingent, in personalty, or to release or extinguish any power which may be vested in her in regard to such freehold or copyhold hereditaments, money, or personal estate, but the power of disposition now vested in married women over all such hereditaments and other property shall remain the same as if this Act had not passed.

2. No woman shall be liable to be taken in execution upon any judgment founded upon a contract made or act done by her during coverture, and no such judgment or execution thereon shall bind or affect any property except such personal estate (if any) as she may be possessed of or entitled to for a present interest during her coverture.

3. Every woman who marries after this Act has come into operation shall, notwithstanding her coverture, have and hold all real and personal property, whether belonging to her before marriage or

acquired by her in any way after marriage, free from the debts and obligations of her husband, and from his control or disposition, in all respects as if she had continued unmarried.

4. Every woman married before this Act has come into operation shall, notwithstanding her coverture, have and hold all the real and personal estate, her right to which shall arise after this Act shall have come into operation, free from the debts and obligations of her husband, and from his control or disposition, in all respects as if she had continued unmarried; but nothing herein contained shall exempt any such property from the operation of any settlement or covenant to which it would have been subject if this Act had not passed, or shall prejudice any rights or interest to which her husband or any person claiming through him may be entitled at the date at which this Act comes into operation.

5. The earnings of a married woman in any trade or other occupation carried on by her as a principal separately from her husband shall be deemed to be her property acquired after marriage.

6. A husband shall not by reason of any marriage which shall take place after this Act has come into operation be liable for the debts of his wife contracted before marriage, but the wife shall be liable for such debts as if she had continued unmarried.

7. No husband shall by reason of the marriage be liable in damages for any wrong committed by his wife during the coverture.

8. No husband or wife shall be entitled to sue the other in any action at law for a tort, except in respect of property; and in case any action shall be brought by one against the other, it shall be competent for any judge of the court in which such action shall be brought, on the application in a summary way of the defendant, in case such judge shall think such action frivolous or vexatious, to stay the proceedings thereon, either absolutely or upon such terms as to costs and otherwise as he shall think just.

9. If a wife shall contract a debt as the agent of her husband, she shall be liable to be sued for the same, together with him, but as between the husband and wife she shall be deemed his surety, and shall be entitled to the same remedy over against her husband for indemnity, as in the ordinary case a surety has against the principal debtor; and if a husband shall contract a debt as the agent of his wife, he shall be liable to be sued for the same, together with

her, but as between husband and wife he shall be deemed her surety, and shall be entitled to the same remedy over against her for indemnity, as in the ordinary case a surety has against the principal debtor.

10. In any question between husband and wife as to the title to or possession of property, either party may apply by summons or otherwise in a summary way to any judge of the High Court of Chancery, or (at the option of the applicant irrespectively of the value of the property in dispute) to the judge of the county court of the district in which either party resides, and the judge of the High Court of Chancery or of the county court (as the case may be) may make such order with respect to the property in dispute, and as to the costs of and consequent on the application, as he thinks fit, or may direct such application to stand over from time to time, and any inquiry touching the matters in question to be made in such manner as he shall think fit: Provided always, that any order of a judge of the High Court of Chancery to be made under the provisions of this section shall be subject to appeal in the same way as an order made by the same judge in a suit pending in the said court would be, and any order of a county court judge under the provisions of this section shall be subject to appeal in the same way as an order made by the same judge on an equitable plaint would be; provided also, that the judge of the High Court of Chancery or of the county court, if either party so require, may hear such application in his private room.

11. When a wife having real or personal estate has allowed her husband to receive the rents and profits or income thereof, the husband shall not by force of such receipt be held liable to account for such rents, profits, or income.

12. Where the husband of any woman having property of her own becomes chargeable to any union or parish, the justices having jurisdiction in such union or parish may, in petty sessions assembled, upon application of the guardians of the poor, issue a summons against the wife, and make and enforce such order against her for the maintenance of her husband, as by the thirty-third section of "The Poor Law Amendment Act, 1868," they may now make and enforce against a husband for the maintenance of his wife, who becomes chargeable to any union or parish.

13. A married woman having property of her own shall be subject to all such liability, for the maintenance of her children, as a widow is now by law subject to for the maintenance of her children: Provided always, that nothing in this Act shall relieve her husband from any liability at present imposed upon him by law to maintain her children.

14. Nothing in this Act contained shall interfere with or affect any settlement, agreement for a settlement, or other instrument made or to be made, whether before or after marriage, respecting the property of any married woman, or especially shall interfere with or render inoperative any restriction against anticipation at present attached or to be hereafter attached to the enjoyment of any property or income by a wife under any settlement, agreement for a settlement, will, or other instrument; but no settlement or agreement for a settlement of a wife's own property to be made or entered into by herself, and no restriction against anticipation contained in any such settlement or agreement for a settlement, shall (unless such settlement or agreement for a settlement have been made before marriage) have any greater force or validity against creditors of such wife than a like settlement or agreement for a settlement made or entered into by a man would have against his creditors.

15. Property, whether real or personal, settled to the separate use of a married woman, without restraint against anticipation, shall be subject in equity to the same liabilities as her personal property in possession not so settled would be subject at law under the provisions of this Act.

16. Any woman during her minority may, with the consent of her parent or guardian and of her intended husband, make or enter into any settlement or agreement for a settlement in contemplation of marriage, and the settlement or agreement for a settlement so made or entered into shall be as binding upon her, and those claiming under her, as if she had been of full age at the date thereof.

17. Upon the death of a wife intestate her husband shall take the same distributive share in her personal estate as a wife would take in the personal estate of her husband if he died intestate, and, subject thereto, her personal estate shall go to her next of kin according to the Statute of Distributions.

18. Nothing contained in this Act shall affect the right of any

husband to hold as tenant by the curtesy any real estate to which his wife shall be entitled at her death.

19. This Act shall come into operation on the first day of January one thousand eight hundred and seventy.

20. This Act shall not extend to Scotland.

21. This Act may be cited as the "Married Women's Property Act, 1869."

APPENDIX C.

TABULAR COMPARISON BETWEEN THE ORIGINAL AND AMENDED BILLS.

Sections of the Original Bill.	Corresponding Sections of the Amended Bill.
1	1 (part 1)
2	3
3	4
4	5
5	6, 7
6	17
7	18
8	10
9	11
10	14
11 (part 1)	16
11 (part 2)	—
12	19
13	20
14	21

It is not intended to imply that the "corresponding sections of the Amended Bill" are necessarily the same precisely as the sections to which they correspond in the Original Bill, but merely that they deal with the same subjects.

APPENDIX D.

THE following story is told in the *Manchester Examiner and Times* of June 3, 1869, and in the *Echo* of June 5 :—

"A solicitor in good practice died some years ago, leaving to his sister a small fortune of something under 400*l.* a year. Another solicitor, an intimate friend of the first, and a man of high reputation and peculiarly grave manners, paid his addresses to the lady and married her. Trusting to him, and having no male relative to look into her affairs, she allowed him to draw up her settlements himself, and left them in his hands. Shortly after the marriage a younger woman came to live in the house as a sort of companion or housekeeper. Soon the wife was reported to have a severe illness, and next to have lost her mind. To the few friends who persisted in inquiring after her the husband stated that as she was not violent he would not have to send her to an asylum, but preferred to keep her in his house, where, of course, she was well cared for, and attended by the woman who now took the place of mistress of the house. At the end of seven or eight years, the solicitor died, after a short illness. His relatives then came into possession of the house, and, on examining it, found the helpless wife locked up in a garret in the full possession of her senses, which she had never lost, but having been for all those years imprisoned as a lunatic, with her rival for a gaoler. Her marriage settlement, whatever might have been its provision, had been destroyed, and she was, of course, left to the operation of the Common Law and the terms of her husband's will. By that will, every shilling of the fortune which had once been hers was bequeathed to the woman who had supplanted and imprisoned her, and she was left absolutely penniless. The unfortunate lady lingered but a short time longer in the world wherein she had endured such wrongs, and died in want, her only means of subsistence having been a trifle allowed to her by the woman who had robbed her of liberty and fortune. Such is the possible action of the Common Law. Those who feel indignant to learn that such things can be done under its sanction, should exert themselves to aid the passing of the 'Act to amend the Law concerning the Property of Married Women.'"

VIII.

FEMALE SUFFRAGE, CONSIDERED CHIEFLY WITH REGARD TO ITS INDIRECT RESULTS.

BY JULIA WEDGWOOD.

THE question, Ought Women to have the Suffrage? is one, the answer to which implies a consideration of some of the deepest problems of our day. No one can answer it who has not weighed all the large changes which it is likely to introduce into public and domestic life, one against another, and solved an intricate problem of profit and loss. Few are fitted for such a task—few know enough, and many feel too much. The present writer aims at an office, less valuable than that of the judge, but which is, on literary ground, insufficiently appreciated. It is not the act of a partisan, but of an earnest seeker after truth, to contemplate any large subject, for a time, steadily from one side. No persons are likely to be more onesided than those who attempt to look upon anything from all sides at once; who hurry, that is, from one point of view to another too rapidly to correct their crude impressions of any. I think, therefore, that an avowed intention to present to the reader one side of the question solely is the best safeguard against the great danger of treating it in a onesided spirit. One other preliminary caution must be given. The Enfranchisement of Women is, in this attempt, considered rather for what it implies than for what it is;—as the most obvious and comprehensive symbol of that change which should make Woman, in the fullest sense of the words, a fellow-worker with Man, rather than as an inconsiderable enlargement of the Constituency.

Starting, therefore, from the concession that weighty reasons are to be alleged against the proposed change, that as women are at present educated there is fear that its immediate effect might be an increase of that part of the constituency which is open to unfit influence, and perhaps an addition of strength to whatever is unreasoning in Conservatism, let us yet review all those reasons which should keep the Enfranchisement of Women before us as our goal.

I say "as our goal," and not "as our present desideratum." That it is also the latter I neither affirm nor deny. If we regard it as an isolated fact its objective importance would not, perhaps, be very great. But it is not that now and then the women in a small borough might have a chance of turning an election which we have to consider, it is that in such circumstances a large principle would be admitted which would totally change the position of women. Once give a woman political status, and her admission to any career becomes an open question, the *onus probandi* is thenceforward thrown on those who would exclude her. We may think in many cases this burden would be a very light one, but that is not to the purpose here; what we have to note is, that in the present state of public feeling a woman has crossed a watershed when she receives a right to vote. I consider, therefore, not merely or chiefly what reasons are there for extending the suffrage to women; but what reasons are there for admitting them to a platform whence the ground slopes away without interruption to that which is common with men? In short, Do women really need a wider scope than they have already? What scope have they already?

A woman may write books, paint pictures, go on the stage, teach children, manage a hospital,—we may now add, become a Doctor. This does not seem a narrow range of pursuits. They include within their range some of the most varied forms of mental work. But when we say a woman may do these things, do we use the potential mood in the same sense as we should apply it to the choice of a man's profession? No doubt there are some of these pursuits which are as open to any woman who possesses the requisite talent and cultivation as they are to a man in like circumstances. If a woman writes books as well as a man does, she will find it just as easy to get a publisher to take them as a man does. If she paints pictures as well, she will find the public equally ready to buy them. It is nothing to the contrary that our greatest female writer is known as George Eliot, and that young authoresses who choose a *nom de plume* prefer one which leaves the sex doubtful. We need not enter on the reasons which induce a great and fearless thinker to claim the liberty of speech conventionally only granted to a man, and for her more timid followers it is sufficient to suggest the presumption that a woman's writing will not be so good as a man's—a probability which no one will dispute. But if the inferiority of her powers to his is due in any degree to the conventional arrangements of society, it is not true that society leaves as open to her as to him any career which depends on the full development of those powers. We make the means inaccessible, and therefore practically exclude the ends. It is not immediately to our purpose to dwell on the poverty of the present means of education for women, but some aspects of this poverty have not been sufficiently recognised, and are relevant to the subject before us. I think the positive inferiority of a woman's means of cultivation to a man's is sometimes over-rated, but what hardly can be over-rated is the difference in the facility afforded a man and a woman in setting to work. I do not believe the idlest youth who just saves his degree at College wastes more of his undergraduate years than an energetic girl of the corresponding portion of her life.

For how does a girl pass those precious years of her life, from eighteen to four-and-twenty? Emancipated from schoolroom inferiority, and moving for the first time among her elders as an equal, she enters the enchanting grown-up world, with all its responsibilities—so, at least, she delights to think—and is eager to take up the full burden of the important duties which her imagination creates out of every small conventional opportunity. All invitations to gossip become social claims; she hears it said that she should help her mother; and all that is best in her nature throws its weight into the same scale with frivolous tastes and thinly-disguised self-indulgences. How can she sit reading history in her own room, when her conscience and her inclination whisper in concert that she may be wanted to settle a plan with her parents, or entertain a visitor? We may smile at these temptations, but they are omnipotent with a girl of eighteen. The mother who is willing to further the full development of her daughter's powers at considerable (though not, I believe, permanent) loss of gratification to herself, can, no doubt, prevent this conflict, but this at present requires resolute self-denial. Not, as is conventionally supposed, that she turns to her daughter for help. A woman of fifty rarely needs help from a girl of eighteen; that need has not yet arisen, and it is hardly ever selfishness which is the disturbing element in this relation; but she is anxious, on the one hand, that her daughter should make the most of every chance of pleasure which, as continually varying, she thinks exceptional, and on the other she regards study as something that can be taken up at any time, and may therefore be continually laid aside. She has thus no inducement to encourage that rhythmical and continuous life which, while she clearly sees it to interfere with the sources of innocent amusement, she does not perceive to be the indispensable condition of study. A guest is coming, or a guest is going; or it is a beautiful day, and the girls ought to go out; the books will remain, and the sunshine will not. And the daughter does not discover for some time, that, even if the books will remain, the power of using them is, under these constant interruptions, more evanescent than the sunshine, and when fully awake to this, never knows how far she ought to resist suggestions from her mother. When at length she sees that a stand must be made, if she is to save any power of work, she has plenty of errors to regret on the side of resistance. On Monday she made her book or her drawing excuse for not coming down to a tiresome visitor, and so on Tuesday, resolving to be obedient, she puts aside the book to join in gossip which she likes better than history. I wish I could adequately present the incompatibility of any intellectual work with the doubts and scruples which are born of circumstances like these. It is not that they occupy a large space of time (though they do occupy much more time than any one would imagine who knows nothing of the struggle), but that they keep the attention concentrated on minute and shifting objects, from which, even when released, it cannot return to the large and remote region of intellectual work. I do not say that all kinds of gain are impossible under this experience; there is no trial which may not develope some form of moral excellence, but to expect study to be carried on in such an atmosphere is as if you should expect fine engraving to be done at sea.

This language, which women will understand, will sound exaggerated to men. They know nothing of the experience here indicated. They may, of course, find it a struggle to stick to work in the face of innocent or laudable temptations to amusement, but certainly, at the age we are considering, the theory is that they should work, and nobody ever attempts to invade their hours of study with any social claim. However much they waste their undergraduate years, still those years are spent in an atmosphere of study. Life is arranged with a view to some kind of intellectual achievement; they are, as women never are, surrounded with influences that make it natural for them to devote themselves to mental cultivation. The influence which the anticipations of others exercise over us is subtle and impalpable, but its importance is such that the difference of facility in following out a pursuit to which these anticipations are or are not adjusted, can only be represented to a person who has never experienced it by saying that the largest allowance of outward help is hardly a compensation. When a woman, after such a youth as is here indicated, wakes up to a distinct knowledge of the capacities of her nature, the power of profiting by it is gone. Leisure perhaps remains to her in abundance, but that power of concentrated attention which can only be attained in youth, with which the scantiest leisure is available, without which the most abundant is useless, is for ever beyond her reach.

Surely, therefore, we can only say a woman may cultivate Literature or Art in the sense in which we should say a man may be Lord Chancellor. We mean, that it is not impossible to a nature of exceptional strength of will and power of work. The mental gifts that would raise a man to the woolsack will make a cultivated woman. I am not now inquiring whether this is desirable; I only urge that, when reckoning up a woman's opportunities, you do not forget that they are opportunities in quite a different sense from a man's.

So much is true even of those pursuits where the social code recognises the desirableness of the end, and only makes the means, to all average women, inaccessible. But even more than this may be said of those which are looked upon as questionable in themselves. Most mothers, however high in the social scale, would be glad to see a daughter occupy a position in the front rank of literature, though they might do their best to interrupt the solitude and calm which alone makes vigorous thought possible; but they would be anything but glad, probably, to see her manager of a hospital. And although of late years this has grown more possible, and in average circumstances, under our over-easy filial code, a middle-aged woman would get her own way in the matter; still, I urge,—at what a cost? What a hardening of nature is inevitably consequent on so much strain! What a loss of moral loveliness in the scars that bear token of the conflict! And let it not be supposed that this is a conflict between duty and taste. God forbid that arrangements should ever be made to mitigate the punishment of one who leaves the parent's fading years uncheered by filial care! But a large part of this suffering is inflicted on women who only leave parents not needing them in the least;

parents to whom their removal to the other end of the world by a tolerably happy marriage would give unmixed satisfaction. We visit with almost the same penalties neglect of the most sacred personal claims and of the most ungrounded social conventions, and shackle the movements of a woman whose energy takes any unusual line, as much with the unreasoning anticipations as with the needs of those who love her. What stops her way is not the claim of particular individuals, but the adverse ideal of a social code.

Now, to say that a woman cannot devote herself to any large object without coming into collision with the anticipations of society, seems to me another way of saying that the scope allowed her sex is too narrow. And the undeniable fact that her demand for a larger field of action has been (like most other urgent demands for change) associated with much that is trite, much that is foolish, and much that is in bad taste, so far from being an argument against this conclusion, affords those who maintain it a good illustration; for, if no folly or weakness were associated with the craving after a richer education and a larger sphere of work, it might not unfairly be taken as a proof that the condition of both was satisfactory. As it is, our own exaggeration and distortion affords one proof among many that we need a widening of our horizon, an enrichment of our aims, a strengthening of all that part of our nature which rests on large ideas, a weight thrown into the scale opposite to that of small personal interests. A difference in the power of appreciating proportion is one of the few almost unquestioned distinctions between men and women. Talk over some small family worry with a man and his wife; which of the two will feel it most keenly will be of course a matter of accident; but you will almost invariably find that in one case you leave the sore subject behind you when you have done with it, and in the other you keep looking at it obliquely. A man is mortified, chafed, annoyed,—he gives vent to his vexation, and turns to something else; there *is* something else in the background; mere personal feeling does not exhaust his capacity for pleasure or pain. With a woman it is not so; she can only proceed from her own personal interests to somebody else's personal interests, and the wide, enduring, *common* life, so much less subject to vicissitude, so much more invariably available, is hidden from her view.

No doubt this very difference between men and women may be represented as cause instead of effect of their different political position, and thus made to do duty in a direction precisely opposite to that which is here assigned to it. This is not, however, an objection which need be answered by one who is trying only to set forth the arguments on one side. If there is this inherent defect in woman's nature, that is no reason we should not do everything to strengthen the opposite virtue, supposing nothing is sacrificed thereby. Nor can you ever decide which of two concomitant facts is cause and which effect till you alter one of them.

There are many, though not perhaps so many as there

used to be, who will deny that this strong preponderance of the personal element in women is a defect, who would think it a loss that they should ever stand towards public affairs in the same relation as their husbands and brothers, and would lament any diminution, not only of the positive space which the affairs of their household occupy in their minds, but of the proportion in which these private concerns stand towards larger matters. It cannot be denied that any such change would tend to blunt the edge of contrast between the sexes, and if the ideal of their mutual relation is a picturesque antithesis, no doubt things are best as they are, or rather as they were a hundred years ago, for the picturesque contrast is to a great extent lost already But let those who look at the question through no pre-arranged theory, but through the colourless medium of a simple desire for truth, ask themselves, Do people really effect most in any particular department who understand that department alone? Can we estimate any single thing till we know its bearings towards other things? I believe that very often the only thing sensible women need in order to appreciate some family difficulty is, no more time to think about it. We should come back to our domestic perplexities, after an interval of occupation with something entirely different, as we come back to them after a good night's rest. "Was it only last night this difficulty seemed so insuperable?" we have often asked ourselves: "how simple it is, after this interval of oblivion." And more effective than any mere oblivion is that different action of the mind which we attain in turning from small to large interests. Let no one attempt to estimate this kind of gain by marking the degree in which intellectual pursuits are a refuge from practical worries. The smallest thing to be done outweighs, in its claim upon the attention, the largest thing to be known; and though study is a shelter from all those cares which we literally create for ourselves, those who turn to it in the hope of escaping the pressure of some real though small practical difficulty, will be apt to feel as if they had leant upon a broken reed. When these difficulties have taken a strong hold upon the mind, we need the help of some peremptory external demand in order to enable us to measure and rightly deal with the interests thus interrupted. Seen through the microscope of prolonged attention, the hasty word becomes an expression of hopeless alienation, the trivial fault expands to the dimensions of a sin needing profound repentance. And so women very often do harm in proportion as they are conscientious. Men far more easily forgive an explosion of bad temper or a display of gross selfishness than that aspect of Christian forbearance and resignation with which their shortcomings are often met by women who would make almost any sacrifices for them, and who simply need a background of large interests in order to turn their conscientiousness to good. This mistake is seen more ordinarily in the form of a cowardly suppression of all criticism, and abnegation of all influence; and perhaps this is not its least injurious form. Especially in the case of a mother and son, I believe much is lost by a woman's incapacity to look at faults lightly—much to her, and yet more to him. "If I had not preached to my son *then*, he would have been so thankful to listen *now*"—words I once heard from a conscientious mother—indicate an experience quite as injurious to men as to women.

I think, therefore, that that domestic life for the sake of which people are anxious to curtain off large interests from women's lives, would gain by the admission of those interests. Yet I could not concede that if it were not so, this would be an ultimate reason against their admission. We deceive ourselves with names in this matter. "Domestic life" means marriage; and while the attraction of one human spirit to another lies in a region much deeper than the influence of the social code can penetrate, the attraction of an outward framework of life might be diminished with no loss to any one. All high aims gain when they are disengaged from adventitious attraction, and those who think the office of wife and mother the highest, will be the most anxious to cut off every temptation for any one to enter upon it whose motive is a dearth of other interests. When stated in plain terms, indeed, the opposite view is absurd; no sane human being would seriously maintain, as an objection to an innovation, that it would make us pause before entering upon the most solemn responsibilities of life.[1]

[1] I retain this sentence, in spite of an assertion in the article "On Female Education" in the number of the *Quarterly Review* for April 1869, to the effect that "Our object is to entice our golden youth into matrimony by the exhibition of a useful and womanly character," which I confess does not appear to me

But people judge of truth and error so much by association, they are so little in the habit of looking at facts except in bundles, and the bundles are sometimes made up so arbitrarily, that it behoves every one who approaches a subject familiarized by long conventional handling to be resolute in refusing all assent to words which do not attach themselves to concrete fact. And those phrases which come to us with the subtle perfume of dignified and peaceful association, and bind together the ideal of Woman and Domestic Life, seem to me in one sense equally true, and in another equally false, for every human being, man and woman alike.

Surely, so far as any of us, woman or man, knows nothing of the family life, so far he or she is the less of a human being. I see no difference in this respect between the dweller in clubs or in convents. Both have surrendered one large source of knowledge and spring of action; they cannot put in its place anything which shall replace, even if it should excel, what they lose; and as every loss is less hurtful in proportion as we are conscious of it, they had better be made aware of this. But to consider that this applies specially to women appears to me an error so hurtful, that it is necessary for one who would speak of this subject at all to discard all conventional theory, however graceful, and confront the actual fact, viz. that the extremely unequal influences by which men and women are drawn towards married life indicate

to form any exception to the class to which I have supposed such statements to belong. Perhaps the character formed with this object, whether useful or not, might not be specially womanly.

a disastrous side of our stage of civilization. It is not necessary to any considerable extent to illustrate a statement which will be accepted by every one who thinks not of abstract wives and daughters, but of the real women he knows; yet, inasmuch as decorous theories of maidenly life form to so many minds a *cul-de-sac* to all speculations on the subject, it is not out of place here to point out some of the inevitable results of a social framework which makes marriage woman's only career.

The most obvious, perhaps, though not the most important, is that it makes friendship between men and women, for average specimens of both, impossible. We all know instances of such friendship, no doubt, and in their power of enriching life they make so much impression upon us, that we are apt to forget they belong only to the exceptions of humanity. The fact that a man with nothing particular about him should be on terms of intimate friendship with a woman with nothing particular about her, is, I venture to say, unheard of. Why is this? Not that commonplace men and women are incapable of mutual understanding—some of the most affectionate brothers and sisters rise to one's imagination to disprove the idea; but that it needs exceptional force of character for a woman to hold at bay the idea of marriage wherever it is possible. To welcome it is easy, to determine against it is easy; but to leave it out of sight—the only basis for friendship—is, to the average girl, whose future is a blank but for this prospect, impossible. It is not only single life which is impoverished by this impossibility; you cannot systematically discourage tastes and capacities in every region but one, and find them in their full development in that one. To deny men and women common ground except on the footing of man and wife is in a great measure to deny it to man and wife also. However indispensable a husband and wife may be to each other's comfort, if their contact is only at a single point, if their intercourse is confined to their relation, and their mutual sympathies find no exercise in any direction but that of their common needs, their conjugal happiness is apt to grow flat and dull as the advancing years strip life bare, and to be very narrowing while it is intense. All mutual affection is so good a thing that we only estimate the poverty of this form of it by comparing it with a marriage which is also a friendship; but in marking this descent we shall recognise how much marriage loses in being made the sole opportunity of communion between the two halves of mankind.

A yet more hurtful result of the theory which regards domestic life as more sacred for one of these divisions than for the other, is, that it introduces a great unreality into a large part of a woman's life. At the age when a man's efforts, if they are worth anything at all, become definite, earnest, and persistent, she suddenly finds the spirit die out of all the aims of her life, and an anticipation which must not influence a single action destroy the interest of all. She may try to reach history, or teach poor children, or cultivate a musical talent; but for a certain interval all is vague, and difficult. The question "Is this to go on?" takes the edge off every pursuit, and drains off interest to a possible future which has no continuity with the present. Most of us have chafed under the provoking impossibility of employing an odd quarter of an hour while we are kept waiting, trying to read or write, and wondering all the while whether it is too late for So-and-so to come now. Something like this, counted by years instead of minutes, is the common lot of the average girl; but the special aggravation in her case is, that the time thus spent is not only wasted and unsatisfactory, but unreal. She has to ignore the possibility which may change her whole framework of life as nothing changes a man's life, and to profess an entire absence of anticipation as to the one event which for a time fills her whole horizon. This is a great evil, and it is an evil to which nothing corresponds in a man's career. His nature is quite as incomplete as hers apart from the discipline of conjugal life; but he is not taught to look upon that life as his vocation, and so he can take it when it comes naturally, and till then let it alone. Now what I would here emphasize is, that this contrast is the result of a theory and not of a fact. That women spend the best part of their lives in preparing for an event which may never happen—an event for which the very worst preparation is to hanker after it, while the very best is to be strenuously occupied with something different, is the result, not of God's decision that one form of life should be *happier* than another, but of man's invention that it should be deemed more *womanly*. A busy lawyer is not necessarily dissatisfied because the bar might, and does not, lead to the bench; but we in the analogous case infuse dissatisfaction into the lower position by insisting that those persons who remain in it have not fulfilled their vocation at all. An error so wide-spread and deep-rooted must rest on causes too subtle to allow us to hope for any except a very gradual removal; but I firmly believe that the first step in this direction is a choice of careers for women; and among all the advantages which may be looked for in opening an enlarged scope to them I regard it as not the smallest that it gives them something to surrender on marriage.

To say, then, that "Home is the proper sphere of woman," that "No education of women is valuable which does not fit them for domestic life," to use any of the well-worn formulas, in short, is to say that you must bring girls up to hanker after husbands. Of course all women, as well as all men, are born into a family; but if a woman is educated with a view to domestic usefulness, she will almost always feel her sphere inadequate till she has a home to rule over. You may call it domestic life when half-a-dozen grown-up sisters live together with a sufficient staff of servants; but I can hardly fancy a state of things less favourable to happiness or concord than that they should all try to find occupation and interest in the affairs of the household; grave faults of temper or feeling would not produce more irritation than the tendencies which would be thus fostered. This is not a real danger, the facts of life are too strong against it; but the alternative of that vague, half-conscious craving after a household of one's own, which I have already spoken of, is real enough. It is true that there comes a time when most people need from their children the same kind of attention that they have given them, and to satisfy this demand is occupation enough, not only of heart and mind, but of time. But it is not a claim that could be met by a daughter who had spent middle age in a fever of fuss over trifles. What old people need, almost more than even love, is calm. The truth is, that it is the filial relation which would be most enriched by widened interests. For a time mothers need nothing from their children than that they should grow,—to watch and guard the development of life is enough employment for the whole being, and while this employment lasts, the parental relation is on the whole a happy one. Associations of difficulty or disappointment with the life of the nursery or school-room are rare; they take their rise from the period when the children enter on common ground with the parents. Why is this? Because in early life there is, and in middle life there is not, a function to give the relation of parent and child active and healthy exercise. The time of mere growth comes to an end. Of course, our whole life is a period of development; but when youth is past this becomes no longer a thing to watch; one phase of the relation is past, and it is time that another should begin,—the limits that were enough for every desire before now cramp the whole nature. If the parents now immediately began to need the attention which they had just ceased to give, all would be well where the relation has been happy, but during that interval of mutual independence through which most homes have to pass, there comes a grievous strain on temper and forbearance, because both parties are trying to live in an exhausted receiver. Generally it is about the time when the parents are entering that stage of life when the outer circle of interests begin to wither, when the life of the heart is alone active, and intellectual tastes need to become vicarious. What they now need from the young is not help or service, but opportunities for sympathy, and for participation in interests which they cannot carry on alone; and their children's incapacity to suppply this need is what so often spoils the relation. We see this forcibly illustrated in the improvement of intercourse between a mother and daughter that generally takes place after the marriage of the latter; it is not only that they see so much less of each other, or that married women understand each other best; it is also, and I believe chiefly, that the younger woman now brings the elder fresh food for heart and mind. We see the same kind of contrast in the different capacities of a daughter and a son; how much of her dutifulness it takes to compensate for the touch of external life he has the power to bring with him! The half of mankind who are not educated for domestic life are the half who have most power to enrich it.

If, in answer to this attempt to show that women at least would benefit from a change which should remind them that domestic life does not exhaust the possibilities of existence, and open to them some of those alternative possibilities, it should be asked, "Are you prepared to test the value of this change by the condition of those who have approximated to it already ?" I answer, unhesitatingly, No. I would never allow that this or that "cultivated woman," whose cultivation seemed chiefly to have developed the unfortunate tendencies of her sex, and this or that "strong-minded woman," whose achievements in any unfeminine direction unquestionably failed to compensate for her loss of all womanly grace, afforded any arguments against opening to their sisters the region in which they had been unsuccessful. Putting aside the important but obvious consideration that human character is too complex a thing to allow of large inferences respecting it to be drawn from individual cases, I deny that the failures of those who struggle through difficulties and discouragements to reach an object afford ground for any conclusion as to the value of the object, or the practicability of removing hindrances in the way of pursuing it. It is a fertile source of misconception in this matter that we call women cultivated if they are only intellectual; few people, for instance, would hesitate to apply the epithet to a woman who merely read all the new books that were much discussed in the intellectual world, though every one would feel this to imply a very poor ideal of cultivation if it were applied to a man. No doubt, any one who has read the best books of the last twenty years has acquired, if it can be retained, no contemptible mass of information; but to let the ideas of the day float into one's mind just as the current of popular interest shall turn is not what we mean by culture when we bring the word into connexion with large hopes for our race. To bring the mind into contact with any of the great problems of humanity, to brace the intellect in the atmosphere of any true investigation, to make any region of thought, however small, really *known*—this, which is the function of Education in the full sense of the word, has not been fulfilled in the case of nineteen-twentieths of those who are called cultivated women. "And of how many men?" it may asked. In comparison with the apparatus of a man's education, lamentably few indeed. "Strait is the gate and few there be that go therein," is true no less of the intellectual than of the spiritual life. But it is only those few, when speaking of men, whom we should select to illustrate the advantages of culture, and we shall never see facts as they are till we accustom ourselves to apply the same measure to both halves of mankind.

Now, it is perfectly explicable that persons in whom a capacity is awakened and not satisfied, should contrast unfortunately with those in whom it is not awakened at all. These latter, as far as they go, are complete. The faculty that has never been trained is a source of pure disorder. There is a knowledge of the truth says Plato,[1] which gives rest to the soul, "and thus saves our life." But the mere capacity for this knowledge gives the soul, not rest, but restlessness. Incomplete specimens of any kind of advantage are not only insufficient as premisses for a conclusion; they are apt to suggest conclusions the very reverse

[1] In the 'Protagoras."

of the truth. It is consummate guilt which is most able to simulate innocence, and the most profound emotion the human heart can harbour which in its outward aspect most closely resembles indifference. In like manner it is perfect cultivation which returns to the simplicity of a mind in which the yearning after cultivation has never been awakened. To judge the advantages of education from a mind in the intermediate stage, is like tasting vinegar to see if you like wine.

This is one reason why you cannot estimate the advantages of opening a wider field for women from a comparative view of those who do and do not avail themselves of such possibilities in this direction as already exist; but there is another, which is even more to the purpose of the present Essay. If our standard for man's and woman's education were on a level, if it was the natural thing for an intellectual woman to give as much time and energy to study as it is for an intellectual man, those exceptional natures to whom it is enough to pursue Truth for her own sake would, no doubt, be fully helped and encouraged; but women would still want that stimulus to thought given by its connexion with the world of action which raises and widens second-rate men. This influence is not to be judged from its activity during the period of education, strictly so called. You could not tell in looking over the exercises of two schoolboys which of them was heir to a large property, and which only to hard work. Follow them to College, and there will be some difference, to judge from the praise one hears bestowed on a rich man who attains Academic honours, though no doubt any strong bent of mind would throw it into the shade; but in the mature world this difference becomes striking and decisive. I remember the Review (in one of our most respectable Quarterlies) of a book written by a man of family and fortune, in which the position of the Author was dwelt upon by the critic almost to the exclusion of all discriminating estimate of the value of his work. This was not mere vulgarity; it *was* the most remarkable thing about a not particularly remarkable book, that it should have been written by one who was without all the motives to intellectual exertion which appeal to the secondary and indirect regions of intellectual dominion; most people in the position of the writer would have let that amount of mental capacity which he had exerted, lie dormant. Now something of this kind is true of the whole female sex. It does not apply to Literature; a woman has the same motive for application here as a man, but she has no other channel in which to turn the energy that is developed in intellectual pursuits, and this energy is continuous in the greater number of minds only on the condition of finding some practical application, some channel between the life of thought and the life of action. Therefore when a woman attains to middle age, and finds that no change of mental exercise is possible, the powers which she has up to that time expended on study either wither away or become a source of disorder; and there is no surer source of discomfort to every one concerned than that restlessness which is the characteristic of any function unemployed, in man or woman. How many a woman who begins with a strong taste for Science, finds it wane, as the advancing years open no vista into cognate regions where there is something to be done. Would not she bring the medical profession just the kind of interest and knowledge which it can absorb most effectually? Might not a taste for history, not strong enough to suffice to itself after the natural time for learning is past, in like manner revive in some practical form? It is more difficult to illustrate this suggestion, because any application of legal knowledge is further from conventional ideas of woman's occupation than the business of the Physician; but I may perhaps instance the post of Guardian of the Poor, as a noble opportunity for a form of beneficent activity, which, while it lies close to all women's acknowledged and sanctioned occupations, yet opens a field which no one could worthily occupy who was not prepared by intellectual training. And let no one say that it is an unworthy view of the intellectual life to regard it as a feeder to life only in a secondary sense intellectual, that the culture which is sought as a means, and not as an end, is something low and poor. It is not the highest; those who love knowledge for its own sake, must take rank before those who love it for the sake of its practical application; but intellectual interests, avowedly preparatory and subordinate to some practical aim, are widely different from—have, in fact, nothing in common with—the vulgar spirit which estimates all knowledge as a round in the ladder for "getting on." There is no self-reference, no vulgar utilitarianism, in the demand for some practical sphere on which the energy may be turned which was trained in intellectual pursuits. It is the natural fruit of the average intellectual development, which, like that of some of the lower animals, finds a different atmosphere necessary for its earlier and later stages.

For a double reason, then, you must not judge things as they might be by things as they are. On one side our specimens are misleading; on the other, there are none. I repeat it, for it needs insisting on, we have before our eyes no specimens at all of the kind of female character which would be produced by study, early begun and continuously carried on, with a view to some course of practical life. That this might be no exceptional education needing the apology of very peculiar circumstances, or of some taste so marked as almost to deserve the appellation of genius, but, like the study of music, for instance, the natural course of things where there was no reason against it, is in the opinion of the present writer the strongest motive for furthering any change which should give women wider influence. It is idle to speculate as to the price we must pay for this gain; it is at least vain to endeavour to deduce it from measuring the loss and gain of those individuals who break into the paths we design to open. We cannot judge how much or how little of the grace and refinement of woman's life must be sacrificed if we would widen its scope and increase its efficiency, by watching the course of those who have roughly and hastily to do this for themselves. Those who have to fight for a position, afford us no inference whatever for others who would take that position naturally and easily. The women who are warped and strained by the effort of holding their own against the aggression of the world's hostility or suspicion, or embittered by the heart-piercing discovery that divergent opinion has the power to tear away deep-rooted affection, afford no rule for women who, in other circumstances, shall follow in their paths, and do their work without fighting their battle, any more than the dwellers on a frontier that has been the battle-field of former generations must still work with arms by their side. The most salient point in the experience of one set of workers is that which it is our object to remove altogether from the experience of their successors.

This object, if the foregoing reasoning have any value, is surely not a small one. Nevertheless, when such a change as the admission of women to the Franchise is demanded as a means to this end, I can conceive that many people will be impressed by a sense of disproportion, and some even of absurdity. "To give a few morbid women something to think of every four or five years," it may be said, not unnaturally, though most unjustly, "you are asking us to add to the electoral body material avowedly the most corruptible which it could receive. The Chinese epicure who, according to Charles Lamb, burnt a house to roast a pig, was not guilty of a measure more preposterous, in the true etymological sense of the word, than you are asking us to concede."

Such an antagonist, I believe, may be met on his own ground. But before inquiring whether in the change we advocate women would not be givers as well as receivers, let me ask our objector if it is a small thing to elevate or widen the minds of those who form, not only half the population, but the educators of the succeeding generation. Let him try to represent to his mind that educational measure which should rival in importance any improvement of the influences which act upon the minds of young children. What measure of University Reform, for instance, could spread over so wide a surface, could penetrate to so great a depth, as one which should bring the nursery under the control of wisdom? Is it held that folly in this region does no harm? that sense is wasted on babies? Such a plea needs no refutation beyond its clear statement; the memory of every human being, if it were sufficiently far-reaching and accurate, would supply material for an answer.

If this were all we had to say, it would be enough, not indeed to establish woman's *right* to the Suffrage,—the question is not here regarded from that point of view,—but enough, surely, to make out a *primâ facie* case for its concession as a measure of expediency, which is all that the present Essay attempts. But this is not all that may be said in favour of its object. It may be urged that women, to some extent even as they are, to a very great extent as they might be, would supply an element needed in our political life, and that from their taking a share in it men would gain, not only wiser wives and mothers, but fellow-workers who had a kind of wisdom which they lacked.

For those who regard Female Franchise as a *right*, the whole of the present train of reasoning must take the aspect (without being in the least invalidated thereby) of a series of supplementary considerations, such as, no doubt, might always be brought forward to enforce the expediency of conceding every right. A share in the government of a nation does not appear to me a subject of right, for either man or woman, in any other sense than as it may be for the interest of the majority that that particular individual should possess it, and those who take a different view of the nature of that political right will at least agree with me in regarding national welfare as its infallible test. Now surely it is an unquestionable truth, when we look at it through an atmosphere free from the mists of prejudice, that a nation's welfare is furthered in proportion as its laws, which can express the wishes only of the majority, absorb and imply the knowledge of the whole nation, and the decision of the strongest side is sifted through every objection that the weaker can bring to bear against it. Can we say this is the case while one large fundamental division of the nation is shut off from contributing that special knowledge which, unless in some exceptional way disqualified, every equally distinct class would be allowed to possess?

The theory of a Representative Government is that the governing body should represent, as in a convex mirror, the views, opinions, desires, even prejudices of the governed, in so far as the latter have, by the possession of a certain amount of property, given a pledge that they have something at stake in the matter; but we refuse to admit to this representation exactly that half of the community whose acquisition of property gives the strongest proof of all those qualities for the sake of which we make property the test of the constituency.[1]

Of course, if women are either exactly like men, or simply men minus something or other, they could add no light to that already possessed by a male constituency, but I know of no one who seriously believes either of these things. There is need very often for showing the falseness of a theory which forgets that

[1] We must not forget that it is a real hardship to working women, that property is for their sex thus shorn of its full advantages, and that this hardship is greatly increased by the last Reform Bill. Of course, so far as the Franchise goes, a female tenant has no chance against one who will bring a vote with him; and the Bill which introduces household suffrage discourages female householders altogether. I do not relegate this observation to a note because I consider that the evil it refers to is slight—it seems to me, indeed, the one unanswerable argument in favour of Female Suffrage—but partly because it lies so far out of the region with which the text is occupied, and partly because to treat it adequately requires a knowledge which I do not possess: I only remind the reader in this note, that our present arrangements seem expressly designed to discourage women who remain single in order to take charge of an aged parent; to increase the number of unsatisfactory marriages, the preponderance of which among the poor must strike every one who compares the average union in their rank and that above them; and finally, to throw every obstacle in the way of one field of employment for women—the management of a little shop or farm, which would present a valuable intermediate ground between the resources of domestic servants and the lower grades of governesshood.

both men and women have the characteristics of a common humanity, but any protest against the opposite view, that they have none but these, seems to me entirely superfluous. Nor do I think many people need to be told that "woman is not lesser man." Even those assertions of the radical inferiority of women to which rough practical thinkers have been provoked, perhaps, by the extravagance of some among women's advocates, are not really inconsistent with the admission that women are capable in directions where men are not. Any further discussion when this admission is given is irrelevant to our purpose here, otherwise I at least should be anxious to concede that in all joint action between men and women there does seem a predominance on the part of men which is not likely to be altogether the result of human arrangements. Do not let it be supposed that every one who pleads for an enlargement of the sphere of Woman is thereby committed to the advocacy of her independence. When seeking to obtain for one half the nation a better education, and a career in which this education should find its fitting issue, we need neither assert nor deny that they should retain towards the other half that degree of dependence, whatever it may amount to, that they have at present. The dangers here lie about equally on both sides of the path. That combined cowardice and indolence which shrinks from all responsibility, and from the effort of initiating action, is as much temptation to some characters as the pride and self-will which rejects all control is to others. There is a part of our nature to which dependence is a temptation, and there is a part to which independence is a temptation, and men and women must be prepared to resist both.

Leaving the irrelevant question of authority open, therefore, let us come to common ground. The strongest opponents and the warmest advocates of Women's Rights would probably agree that women are distinguished from men by the predominance of that faculty which is, on the intellectual side, insight, and on the moral, sympathy; judgment or justice, according to our point of view, being the analogous faculty in the case of men. It may appear a fanciful comparison, but I should be inclined to compare the difference between the two natures to that between Greek and Gothic architecture, one fine in outline, the other in detail. Now, is there no room in those relations which we label Politics (and in so doing disguise from ourselves that they are no more than relations between human beings after all) for this sympathetic insight characteristic of women? If questions of imperial policy appeal rather to the masculine mind, as needing a judgment of proportion and not of detail, surely they do not exhaust—they less and less tend to exhaust—the exercise of national activity. A large and increasing proportion of this activity is occupied in directions which, if a few people were concerned instead of a great many, we should say were specially woman's province. To care for the sick and poor, and to teach children, are accepted as the special duties of women when we count by units.

Does it make the difference of depriving her of her special qualifications for judgment that we count by thousands?

For the political life of our own day, those qualities which are conceded to be markedly developed in women are needed in a special degree. Take one question certain to occupy the attention of Parliament at no distant period—that of Education. Surely, if we wanted to know what children were likely to learn best, and how to set about teaching it, we should, *cæteris paribus*, turn to a woman rather than to a man. One might endeavour in vain to recall among a pretty large acquaintance any woman who had no experience whatever of teaching, while the difficulty with men is the other way; except in the Church and the body of professional teachers, you will hardly find a man who knows by experience what it is to endeavour to communicate knowledge. This is only one side of a large and complex subject; but it will not be contended, either that it is an insignificant one, or that it does not specially belong to a woman's experience. Much the same may be said of Pauperism. Women know the homes of the poor in a manner and a degree which men do not know them. When we see the patent harm done by rich benevolent ladies, when we watch their influence in extinguishing all idea of independence and encouraging a number of people to leave off all exertion, and bring into the world large families to whom the idea of working for their living is actually never presented,—when we are awakened to the enormous evil which results from women's habit of looking at the great facts of life as exceptions, instead of as coming under a general law,—we may be inclined to think that legislation is required rather to shut off the influence of women on the poor than to give a larger scope to that influence. Here, as often elsewhere, I believe that the true need is to increase that power which at first it seems necessary to diminish. What we want is to give women a sense of *responsibility* in dealing with the poor. It is so painful to see squalid misery, however well deserved; it is so pleasant to hear words of gratitude, however shallow, and watch a gleam of relief, however temporary. What is to teach us to withstand the temptation of winning this cheap pleasure for ourselves, and restrain us from interference with those laws which for the masses—and for the masses only—bind together misery and sin? Nothing, I believe, but making us feel our responsibility, as parts of a nation, in yielding to these temptations. It needs the sense of a national life to bring this home to us; no sense of individual justice will support us under what we have to witness of suffering and degradation. Nothing but the sense of a common life, to be purified through individual suffering from the evils which those individuals have not always brought upon themselves, will strengthen us to confront our duty in regard to those evils. As women attain a political position, they will, perhaps, awaken to the perception that some among the best of them have done their utmost to transmit from generation to generation an ignoble tolerance of debt, and to shut out from the homes where Englishmen are trained the bracing air of independence. They may come to see that they have endeavoured to interfere with that beneficent discipline by which a nation is taught uprightness, endurance, and thrift, and have helped to spread the rot of pauperism through the heart of oak that supports the dignity and greatness of England.

And, enlightened by this sense of responsibility, the very power of sympathy which makes the action of women so often injurious as things are now, would prove a channel of actual knowledge. Some years ago, when village savings-banks were first introduced, a friend of mine, upbraided for the information she gave the depositors that the savings of the wife were the legal property of the husband, tried to turn the poor women's indignant dismay against the true offenders, the framers of the laws. "Ah, ma'am!" was the answer, "then the Parliament can't know what husbands we have in *this* part of the country." It is not only to ignorant labourers' wives that such a belief has suggested itself. The following extract is taken from a volume of Essays, which, as "Questions for a Reformed Parliament," naturally affords us specimens of the kind of subject which may test women's capacity of special understanding. After speaking of the incapacity which an assemblage of rich men have for apprehending the needs of the poor, the writer[1] goes on:—"This inability displays itself every day in almost every department of legislation, but most visibly in the action of the House with regard to the Poor Láw," and to some other matters with which

[1] Meredith Townsend, *Essays, &c.*, p. 67.

we have no concern. "The Poor Law, as it now stands, was framed by the Reformed House, and was, on one side, an immense improvement upon the ancient system. But its working was from the first impeded by two mistakes, strikingly characteristic of an assemblage too rich to feel where the shoe pinches the poor. The initiation of administering relief was confided exclusively to the ratepayers, and no distinction was taken between the willing and the unwilling recipient."

After going on to illustrate these two mistakes, the writer continues—"It may be admitted, that no representation of paupers was possible at the Boards. But it was quite possible to represent the State as an impartial arbiter, and a really sympathetic House of Commons would long since have done it. As it is, the pauper is left to the ratepayers, without any trustworthy arbiter between him and them."

Do not those words indicate work for a Female Constituency? I venture to say, that no man could enter into the claims of paupers as a sensible, experienced, business-like woman who knows the inside of a workhouse. It will be fresh in the memories of some readers, that when a disclosure of the mismanagement of workhouses was exciting general indignation some time ago, a Poor Law Inspector excused himself for not having noticed the cruel neglect to which the sick were subjected by saying, that none of them had told him of it. "How was he to know of these things, if no one would mention them to him?" Of course this is not brought forward here as an instance of average discernment on the part of a man ; it was indeed by a man that the state of the sick was discovered and exposed. But it would not have occurred to a woman to justify her indolence by assuming that the way to be awakened to the presence of disease and filth was by being informed of it. Her eye for detail would not have let her assume such an incapacity for perceiving these things, however much her interest might have demanded such an assumption. That, as matters stand now, this superiority of insight is more than counterbalanced by her inferiority in a sense of proportion, that even a careless and languid estimate is less injurious than the exaggeration of a partisan, is true enough ; but it is a truth relevant only to the contrast between responsible man and irresponsible woman. We have yet to learn what might be the result on the minds of women of a sense of power in dealing with abuses. That sense of difficulty, of there being two sides to a question, which seems so wonderfully remote from their minds, is brought home to us with wonderful rapidity and force, when thought and feeling have to issue in action. And let it not be said that the influence of a vote is too trifling to possess this large educational power. The above remarks may perhaps apply more especially to that varied form of contact with the working of our institutions to which the Suffrage is likely to lead, than to the effect of the Suffrage itself ; but you cannot measure the margin of association that gathers round such a fact as a woman's admission to political status,—you cannot estimate what women might do as voters, by adding to what they effect already the power of giving a vote now and then. There would be a complex action and reaction of their own responsibility and consideration from others which we cannot measure, but which we may be sure would result in no contemptible influence on all those institutions with which they have been accustomed to meddle so helplessly and capriciously. At the same time, a large part of this contemplated action lies close to all that is accepted as Woman's Work. One cannot fancy a less objectionable attempt, from every point of view, than for such a body as the Ladies' Workhouse Visiting Society to prepare a description of any failure in the working of our Poor Law which might form a basis for legislation; but as matters now stand, it would be an effort rendered futile partly by want of knowledge, but still more by the habit of looking at facts in reference to feeling and not to action. The only new element which we need infuse into benevolent zeal in order to turn it to national gain is the sense of responsibility.

Both Education and Pauperism, then, offer a field in which it may be believed that women, endowed with political rights and with all which these imply, would do valuable work. Is there any other subject on which they may be supposed to be specially qualified? I believe it to be the case with the most important of all. What form the national recognition of Divine guidance is likely to assume in the future few of us have any conception; it is not certain that the form is likely to be changed in the lifetime of the present generation. Yet it is not improbable, and no one can say that the young may not live to see the day when the Church of England will mean something quite different from what it does to-day. I am aware that the influence of women in any matter of Religion would be regarded by men with a contempt which would save them from dreading it. As women are now, the feeling is not altogether unjust. I fear some among the noblest of us have not awakened to the knowledge that truth demands our undivided allegiance, that the love of light as light, and not merely as the needful condition of doing one's work,—a love rarer among human beings than any other virtue,—is rarest among women. But it is not less true that women have a keener vision for the spiritual world than men, and that their guilt in refusing to gaze into it fearlessly is greater. Surely all that many a man has of religion is a reverence for something which fertilizes the life of his mother or his wife, a glance towards that unseen thread of water in the valley which keeps its margin fresh and verdant. It is always felt as a loss to an individual that he should have been wholly cut off from such influence as this. Is not this equally true of a nation's development? I am unprepared to illustrate this suggestion; I can only point on the one hand to the influence of a religious-minded wife on a worldly-minded man, and on the other to the thinly-disguised Paganism which, in our national councils, always seems to emerge into distinctness, or transform itself into something unreal, on every occasion when Religion is in question, and urge that something analogous to the highest influences of private life must be possible on the larger scale.

Such are the reasons for which we urge the admission of Women to political Power. It does not fall within the scope of the present Essay to attempt any estimate of those reasons which might be adduced against it, but we are not precluded from noticing the obvious difficulty which presents itself to people's minds with the idea of Female Suffrage. If you go so far, it will be said, why not farther? If we are to admit women to the Electoral body, why not to the Representative? If they are to be Physicians, why not Lawyers? If they are to be educated like men, why not send them to Oxford and Cambridge? And if the second step is in all these cases felt to be undesirable, ought the first to be taken? Can it be desirable to smooth the paths of human beings to the edge of an abyss?

It might easily be shown that this objection no more applies to the admission of woman to the Franchise—the only right of property withheld from her—than it does to the admission of woman to the Throne. The possession of supreme power by a class—a possession which belonged to women when a Queen was a governor—implies the possession of subordinate political power by that class also; and if there happened to be no such things as Queens, the position would strike us as far more anomalous and appropriate for women than the position of female voters does now. But this extension of the Franchise is here advocated on grounds which do bring it within the region to which this objection applies. We urge it, not for its own sake only or chiefly, but for the sake of results which do, apparently, tend in the direction which is felt so dangerous. And as it is not here based on the ground of justice, we are cut off from the refuge, *Fiat justitia, ruat cælum.* If the sky is to fall, it cannot be justice which seeks to act.

For my own part, I believe that natural selection, in this region as in most others, may be left to do its work without any interference from us. This will be enough, we may be sure, to apportion to Woman those tasks which she can perform better than Man, and to cut her off from those in which he excels her; an occupation for which the two have a quite equal facility does not, I am certain, exist. I can fancy, for instance, that the Medical Profession might be proved to belong so entirely to woman's province, that the exclamation of a little child educated by an American lady-physician, "Only think! there has been a Doctor here, and *he was a man!*" might represent a general feeling. I think, moreover, that a woman's natural shrinking from any actual collision with those to whom she must, on the last resort, make the appeal of physical weakness, may be fairly trusted to hold her back from any profession or office in which, as in the Bar or the Senate, she must meet men as opponents. Her peculiarities of capacity on the one hand, and her insurmountable incapacities on the other, mark out a distinct path, which no arrangements of ours seem to me required in order to narrow. But a more satisfactory answer to such objections as these lies, not in any speculations as to the safeguards which in future generations will preserve woman from anything unwomanly, but in the conviction that, for creatures as shortsighted and conventional as we are, it is not wise to abstain from any step which we can clearly perceive to be expedient, because it seems likely to lead to another which is inexpedient. Most of us can recall, probably, some curiously wasted anxiety or precaution in our own lives, which, when the period to which it referred is past, we cannot remember without a smile. We have been afraid of finding life empty, and it has proved oppressive from its fulness of interest and work; or we have braced ourselves to endure searching criticism, and have been mortified by utter neglect. The experience of the race is so much more searching than that of the individual, that whatever is universal in such prevision on the part of any one of us is doubly and trebly unwise with regard to the race. It is not for us to estimate the temptations of the generation which is to come after us; we have to beware that we bequeath them no errors of our own, but we are not to abstain from any change which seems beneficent now from any fear that it may turn to misfortune when garnered in the past.

Is it a vain hope that the admission of women to higher culture and wider responsibilities may be a measure fertile in wide-spread and deep-reaching good? that it, and that widening and deepening of the life of one-half of our race which it implies, may make marriage nobler and more complete, a union of mind and soul as well as of heart, may enrich and strengthen the mother's influence, and give single life dignity and strength, and that the powers thus developed may find their way to a fuller and richer political life, like some beneficent Nile-stream admitted to fresh pastures? We may, we probably must, expect too much from every great change. We have been reminded lately, by one of the most eloquent and thoughtful of our public men,[1] that Christianity itself would hardly bear to be tested by any results that are obvious to us, and the very greatness of the hopes inspired by any change that affects so large a proportion of humanity may be an occasion of inevitable disappointment. But all the greatest benefits which have been won for our race have come through the instrumentality of those who were striving after good that was, for the time, unattainable. If we aimed only at what we could reach, we should reach nothing. It may be, for nations as for individuals, that they should not find the blessings they expect where they look for them; but we know in the case of each individual, and we can see it perhaps even more clearly in the lives of nations, that this disappointment is often the prelude to our greatest gain: that the good which is the unexpected result of earnest search, is far better than that which was its motive, and which we have been taught to renounce.

[1] See Sir J. D. Coleridge's speech on the Irish Church Bill.

IX.

THE EDUCATION OF GIRLS, ITS PRESENT AND ITS FUTURE.

BY ELIZABETH C. WOLSTENHOLME.

WE are, it appears, on the eve of great educational reforms. We have been told, and by voices we cannot disregard, that instead of being, as we fondly believed, amongst the first of European nations in matters of instruction, we are so far fallen behind the onward march of other nations that it is now the special shame of England to possess almost the worst instructed people in Europe. The unscientific temper and spirit of our upper and governing class, the Philistinism of our middle class, and the sordid and brutal ignorance of multitudes of our working people, have been conclusively shown to be due either to defects of education or to its still more melancholy absence. The cry is everywhere loud for amendment. Schemes of University reform and extension, schemes for the re-organization of our secondary instruction, theories of very different degrees of merit as to the just plan and scope of a comprehensive system of national education, are now before the world. If the day of much talking is the precursor of the hour of action, then the hour of action is near at hand. And yet, even amongst our reformers themselves, there appears to be little agreement as to what we can and ought to do by instruction. One authority has very recently told us that the first object of all instruction should be to fit a *man* to earn his own livelihood. Another tells us that it is the function of education to correct all narrow, special, and professional tendencies. A third, that the primal and direct aim of instruction is to enable a man to know himself and the world, all other being at best but subordinate aims. Are these views really so antagonistic as those who hold them seem to believe? Is there not a meeting point in which all are reconciled? Is it not plain that honest industry is of itself a part, and a most important part, of the highest education; that genuine work is the most perfect method of culture? Surely it is time that the dignity of labour in this sense should be recognised, and that such instruction should be given to all as shall substitute living, thinking workmen for mere machines. The industrial and economic advantages of this are clearly enough perceived, and a more rational system of instruction is urgently demanded on these grounds. Of at least equal importance is the enormous intellectual gain both to society and to the individual workman. And again, is it as a matter of fact the case that the best workman, the one who has had the fittest training for his task, is in any true sense narrow, special, or professional? Is it not, on the contrary, the case that where the intelligence is the clearest and quickest within the range of the daily avocation, intelligence and sympathy will be widest and deepest beyond its bounds? Where mere routine enters the least into the daily order of life, the life outside that daily order will be most intense and vivid. And again, how can a man rightly choose his daily task unless he has first learnt to know himself and the world? Such knowledge, as Mr. Arnold says, is "the only sure basis for action." Nothing else can secure for us that just economy of individual aptitude which is the key to all the success of the future. Nothing else can secure to us that wise use of special aptitudes which shall give to each man access by his own particular gateway to intellectual life and vital knowledge. Unless some such reconciliation be possible, our hope of securing an educated people is indeed a vain dream.

But in all these discussions we hear singularly little of the education of women. "The air is thick," says a Quarterly Reviewer, "with schemes for the education of women;" but these schemes lie quite apart from the general discussion of the subject, and have been conceived in the interests of women by women themselves. In the remarkable volume of "Essays on a Liberal Education," which we must regard as the manifesto of the most advanced educational reformers, one solitary paragraph is devoted to the education of girls, and to a casual plea that what they learn at all they should learn well. From Mr. Arnold's interesting volume on the Schools and Universities on the Continent, we gather a shadowy notion that there are such things as girls' schools, that the teaching of the girls is on the whole the best where that of the boys is the best; but that everywhere and at all times it lags very far behind. Mr. Arnold concludes his volume by the sketch of a very comprehensive plan of re-organization for English instruction, but throughout that plan there is no expression of a wish that girls should partake of its benefits. On the contrary, if we are to judge of his intentions from a footnote elsewhere, he would seem to desire expressly to shut out girls from any scheme for the improvement of public or school instruction.

The Schools Inquiry Commissioners, whilst readily yielding to the representations that girls' schools fell naturally within the scope of their inquiry, and bestowing great pains and attention, both directly and through their Assistant Commissioners, on the investigation of the problem of Female Education, were yet unable to treat it otherwise than as a separate and secondary matter. We do not complain of these things. They are but natural, perhaps inevitable, in our present imperfect state of civilization, and they are only referred to here in order to show how necessary it is that women should speak for themselves, and claim to be considered, not as a separate community, but as a part of the whole. The aim and office of instruction are surely the same with women as with men. Their claim to right instruction rests on precisely the same grounds; their need of it is as great, perhaps greater; nor has it ever yet been proved that the nature of women is so radically different from that of men that the methods of instruction which we pronounce unscientific, uneconomical, and irrational in the case of men, can be pronounced scientific, economical, and rational when applied to women.

It will not come within the scope of this paper to consider the great problem of National Education in its broad sense, including the instruction of all classes, and emphatically the elementary instruction of our wage-receiving class. All that need be said on this head is that when that question comes fairly before the nation, and the time for decisive action has come, as it must come very soon, it should be remembered that we are not one nation of Englishmen and another nation of Englishwomen, but one nation of English men and women, and that, as a matter of the soundest national policy and a means of the highest social well-being, it is imperative that Englishwomen should be as well instructed as Englishmen. But in the more limited part of the subject, with which alone we have here to deal, it is easy to show that, what for want of a better word we must call the secondary instruction of girls, is even more confused, more fragmentary, more worthless than that of boys, and stands in even more urgent need of a thorough and comprehensive re-organization, whilst the higher education cannot as yet be said to have any existence. Its shadowy form floats before the public eye, as Carlyle pictures the German Adam to have done upon the stage "going to be created."

It is almost impossible to convey to any one who has had no experience in teaching girls any notion of the wholly unsystematic and confused state of their education. A lively, we *wish* we could say an exaggerated, sketch of some of its most striking defects is to be found in Mr. Bryce's valuable report presented to the Schools' Inquiry Commission. The great majority of English girls are educated either at home with the help of governesses and masters, or at exceedingly small schools, whether day-schools or boarding-schools. Parents prefer these small schools because they believe they approach the most nearly to that which is their ideal of instruction for girls, and what in theory is very beautiful, home-education; but in nothing whatever is there a greater divergence between the theory and the actual, and in many cases the only possible practice, than in this matter of home-education for girls.

Before, however, entering upon the consideration of special defects of the education of girls as carried on at home and in these small schools or quasi-homes, it will be worth while to notice some defects which affect all schemes and methods of female education alike, and the correction of which must attend any considerable reform in mere organization. The first of these defects which require reform concerns the parents, the second concerns the teachers. It is simply true as a general statement that English parents, who are apathetic and irrational enough about the education of their boys, are much more so when the education of their girls is in question. Here and there a mother devotes herself to the right training of her daughters, superintends judiciously the teaching both of governesses and masters, or supplements and sustains the efforts of the school teacher;

and here and there a father interests himself in developing his daughter's powers, and is anxious that she should be a thinking creature and not merely an accomplished nonentity. But how few these cases are every teacher can bear melancholy testimony. In the wealthy classes frivolity and fashion rule. The mother devotes herself to society, and social duties and social pleasures are found incompatible with other obligations, whilst the girls themselves are too lightly and too early whirled into the same vortex. Fashion has stamped its approval upon certain external accomplishments and graces. The period during which social triumphs can be achieved is short and fleeting, and these accomplishments and graces, right enough and beautiful enough in their own place, must be purchased at the sacrifice of all else. Such a mother has simply no notion in what true education consists. It is not often that one can be found so simply ignorant and silly as the mamma who begged that her little daughter might not be troubled with the halfpennies and farthings in her arithmetic, because, as she said, "she can have no use for it when she marries; her husband and her housekeeper will do all that." But the spirit of that mother is found everywhere. The suppressed thought most frequently is, "It will not help her to get married;" and thus we are brought round to the consideration, that the primary cause of the bad education of women is to be found in the bad education of men themselves. If we seek to improve the education of women, we must improve that of men. If we improve that of men, we shall sooner or later improve that of women also; but the advantage is greatest every way if the two reforms proceed hand-in-hand.

In the less wealthy middle classes the pressure of necessity is often very heavy, and the instruction of the girls is the first expense in which it is commonly thought curtailment is possible. As in the case of the wealthier classes the wish to make girls brilliant and attractive during a certain short period of their lives is answerable for much folly; so in this class the fact that the education of girls has no immediate commercial value is the great hindrance to a better education. We cannot appraise the value of a cultivated mind. Presumably, therefore, it has no value. A certain amount of education, or at least of instruction, is essential to a son's success in life, and, fortunately for boys, some of the subjects in which instruction is thus essential may be made educational instruments of no mean value. But what success in life is possible to a daughter? The son must make his own way in the world. The daughter must have hers made for her by somebody. It is thus that the question of education or no education is regarded. The period of a daughter's systematic instruction, if systematic instruction for girls *is to be found*, is perpetually interrupted and cut short at both ends. If there were no other plea than this for the free admission of women to industry, we should hold that this plea was sufficient. Industrial occupation is more than the supplement of education to women of this class. It is the only condition upon which they will be permitted to be educated. Other reasons, and ostensibly more urgent, there no doubt are, but this reason is in very truth the most weighty of all. Let us but consider how it works. A woman must remain ignorant because, to her, knowledge has no practical, that is, commercial value. She is idle because she is ignorant. She becomes frivolous or vicious because she is idle. And for how much of the misery of the world idle hands and wasted brains are responsible it would be hard to say. This we can only suggest as a point needing far graver consideration than is often given to it. So, too, it is worth considering how enormous a power for good all this energy might become if economized and trained. How to deal with these difficulties in the case of parents is the standing perplexity of teachers. We must confess that we see no hope for immediate reformation. It is only by the greater extension of education itself that education will come to be rightly valued, and in this way the task of the teachers of the next generation will be a far easier and pleasanter one than that of the teachers of to-day.

But if the teachers cannot reform the parents, they may at least reform themselves. Mr. Bryce says: "Teachers," that is, women who teach, "have two defects; they have not themselves been well taught, and they do not know how to teach. Both these defects are accidental, and may be remedied." These are not slight defects. The charge against teachers could not well be graver than that they are ignorant and incompetent, and yet it is quite true that these defects are "accidental, and may be remedied." It is not the fault of the existing body of the teachers of girls that they themselves were badly taught. It is not their fault that they had no right training in teaching as an art, and have never been led to look upon education as the practical application of the highest science. But it will be their own fault if they do not discover these defects for themselves; if they do not apply the remedy, and if they do not make it impossible for such a charge to be justly brought against the teachers of the future.

The elder teachers can indeed do little more than perfect themselves by private study in the various subjects which they profess to teach, and aid the younger teachers by their experience, encouragement, and sympathy; but for the younger teachers facilities are already offered, or will shortly be offered, of which if they do not choose to avail themselves they will be foolish and almost criminal. Stimulants to private study, and direction in that study, are now accessible in most of our great towns, where the Lectures to women have been successfully established. Whatever shape these Lectures may ultimately take, and whatever their bearing upon the education of women in general, there can be no doubt of their great value to teachers, not merely, nor even chiefly, for the direct instruction which they afford, and for the suggestive lines of study pointed out, but by helping them to the best methods of teaching, by bringing them into contact with the best living teachers. Those who have had the opportunity of listening to Professor Huxley's Lectures at the London Institution—lectures the mere syllabus of which is a most instructive lesson in teaching

—will readily perceive of what immense value such aids must be to the teacher. But incidental aids of this kind will not alone suffice. It is absolutely necessary in the interests of education that teachers should secure the highest special training for their special work, and that they should master the secrets of combination and co-operation. Whilst a general high culture is essential to a teacher, it is equally necessary to do away with the superstition that any one person can teach any and all subjects equally well. Here more than anywhere else is it necessary that there should be that economy of individual and special aptitudes of which we have before spoken. It is not less necessary for women than for men, for girls than for boys, that those who teach should be "masters of their business—that each shall be set to teach that branch which he has thoroughly mastered, and shall not be allowed to teach any that he has not." But this presupposes that teachers will be prepared to submit themselves to definite tests of their qualifications, as well as to the specific training which is necessary. For women in general such tests of attainments have already been provided by the Universities of London and of Cambridge[1] in their recently-devised Examination schemes. The Cambridge scheme in particular lends itself to the present necessities of teachers in a manner which will make their acceptance of it almost a matter of certainty. The examination falls too early this year—too soon, that is, after the publication of the scheme, and in relation to the usual distribution of the time of teachers—to afford

[1] More recently by the University of Dublin.

any conclusive test as to their readiness to avail themselves of its provisions. If they should permanently refrain from doing so, the fact would have a painful significance.

Whether under the provisions of the Endowed Schools Bill *Special* Examinations for teachers will be devised, and if so, what form these Examinations will take, it would be premature even to guess. But after all, no test of attainments, however necessary and however valuable, will suffice for the equipment of a teacher. It ought to be a recognised part of every teacher's duty to familiarize herself with the great educational experiments of the past, and with their results; with the experiments now being made in other countries; and, above all, with the experiments which are being made at home. Actual practice in teaching under the eye and direction of an experienced teacher would be invaluable, and some machinery by which this shall be made possible ought now to be recognised as a pressing educational necessity. It would not be difficult to point out ways and means of securing such training. How important this is every teacher who has blundered through many wrong methods, and who has felt the consequent vexation and disappointment, as well as the absolute loss to pupils, can abundantly testify. One other point may here be mentioned: it is more than ever desirable that those women who devote themselves to teaching should do so with deliberate intention. It is a matter of grave concern, that in the case both of men and of women who teach this should so seldom be done, and that the work of a teacher should be constantly taken up as a mere temporary occupation pending something better. No high professional skill can be hoped for so long as this is the case, and in no profession whatever can skill and experience be more desirable and important.

But however much may be done by an improvement of the qualifications of teachers themselves, we cannot look to this for the whole of the advance we desire. Without better organization, without a better relation between all the parts of the scheme of our instruction, the ablest and most highly-qualified teachers will accomplish but little. The present general practice of education, either at home or in very small schools, is inconsistent with any *wide* diffusion of a more thorough instruction. No doubt this is the best thing possible in particular cases; but even in the best cases of the kind the waste of power is enormous.

The objections to education exclusively at home and to education in very small schools are so nearly the same that it may be convenient to treat of them together. The small school has indeed the disadvantages of home instruction, with some of its own superadded. The notion of many people on this subject is, that if mothers and governesses were what they should be, home education would be the perfect ideal of education for girls. Yet it is not too much to assert that education at home, understanding by education thorough systematic instruction, is in any but the very small minority of cases impossible. It is idle to deny the immense value of home influences. The ideal of girls' education, and of boys' also, appears to demand the just admixtuı public instruction and of private and domestic influence. The problem is a difficult one, perhaps the more difficult because we do not yet appreciate its difficulty; but also one not incapable of solution. In the case both of the home and of the small schools, the first fatal defect is that one person must either teach many subjects to different pupils in different stages of progress, or that separate teachers must be engaged at an expense which is beyond the reach of any but the very wealthiest. A very small result is produced by an expenditure of power, of time, and of money, wholly incommensurate. Take the case of a governess in a family with three or four children of different ages. She is expected to teach something of perhaps a dozen different subjects to each of three or four pupils, each of whom requires separate and individual instruction. But individual instruction in such a case means no instruction at all. It means giving an infinitesimal fragment of time, and a divided and distracted attention to each of the pupils and subjects in turn; or if anything more real is aimed at, it is only accomplished at a cost of time, of labour, of brain, and of nerve, which no human creature should be asked to undergo. Even in the more fortunate case of the governess whose pupils are of much the same age and the same attainments, the effect is pretty sure to be depressing to the teacher, and monotonous to the pupils. The teacher's powers are never roused and stimulated as they are under the effort necessary for collective or class-teaching, and the pupils have no standard of comparison outside and beyond themselves. Moreover, we believe it to be mischievous to both teacher and pupil that the latter should be so exclusively under one predominant influence, and that the former should be so constantly in the attitude of a critical study of the same type of character, the same defects, or even of sympathy with the same excellences.[1] Of course when masters and other teachers are in attendance this evil is to some extent remedied, but then another difficulty arises. Unless the governess is sufficiently cultivated both to supplement and superintend this additional teaching, it fails to become education in the true sense, and remains mere instruction on detached and unrelated subjects. No doubt this is a defect of school teaching also in our present state of confusion; but it is one of the defects most easy to remedy. For the full development of character the free play of a variety of influences is most desirable. In a home of real refinement and cultivation a thousand subtle influences are daily brought to bear upon the children which are of the greatest importance, and which it is the height of folly to forego. The education of the feelings is here carried on, informally, but most effectually. This, which is *the* valuable part of home-education, ought not to be lost. To send a girl from such a home to a mere ordinary fashionable

[1] A friend writes: "A master whom I knew got a boy or two removed from his own class into that of a master of a different temperament. His class, which had hitherto gone ill, went well. He said, 'I felt I only had to *eliminate the personal equation.*' But a governess such as you describe has no chance to eliminate the personal equation."

boarding-school is a high stretch of imprudence; but this is probably not necessary.

In the case of small schools all the difficulties of home instruction are found, if possible, in a somewhat aggravated form. Let us take the case, a very common one, of a school with from twelve to twenty pupils, their ages varying from six or eight to eighteen, and let us imagine what one, two, or even three teachers can do in such a chaos. For our present purpose it does not matter whether these schools are boarding-schools or day-schools. In the case of the cheap schools, the one or two teachers must suffice for the needs of all the pupils. In the case of the more expensive ones, a larger staff of teachers, either resident or visiting, is provided, but at a cost which makes the fees, though excessive to the parents, scarcely at all remunerative to the principal teacher. It would be interesting to learn what is the average rate of *profit* upon her capital of a schoolmistress, to say nothing of remuneration for her labour. If one could set the case of the very few who acquire a small independency over against that of the many who struggle on encompassed by difficulties, and of those who are utterly ruined, we should probably find that the average of profit was nothing at all. There are reasons for this in the present state of female education into which it is not necessary to enter, and it is only mentioned here to illustrate the wastefulness of our present educational confusion. But whether in the case of the less expensive or of the more expensive schools, this difficulty is added to most of the difficulties of home instruction, that not only are the pupils of all ages and at all stages of progress, but that they come and go in the most bewildering manner. A girl of sixteen will perhaps come to school and prove on examination more backward than another child of twelve. It is injurious to both to teach them together; to provide separate instruction is again to multiply difficulties. One would scarcely expect to be believed, if one gave the simple natural history of such a school, and showed how fitful and how irregular is the school instruction of most girls. We wonder much how many school-mistresses ever framed a consistent course of study which should stretch over six years. We wonder still more how many have successfully carried it out in the case of even one pupil. Either those pupils who stay longest at school are sacrificed to those who casually come and go, or these latter, and these are the far greater number, must be sacrificed to the interests of the very few. The burden laid upon the teachers of small schools is indeed greater than anyone can bear, and it is no wonder that even able and earnest teachers begin to feel, after years of such experience, that the remedy is not in their own power. It is not in the power of any *one* teacher to remedy this evil, but it is within the power of combinations of teachers working together in the interests of education and working judiciously, with the aid of public recognition and encouragement, gradually to extinguish it.

The experiment of large schools for girls has already

been successfully tried, and the results are conclusive as to the superiority of the system (so far at least as concerns day-schools), from whatever point of view we regard it. Their superior economy is obvious. But this economy cannot be estimated simply in terms of money. The school reacts upon the teachers, and their teaching becomes more spirited, energetic, and successful. The lower fees at which such schools can offer really good instruction, enable intelligent parents to avail themselves of the advantages of a longer school period, and in such schools alone have we as yet been able to reap the advantages of a graduated, systematized, and comprehensive course of instruction. Morally, we believe the gain to be also great. It is possible in such schools to substitute government by a healthy public opinion for government by a personal will; the free play of extensively varied influences is secured, a freedom which tends much more to the naturalness, independence, and variety of character than any system of more exclusive influences. Classification is easy, and the stimulus and support of companionship in study are more fully afforded.

The case of large boarding-schools is different and much more difficult. Perhaps the best that can be said of them is, that the inherent evils may by skilful teachers be reduced to a minimum, but it can never be considered very desirable to bring together great numbers of young people and to throw them into the intimacy of an English boarding-school, without far more careful oversight than it is easy to secure, whilst any approach to the system of perpetual espionage would be at once hateful to our English notions, and, as we believe, fatally mischievous to both teachers and pupils.

If these are the evils, what then are the remedies? We are not in Utopia, nor do we propose to shadow forth Utopian dreams, but sober, practical measures, which, if not possible to-day, may perhaps be so to-morrow. By connecting the home life with some one or other of the forms of collective instruction of which we shall hereafter speak, the home influences might be preserved, and another set of influences, little, if at all, inferior in value might be added. We want first, in every considerable town in England, a High School for girls—perhaps a High School and a Secondary school, under Municipal or Government control, which should offer the best possible education on very moderate terms. The school ought to be such that it should serve as a model to all those private establishments for which in the future, as at present, there will no doubt be abundant room. To such a school as this it would be very easy to attach all manner of appliances and apparatus in the way of lectures or special classes, which might be attended by pupils from private families or the smaller schools. If we could not in every town find a Professor Huxley who should make Physical Geography fascinating and simple to schoolboys and schoolgirls, and incidentally teach teachers how to teach, others might yet be found who would in their several ways perform a similar service.

II. If the small schools, whether as day or boarding

schools, are to continue, teachers must find out for themselves some plan of co-operation which shall make their labour richer in results. If four or five teachers would work together and make of each small school one class, each working up to each in a graduated and progressive course of instruction, the matter would be simple enough. So far as the teachers are concerned, we believe this might be done at once. The difficulty is with the parents, who would be apt to suppose that teachers were working from interested motives, and whom it would be impossible to bind down by any formal agreement. If however such progressive classes or grade schools cannot be established, we see no remedy for the crying evil of the small school system, except in the gradual amalgamation and absorption of these schools themselves. Under a comprehensive national system this would be very easy, as a matter of private arrangement exceedingly difficult.

III. As there will still remain many parents who cannot make use of the day-school, but either of choice or of necessity must send their daughters to study away from home, we would suggest the establishment, in various country districts, of schools corresponding to the high schools of which we have spoken, a central institution, that is to say, with its complete staff of teachers and professors, but in which there should be no resident pupils. The officers of the institution should not take boarders because their work in the actual school hours would be sufficiently exhausting, but boarding-houses should be opened, and regularly licensed, the only persons allowed to keep such boarding-houses being ladies (wherever circumstances favoured it, married ladies) of education and refinement. The number of boarders should in every case be limited, and the person licensed to the boarding-houses should stand in the relation of friend and private tutor to the boarders. By some such plan the gravest evils of large boarding-schools would be escaped, and the economical and social advantages of collective instruction be secured.

IV. We need the establishment first of one, and ultimately of many such institutions as the Hitchin College for Women. It would seem almost unnecessary to argue this point. If the education of women is ever to advance beyond its present low level, it must be by the creation of means which have never yet been employed. Systematic instruction for women in any way analogous to that which the Universities supply to men, and which is likely in the future to be supplied more fully, and at more numerous centres, has never yet in England been offered to women. That there are many amongst us who would gladly have profited by this higher education we know too sadly. That there are now those eager and desirous to avail themselves of it, is perfectly certain; but whether such a demand exists or not, it is plain that it ought to exist and that we ought to set about creating it if it did not. Such provision is necessary in the first place for teachers; for the rhyme is as true to-day as it ever was:

> "But little way her knowledge reaches
> Who knows no more than what she teaches."

And yet, such is the irrationality of our present methods that we constantly find our teachers teaching what they do not know, and, most lamentable of all, wholly ignorant of their own ignorance. Now the very first step towards improving away these ignorant teachers is to send out as teachers as many women as possible of genuine attainments and high cultivation. Some such women there are to be found already amongst the ranks of teachers, but they have come by their attainments in almost every case by the slow and difficult process of self-instruction. Possibly character may have been strengthened and faculty matured under the process, but at a cost both to themselves and others which they would thankfully have been spared. If such women could give the history of their own efforts and failures, we should find in these the very best plea for making the higher education easily accessible to women. Which of them could not tell a dreary story of efforts wasted upon wrong methods of study, of time lost in reading inferior books, which the slightest suggestions of greater knowledge or experience would have saved them? There is not one amongst them who is not conscious of painful gaps and shortcomings, defects which are perpetual hindrances to her best and most earnest work. But this is not peculiar to women who teach. All those women who, from whatever cause, have been led actively to interest themselves in the pressing social questions of the day, must have felt the same miserable want of an instruction larger and deeper, and a mental discipline more bracing than has been permitted to them. The difficult social problems of to-day are not to be solved by mere native kindness of heart, still less by unassisted common sense. Never was there a time when there was so much work waiting to be done which demanded the highest faculty, perfected by the best possible training. Our schools cannot supply this want of good training. We have shown that they are not adequate to the work already imposed upon them. The cases are very few indeed in which by a special happy combination of advantages a woman can secure at home the systematic culture which is most desirable. It is not probable, indeed it is not possible, that such an experiment as this should supply all that is necessary for the higher education in an age of educational ferment and innovation like our own. But as *one* experiment, and a most valuable one, we earnestly wish it complete success.

V. But for the multitude of women who cannot avail themselves of such an institution, or who would not if they could, who want systematic instruction brought to their own doors, or who have only time and opportunity for some measure of the higher culture, which fragment they would yet most highly prize,—for these, for the young mothers seeking instruction, for the teachers engaged in their profession and wishing to continue their studies and to supplement their own fragmentary education,—for all these we must look to the development of the Lecture system at work in many of our large towns. These courses of lectures, distinctly educational in character and supplemented by examinations, have already proved of essential service. Whether ultimately these lectures will develop themselves into genuine local colleges, offering the highest instruction attainable to women, whether they will form an important part of those educational agencies of the future which are to affect not only our women but our men, it is premature to say. Those who work most earnestly for them, and are most interested in their success, are of all people the most unwilling that they should be prematurely systematized, or should ever become crystallized or stereotyped. But we do see in these beginnings the germs of something far greater, of something indeed capable of almost indefinite expansion and development; for wherever the zeal to teach and the desire to learn have manifested themselves in a remarkable degree side by side, as they have done lately, in our lecturers and pupils, *there* is a vitality which is only struggling to invest itself with a form—there are the elements of organic growth, which our want of skill may thwart or distort, but cannot kill.

It would be wrong to bring this paper to a close without something more than a mere passing reference to the great educational measure of the day. The Endowed Schools Bill is not a source of unalloyed pleasure to some educational reformers, who would have preferred that it should have taken its place as part of a larger national scheme. But taken by itself as a part measure, and as a promise of the future, no one who cares for the real advance of education can afford to be indifferent to it. Least of all can women be so. If that measure, or any modification of it, whilst retaining the saving clauses which secure to women a share in its advantages, should ever become law, it will be the fault of women themselves, if they do not use it as the most powerful lever ever yet applied to raise the education of women. It will be their duty under the provisions of the temporary part of the Act to claim for girls, wherever grounds of right or of expediency can be shown, their share in any and all educational endowments, to insist that the necessities of girls shall not be forgotten. Forgotten, we say, since in the misappropriations of the past it is certainly not wilful injustice which has been at work. It is with this, as with much else that is painful in the position of women,

> "Evil is wrought by want of thought
> As well as want of heart."

Since the Endowed Schools Bill was first brought before the House of Commons, a very important change has passed over it. Power was given to the Select Committee to which the bill was referred, to divide it into two parts. This has been done, and it is only the first and least important part of the bill which has passed the House of Commons, and will, it is hoped, speedily become law. This part of the bill will make possible a thorough reform and re-organization of our Endowed Schools. It will lead to the right and economical use of educational funds which have been scandalously misapplied. It will bring up the existing Endowed Schools to a far higher level of efficiency. Let us hope that it may ensure the acceptance of a larger and broader system of culture than many of our Grammar Schools, adhering too servilely to the traditions of the past throughout a changing present, have hitherto found possible. But after all, we have here only the machinery for a temporary and partial improvement. Some schools will be immensely improved, the majority will be left pretty much where they are, and no machinery has been provided for securing the continued efficiency of even the improved schools. The most important part of the measure has been postponed; but will, no doubt, be brought forward next session, perhaps with modifications; but shorn, let us hope, of none of its most just and wise provisions.

The provisions for the establishment of an Educational Council, for the examination and registration of teachers, for the registration and inspection of schools, are primary necessities in the present state of education. This part of the measure concerns all schools, and not simply the Endowed Schools; and although no coercion can be employed in the case of private schools to enforce inspection and registration, a considerable amount of moral pressure can scarcely fail to be brought to bear upon them. The best and most earnest teachers of private schools know too well the advantages of external and impartial examination, to allow such opportunities to remain unimproved. No sacrifice of independence is involved, no proposal made to impose any rigid uniformity of subjects or of methods of instruction. That such uniformity could ever be desirable is improbable; in the present stage of educational theory and experiment, it would be fatally mischievous; but such uniformity it is not proposed to establish. Every private schoolmaster will be as free to make his own experiments, and to carry out his own methods then as now. Let us add, every private schoolmistress; for it is most important to observe that this part of the measure concerns women as *much* as men, teachers of girls as much as teachers of boys. The teachers of girls may be examined, girls' schools may be inspected, and the extent to which this is done will depend upon the teachers themselves. It is very much to be hoped that in any special schemes of examination that may be devised under the provisions of this bill, it will not be thought necessary to apply separate tests to men and to women, to girls' schools and to boys' schools. Far more desirable is it that a general scheme of examination should be devised, comprehensive enough for both, and elastic enough to suit individual specialities.

It is also very desirable that women should be directly represented on the proposed Educational Council. There are women in England, just as competent as any men who may be chosen, to deliberate on general questions of education, and to give practical effect to their deliberations. There are many who have given more serious attention to the education of girls, and more active help towards its improvement, than any man has yet done. If the counsel and assistance of such women be rejected, there is nothing to supply its place. And those men who care most about the right education of women, are the most ready to admit that they are not competent alone to solve the problem; that they need, at every step, the suggestion and the co-operation of women.

That this part of Mr. Forster's great measure will have a powerful effect for good upon the education of girls, there can be no manner of doubt. To them it is much more important than any possible provision under this year's bill can be. In this year's bill the interests of girls were to some extent provided for by a judicious use of the personal pronouns. Their claim to *some* share in the educational endowments of the country was fully recognised. The Select Committee improved in this respect upon the original terms of the bill by giving greater prominence to the claims of girls. A new clause, Clause 12, was also introduced, providing that, in framing schemes under this bill, provision should be made, as far as conveniently might be, for extending to girls the benefits of endowments. By this clause, the claims of girls are fully admitted, but a wide discretionary power is left to the Commissioners under the terms "as far as conveniently may be."

Grave questions arise here as to the proportionate claim of girls and boys. A very interesting discussion took place on this clause in the House of Commons, on the 14th of June, when an amendment was moved by Mr. Winterbotham, M.P. for Stroud, to the effect that the words "equally with boys" should be introduced after the word "girls" in this clause.

It should be noticed that the clause, even with Mr.

Winterbotham's amendment, does not necessarily imply that girls should take equal shares with boys in all existing endowments. As a matter of natural right it might be fairly argued that girls have a claim to a full half of whatever money is nationally devoted to educational purposes. The women of the country outnumber the men, and whatever may be said of girls in general, and of their need of and capacity for education, it is clear that in the class most largely affected by the Endowed Schools Bill, the educational needs of girls are, even as a question of simple industrial advantage, quite as great as those of boys. It is in this class that the enormous excess of unmarried women—women who must support themselves by their own independent exertions—is to be found. The practical exclusion of girls from the highest educational advantages offered to this class is in very many cases equivalent to a sentence of lifelong pauperism and dependence. It is to the last degree indecent that women should be dependent on marriage for a professional maintenance. It is highly inexpedient that they should be restricted to a few avocations for which it is presumed that the slightest possible education—or none at all—is adequate. Yet such is the practical result of the exclusion of girls from the higher education. It is not permissible to assert with Mr. Beresford-Hope, that the education required for girls is less extended than that which ought to be imparted to boys, unless it can be conclusively shown that society as a whole, including that very important element the girls themselves, is the richer, the happier, the better for such restriction. It cannot be asserted that this has ever been shown. It is clear that men do not know the material destitution which so largely exists amongst this class of women. It is assumed in the face of the most patent facts that all women marry and are provided for by their husbands; whilst nothing is more plainly to be seen by those who will open their eyes, than these three things:—1. That a very large minority of women do not marry. 2. That of those who do marry, a very considerable proportion are not supported by their husbands. 3. That upon a very large number of widows (more than one-third of the widows in the country), the burden of self-maintenance and of the maintenance of their children is thrown. It is an absolute necessity of our present social condition that women should have as free admission to professional and industrial training as men; that there should be no monopoly of sex, and no protective duty on either side. Natural differences and natural fitnesses would then assert themselves, and men need not for one moment fear that in any work for which they have special natural advantages they will ever be driven out of the field by women. The injustice to women consists in appropriating to men all the artificial and acquired advantages of education and training. Of the economic gain to the community it is not necessary here to speak. But equality of education must precede equality of industrial training. The former is the foundation upon which the latter must rest. Experience has conclusively shown that in cases where it has been sought to give a sound industrial training to girls or women, their defective early education has always been the most miserable but the most effectual hindrance.

But admitting for a moment that no industrial advantages resulted to the country from the better education of women, that the women themselves can be materially provided for without any exertion of their own, that men are and ought to be the universal bread-winners, does it then in the least follow that a more restricted education will suffice for the needs of women, than would be found adequate to the necessities of men? It would rather then appear that the material burdens of society being borne by the men, to the women it should belong to provide for its moral and intellectual development. If we would have a rational and just morality, a religion free from bigotry and superstition, or the reality of intellectual culture diffused to any great extent throughout society, we must look for these results to the education of women.

Nor again is it for those who boast of the sanctity of our domestic institutions to admit that a slighter culture on the part of women than of men is the just basis of such institutions. The influence of the mother is probably the most real and pervading influence in the world. The influence of the wife can be far less accurately gauged, but it is an influence that not even the highest culture can afford to despise; it will degrade where it does not elevate. "The possession of a wife, conspicuously one's inferior in intellect, is, like other high privileges, attended with a few inconveniences, and, among the rest, with the occasional necessity of using a little deception."[1] How profoundly true this is, and how fearful a source of demoralization we have here, is painfully manifest to any acute observer of life.

The arguments or assertions which we have been dealing with were actually used by opponents of the claims of girls in the discussion on the Endowed Schools Bill; but those who held such language met, happily, with very little support or encouragement. It was remarkable how anxious nearly every one who spoke was to express sympathy with the advancement of women's education in general, and with the notion of giving girls a large share of the endowments. But there was an evident reluctance to admit any arithmetical equality of claim with boys.

Before discussing this point, it may be well to remember that from the enormous revenues of our ancient universities, women draw no educational advantage whatever; that in the liberal provision made for the higher education of men, no room has hitherto been found for a consideration of their claims. No institutions parallel to the nine great public schools have ever been founded for girls. Of the particular educational endowments contemplated by Mr. Forster's Bill, girls have only a most insignificant share. The statistics furnished to the Schools' Inquiry Commission, show that about 3,000 girls are educated in what may be

[1] The Mill on the Floss.

called public schools—that is, either proprietary or endowed schools. Of the 1,100 girls returned as under instruction in endowed schools, about 500 belong to the class which attends our national schools. The remaining 600, then, represent the class of girls corresponding to the class of boys who frequent our Grammar Schools. No doubt this enumeration is incomplete, and there remain schools which the diligence of the Assistant Commissioners did not succeed in bringing to light; but these figures show very plainly how insignificant is the help given to girls in the matter of education, and this inequality in the treatment of girls and boys is no modern novelty, although its evil results are, perhaps, more apparent now than at any earlier period. A claim for girls has frequently been preferred on historical grounds. It has been urged that the majority of endowed schools were intended for children of either sex indifferently, and that the appropriation of the schools to the sole use of boys has been an act of spoliation so far as regards the girls. No doubt this is true in a few cases; there are some plain instances of flagrant robbery of girls, but in four cases at least out of five the endowments were distinctly intended for the use and advantage of boys. The very same feelings and prejudices were at work in times past which are at work to-day, and which make it so difficult to obtain pecuniary assistance for any project which has in view the improved education of girls or women—any project, that is to say, which goes beyond the limits of sectarianism, or of a somewhat narrow philanthropy. Even in these directions, what is done for girls is in nothing like equal proportion to what is done for boys. But beyond these limits it is almost impossible, where girls are concerned, to obtain money for any educational purpose. Large sums are every year being appropriated in one way or another for the education of boys; nothing or next to nothing is being contributed to that of girls. Let one case stand by way of illustration. A carefully devised plan, to which we have earlier referred in these pages, for giving to women some of the advantages of collegiate instruction and discipline, has now been before the public for about two years. It was designed that the institution, buildings, and apparatus having been once provided, should be on a self-supporting basis. It was calculated that the building and apparatus would cost somewhere about 30,000*l.*, and an appeal was made for assistance to an undertaking of a truly national character. Of the 30,000*l.* required, about 3,000*l.* have been promised; a sum of course wholly inadequate to the expense of erecting even the smallest building suitable for such a purpose. Students were readily forthcoming, and the College will open in October; but in a hired house with all the disadvantages and waste of power, so perfectly well understood by teachers, of buildings not originally adapted for educational purposes. We cannot help believing that if boys had been concerned, the necessary sum would have been subscribed in a single year. As it is now, so it has ever been, the interests of girls have been postponed, not of ill-will, but of indifference or forgetfulness, to those of boys. We prefer, therefore, to rest the claims of girls on grounds of justice and expediency, rather than on any grounds of historical precedent.

It has been assumed that the education supplied at home is amply sufficient for the needs of girls. It is not necessary to repeat the arguments already urged against this view, since it must be abundantly evident to all who will consider the facts, that as a question of expense alone, home education with the vast majority of girls is simply impossible. The sisters of Eton and Harrow boys may be taught at home, so far as expense is concerned, though even here they are probably at a serious disadvantage as regards solid instruction, but the sisters of the boys who attend our provincial grammar schools cannot be taught at home, and for them there is no provision except in the private adventure school, which may chance to be everything that could be desired, but is just as likely to be for educational purposes utterly worthless. These considerations bring us face to face with the question of the proportionate claim of girls and boys. Mr. Forster remarked in the discussion on Mr. Winterbotham's Amendment, that if they had to set to work to deal with a fresh fund, he quite agreed with his honourable friend that they ought to divide it between girls and boys, but at present the endowments were for the most part possessed by boys. He was very anxious that the Commissioners should consider, in the words of the clause, how far they could extend to girls the benefits of these endowments, but it would be quite impossible that they could do so equally, because that would be to deprive the boys of the education which they were already in the possession of.[1] Although it might be said that the fact of possession does not absolutely cover the right of continued possession, yet it is quite certain that nobody wants to deprive boys of any educational advantages to be derived from endowments. But is it quite necessary that what is given to the girls should be taken from the boys? Is there not room, if the Schools' Inquiry Commissioners can be trusted, abundant room for superior economy of management in many if not in most of these schools, and should all the advantage of this economy be appropriated to boys? Plainly it will be impossible, where the endowment is very small, to establish side by side with a school for boys a similar school for girls. One strong institution is much better than two weak ones, and in the general interests of education it is probably better that there should be one good school, even though boys should appropriate the advantages, than two feeble ones. But these are just the cases in which the experiment of mixed schools might be tried with advantage. If there cannot be the good school for boys and the good school for girls, it seems reasonable to conclude that the one good school ought to be equally for boys and girls. To many of us mixed education appears the only rational solution of our educational difficulties. It is not proposed to argue that a system of mixed education would be of unmixed advantage; it is quite sufficient to

[1] *Times*' report.

show that the balance of advantage is in its favour. On the economic ground the gain is plain. The expense of a double staff of teachers and a double set of school-buildings is at once saved. But the only objections to such an experiment rest on moral and social grounds. Why it should be considered so dangerous and doubtful for boys and girls or for men and women to share each other's serious pursuits whilst they are allowed freely to share each other's frivolities, is a matter of perpetual surprise to those who accustom themselves to look beyond the range of tradition or convention. The strong prejudices of English society on this point have worked very mischievously in many directions besides this of education.[1] Of the saddest results of the separate education and life of the sexes it is impossible here to speak; as a slighter, but still mischievous result, it is sufficient to notice the profound ignorance of each other's real nature and ways of thinking common to both men and women. Certain sides of each other's character are studied perhaps a little too closely and

[1] The experiment of mixed classes—boys and girls—was tried at Liverpool College in the summer of 1868, by the Principal, Rev. G. Butler. A course of lectures on the Schools of Painting was given by him to about 250 boys, the senior pupils of the three schools, and some of the pupils of the Royal Institution School, who attended voluntarily; also to upwards of 100 girls and their teachers. The girls took copious notes, as did the boys, and appeared much interested in the subject of the lectures. No inconvenience of any kind resulted from this experiment, nor did it appear to the pupils as at all strange or unnatural; and it is probable, that to boys living at home with their sisters, and attending day-schools, companionship with girls in study, as well as in their daily life at home, would come easily and naturally. In the above instance, the influence of sisters engaged in the same study as their brothers, was found beneficial.—Editor.

curiously; beyond these all is an unknown land of doubt and mystery, about which vague conjecture is safe and easy since explanation is impossible. We do not deny the charm of this sense of mystery and difference; what we complain of is, that artificial differences should be first created and then mistaken for those real, essential differences which are of the ordinance of nature, and which fit the sexes each to supplement and complement the other. Many a life has been wrecked upon mistakes arising out of this ignorance.

Women are perpetually excluded from the provisions of various kinds made for men, and no adequate separate provision is or can be made for them. The comparative advantage or disadvantage of a mixed system of education can only be determined by free experiment, and this experiment cannot be said to have been yet made in England under fair conditions. Such experiments as have been possible, have been pre-eminently successful. It certainly seems most natural that brothers and sisters should go to school together; that the schoolroom should be the expansion of the home-life into the life of society. Natural reasons against such community of education there would seem to be none, but rather every natural reason in their favour.

But whatever solution of present difficulties may be found, it is plain that the question of the higher education of women is a most urgent one, one which will not bear to be delayed. We plead the cause of women. We ask that the gifts of God may not be wasted, that women themselves may not be robbed of some of the purest joys of life, those of intellectual effort and achievement, and that society which needs their help so much may not be defrauded of their best and worthiest service. Give us knowledge, power, and life. We will repay the gift a hundred-fold. Set free the women who sigh in the dark prison-houses, the captives of ignorance and folly. Cruel tyrants are these ; slay them! With yourselves, people of England, it rests to put an end to that reign of frivolity of which you say you are so weary. Help women to become wise, that they may be just and true. merciful and loving.

APPENDIX.

So few men really understand the material destitution of women, that I am tempted to transcribe a few sentences from letters which have come to me within the last five days, simply premising that these are not picked selections, but specimens of cases hundreds of which could be cited if necessary, and such as are perpetually being brought before those women who interest themselves with the condition of their sex:—

June 16th.—"The negotiation respecting * * * * * falls quite through, I am sorry to say. The hours of work are all right, sixty-eight hours per week; but the salary offered is 30*l.* a year (for every purpose, including board), and the salary is of consequence to Mrs. ——. Can you suggest any other openings? She must emigrate to America as a civil service clerk."

The lady of whom this is written is a widow (marriage the natural provision for women!); an educated woman in the true sense of the word, in the very fulness and maturity of her powers, and though a woman of the highest refinement, one possessed of that energy of character and natural faculty which fit her to act as a pioneer; a lady too who has abundantly proved her administrative capacity in unpaid work of the highest kind. Is it not melancholy that such remuneration should be considered adequate payment for the labour of such a woman?

Granted that she has been specifically trained to no industry, educated labour ought to be worth more than 2*d.* an hour, and the want of special training is the very grievance we complain of,—the want of training, and the monopoly by men of those posts for which such women are abundantly well qualified. With such facts before us, and facts immeasurably worse than these, need we wonder that thousands of women feel that they are an incumbrance in this corner of God's universe, and pray passionately for leave to die?

Another letter :—

June 17*th.*—"I am so sorry that I was obliged to decline the appointment on the terms offered. It would be an idle expense for me to accept a post with a salary on which I could not live and dress myself. Is it not hard for a well-educated lady to begin on 11*s.* 6*d.* a week, less than many a factory girl of sixteen or seventeen receives for her manual labour? . . . If anything else occurs to you which you think might be suitable for me, I shall be very glad to hear of it; but of course I only mean if the employment is anything new, and for the benefit of our sex, as you have too much to do for me to trouble you otherwise."

Another letter, also June 17th :—

"Can you give me any suggestions about the employment of women, or rather *ladies,* who have not enough to live upon, and have not been brought up to do anything? I know so many of that class who would be *thankful* to gain a few shillings a week. Miss King told me of the society in London, but I think something local is wanted. Here (a fashionable watering-place) we have a place where ladies can take their needle-work, but the chance is that it may remain there twelve months before it is sold; if not sold, it is returned, perhaps soiled, and the lady is out of pocket. Besides, work of that kind is *slavery,* the pay for it is so poor."

You who have daughters, wives, and sisters, whom you guard tenderly from present evils, take care that you are not preparing for them graver evils when you are no longer able to provide for them. It would disgrace you, you think, that they should work now, at least outside their own homes, and for any but you. Have you prepared them for the chance, a very likely one, of having no home in which to work? Unless you have done this, cease to sneer at us who seek to make up for your neglect, and cease to wonder that we no longer regard you as a sufficient earthly providence for women. If your affection be anything more than that common form of selfishness which considers women as the mere playthings of men, you will look further into the future than you have yet done, and will prepare differently for the days which may come to all, which *will* come to many of your dear ones.

be driven to the workhouse, or whether they should abandon the care of those for whom they struggle to the Guardians of the Poor. There are some who argue that the country ought to take both charges on itself. Grave objections exist to that theory, but I will not even state them, because the fact is that the country rejects it. The public approves of the proposition that women should work rather than beg, and the public therefore acknowledges that work of some sort must be allowed to women.

But then we are told, that of course this is the case, but that it is nothing new. Women have always had to work, but they worked, say the objectors, "quietly, and in their proper places; and it is only in this generation that they have grown querulous and discontented, and demand new spheres, and want to enter into competition with men in every trade and profession." There is some measure of truth in the allegation, but it may be met with a very simple preliminary answer. The fact is that men have taken away from women the employments which formerly were appropriated to them, and that therefore it is men who force women to claim the right to new openings for their labour. Let us look at any of the older social organizations, even the most rudimentary, and we find in them, it may be a high or a low, but at all events a distinct, place for women. They are, according to the habits of the respective races and the degrees of civilization and wealth, the tillers of the ground, the tenders of the flock, the grinders of corn, the bakers, the cooks, the spinners, the weavers, the tailors, the leather-tanners and embroiderers for the household, over and above all their maternal and domestic duties. In such functions there was room for more than the wives, or there was place for all as wives. Where the rude life of barbarism prevails, every man needs a wife, and so all women are married as soon as grown up. Where polygamy exists wives are in demand above the supply, and they at least are provided for, whether it be the custom for the wives to work or not. When civilization or Christianity abolished polygamy, there were still female occupations for the mistress of the house and the women whom she gathered round her. In Rome, as in old England, the lady sat surrounded by her maids spinning wool and flax, or plying the needle, for use or ornament; or she superintended and directed the heavier domestic labours, in which the strength of men was needed. Within the present century, the women in humble life had always (in some districts they have even still) the spinning-wheel at hand, as a means of support if single, of filling up empty time if married. And when these and such-like avocations were available to women of every rank, they were not only provided with subsistence, but they held that definite place in society, and filled those recognised duties which placed them on a footing of substantial dignity, and forbade the raising of any question whether their capacities were equal with those of men or not.

Not intentionally, but actually, by the progress of science and the new forms of social existence, that position has been taken from women. Machinery spins, weaves, grinds, and even where women can still gain employment in connexion with machine-labour, it is no longer exclusively their own, no longer domestic, but it exposes them to competition and forces them to compete. Other avocations, such as baking and brewing, once the toil of separate households, are now carried on upon a large scale in manufactories, and men have wholly displaced women from them. Meantime emigration, the source of infinite benefit and the relief from infinite suffering, carries off far more men than women; and while it increases the proportion of women left at home, it diminishes the number of the households in which women can find work. The higher standard of comfort now prevalent disinclines men to marry so early as they used in olden times, and the spread of luxury in an equal degree withholds women of the upper ranks from marriage till suitable establishments are offered to them. But every such restraint of marriage diminishes the field open to women of the humbler classes in domestic service. Gradually also some of the coarser and rougher trades in which women have heretofore worked along with men are, either by direct legislation (as in mines, &c.) or by the influence of public opinion, closed against them. Such a fact, certainly, is not to be regretted, but it inevitably swells the number of those who must seek a livelihood in other ways. Again, competition in all trades is so sharp that masters are forced, or at least many think themselves forced, both to cut down the wages of women in their employment to the minimum which the supply of labour makes possible, and to dismiss their surplus female hands whenever the season of the year brings slackness of business. While such causes spread destitution through the lower and middle ranks, the higher do not escape the consequences of the peculiar tendencies of the age. The enhanced competition in display, the recklessness of speculation, the temptation to invest in doubtful securities, bring nowadays many a family to ruin, which in the slower times of our fathers and grandfathers might have lived in comfort if not in affluence. The daughters are thrown upon the world, only to find the market for their superficial accomplishments sadly overstocked; and by increasing the supply, they add to the distress of others while hardly alleviating their own. Thus from every rank and every class of women there rises up the cry that work is wanted and that no work is to be had.

These considerations must satisfy every candid mind that the movement and stir among women is not gratuitous, but is urged by the iron law of necessity. And it will be observed that in thus stating the case I am purposely, in the first instance, confining it to the question of physical necessity, and therefore placing it, if on the most incontrovertible, yet also on the lowest ground. But this simple and elementary view will serve to show clearly the true answer to be made to the objection taken to the competition of women with men. In a sense, such competition is inevitable, unless men will undertake, which they now do not, to support all women without their working at all. Since this is not proposed, it is rather for women to complain that men compete with them. What right, they might well ask, have men to become spinners, bakers, sellers of lace and silks, and of all the nicknacks of women's own attire? Why do they encroach with the help of machinery upon the avocations that are purely domestic, and under the name of free trade upon the employments in which no strength of muscle is required? Their answer is, that they have a right to do anything in any way by which they can make a profit. Well, so they have, but they can clearly have no right to grumble at others doing the same. If men are entitled to sell pins and tapes because they can do it to profit, how can they object to women setting types, painting porcelain, or copying law-papers, if they can do such things to profit? Obviously, when men appeal to public support, demonstrated by public patronage, as their justification in invading the women's kingdom, they appeal to a principle which is a sufficient defence of women, if in any instance they undertake duties hitherto confined to male hands. The public, if it is ready to buy of either, settles the question of the right of either to sell.

The truth is, that there is no middle course between a system which shall map out precise duties, not only to each sex, but to every class and to every individual constituting the State, and the system which leaves to all equal freedom to work at what they choose and what they are fit for. The former system is the system of caste. In its purity it is possible; for it forms a band of brass by which all are bound, and from which none can escape, because all agree to enforce the fetters. Its main defect is that it kills the nation to which it is applied. Modifications of it have been attempted, and some of them still exist in the form of guilds, trades' unions, and exclusive rules of "learned professions." But these never can endure for any length of time, because they are framed for the interest of a few, and the whole public has an interest in abetting their infraction. Their tendency is to make services dear and imperfect, which other persons are ready to render at cheaper price and of better quality; and of course the public supports the interlopers. Either as individuals, or as forming rival societies, the outsiders gain recognition, and break down the barrier of exclusivism. Ultimately, therefore, there is no principle that can live save that of freedom of labour, and the freedom must be complete and universal.

Nor is the result to be regretted, even by the sentimental. It is often, indeed, hard and pitiless in its processes. Men and women may starve when doing their very best, because they have taken a wrong line, in which somebody else can do better. But the cruel teaching saves more suffering than it causes. It points out the departments for which special qualifications are required, and, drawing to them those who are best qualified, it relieves other departments of the competition that would cut down the returns they afford. It divides the workers into groups, not by the accident of birth, but by the test of fitness. So it gives to the world the best service at the lowest rates, and all in turn benefit by obtaining cheaply what is good. But at the same time it gives to each the best remuneration, because each must gain most at the work for which he has most aptitude. Labour is thus employed in the manner in which it can produce the most, and we all are the richer for it. Consider only the difference which would be seen between the nation which lets strong men do rough work, clever men do skilled work, and weak men do delicate work, and the nation which would set the muscle of porters and draymen to weave straw hats, utilize its fools as schoolmasters, and benevolently encourage cripples to take a contract for earthworks on a railway; and we shall recognise at once the true principle and the true merit of the doctrine of free competition.

Now, if we recognise this truth in the case of men as between themselves, how can we refuse assent to it as between men and women? Our assent to it is indeed already given. We do not hire men as nurse-maids even for a family of boys; nor have men yet complained because we do not turn female cooks out of our kitchens in order to instal substitutes of the sex of Ude. Some employments, in point of fact, are virtually confined to women; in others, men and women compete on equal terms. The question then is narrowed to the single point, Why should there be enforced exclusion from *any* trade? No doubt, as I have already acknowledged, it is right in the Legislature to forbid women and children to work at certain injurious trades; just as it forbids men to be employed except under certain sanitary regulations. But we are now speaking of the ordinary run of trades, where there is no moral or physical reason why women, if they choose, should not be employed. Failing such natural reasons, there are two social reasons for the exclusion commonly given. The one is, that the competition of women, if it were allowed, would lower the rate of wages. The other is, that women ought not to be encouraged to renounce domestic duties, and throw off feminine reserve, by mixing with men in what are called the occupations of men.

The former of these arguments is true, if we confine our view to only a limited range of employments and of time. Suppose that in a given trade the workers at present are only men, and that there is work only for so many as are at present employed; it is then obvious that women can only gain admission (apart from any chance individual sympathies) by underbidding and displacing the men. And if such were the case in all the employments in the world, so that there was really no more work to do than what men could do, the argument would be a strong one in favour of letting men continue to be the workers, and imposing upon them the necessary duty of earning all that could be earned, and out of it supporting all women as well as all of themselves. But no one can assert for a moment that the world's work is thus restricted. If men are displaced in one trade by women, there are other trades open.

If in this country there were no trades open, there are the Colonies and foreign countries in which men's labour will be remunerated—not, perhaps in trades, but in cultivating the soil—ten times as highly as in most trades with us. Far from the world being over-populated, it is still infinitely under-populated. Nature offers room for a thousand times more labour than has yet been bestowed upon her. The beginning of all wealth is in her gifts, and human labour is, in the first instance, only spent in appropriating them in a useful form. But her unappropriated gifts are still boundless. In Asia, in America, in the islands of the East and South, there are tracts far larger than Europe capable of supporting a population denser than that of Europe, and which yet are all but unexplored. Even within Europe there are vast regions only half cultivated, and mineral treasures known to exist, but as yet unused. The labour that might be bestowed in acquiring these riches would do more than make the labourers rich, it would make the whole of mankind richer; for each labourer would in some shape redeem more than he could consume, and the surplus would in some shape be available for the consumption of others. When, therefore, we speak of there being a surplus of labour, we may be quite sure that there is only a surplus in some employments, because the labour is wrongly distributed and wrongly divided. There is not, and there cannot be, for more years than the world has yet lived, a real surplus of labour in the world. On the contrary, there is a huge, unsupplied demand for labour; and our blunder is in forcing too much labour artificially into certain channels, and thus artificially depriving ourselves of the benefit it would yield us did it flow in natural channels.

Now, competition of men with men, and of women with men, is precisely the teaching of Nature as to what channels are the most profitable for the work of all to flow in. There are some things that men can do and women cannot. Of course in these men will beat women out of the field. But there are other things that women can do at least as well as men. Whatever needs delicacy, taste, accuracy, what can be done indoors, by the fireside, or in suitable workshops, and what does not need a great deal of manual strength, can, as we all know, be done as well by women as by men. Then why should women not do it? Because some of the men will need to resort to other employments? Then let them. There are employments in which, besides skill, strength is needed, and in which they will have no rivalry. What folly in them to reject such employments in order that they may do a woman's work, and drive a woman out of work! In some things they see this. There are, doubtless, men who could make as good milliners as any woman: there is said to be one in Paris now who is superior in taste as a lady's dress-maker to any woman. But if men were generally to take the making of ladies' bonnets and dresses into their own hands, they can see that they would force just so many women to stand idle, and that they would be fools to do it. The women would have to stand idle, because the range of their employments is limited by their strength and their sex. But if women were to take to printing, or watchmaking, or wigmaking, the men displaced from these trades would find countless other trades or occupations open to them. Are they not then as unwise if they try to prevent women from being printers, or watchmakers, or wigmakers, as if they tried to drive them out of the business of making dresses and bonnets?

I have conceded, for the purpose of illustrating the argument, that in each special trade the admission of female competition might for the moment cause some distress. But let us not be frightened by that apprehension till we have examined its basis. Distress, in any special trade, is caused either by a cessation of demand; or by some sudden modification of labour, such as the introduction of machinery; or by a want of intelligence in the operatives, in not recognising that other fields of labour afford better remuneration. The first cause cannot operate from the admission of women to work. As little can the second; for they must of course pass through apprenticeships, and only a few at a time will become fit for the trade. Besides, it is not the opening of any one trade we are considering, but the opening of many, among which women workers would be distributed in comparatively limited numbers. But the third cause of a fall of wages ought not, and with diffused education cannot, occur in any special trade. If it is recognised that girls are being apprenticed in some trades, the obvious effect will be to lead parents to apprentice a corresponding proportion of their sons to some other trade where wages are likely to be better; or to lead a certain number of young men, married or unmarried, to emigrate instead of entering any occupation at home. Both male and female work will in fact, when dealt with alike, form one fund, which will be apportioned, according to the irresistible laws of political economy, in such a way as to equalize the rate of wages in proportion to skill, trouble, and risk. Only let there be no artificial favour or compulsion, and labour will leave the avocations that are poorly remunerated, and betake itself to those that are better. Nor can there be any general fall of wages so long as emigration offers still better returns, and while there is intelligence in the country to understand their existence. The addition, then, of female labour to male in all suitable avocations, would be so much addition to the wealth of the world; and being both gradual and widely diffused, it could not exercise any appreciable influence in diminishing wages in any trade to which it might be admitted.

If, therefore, these words should reach any members of a Trades' Union which at present resists the introduction of female labour, this is the suggestion I should wish to make to them: Is it better for you, as fathers and brothers, that your girls and sisters should grow up in idleness, or that they should be allowed to be apprenticed in your trade, or in some other trade? If you cannot support them, and make sure of there being some one else to support them when you are dead or disabled, what are they to do? Become servants, or milliners, or dress-makers, or ballet-girls, or go on the streets? You know that every one of these employments, down to the miserable last, is so overstocked, because there is scarcely any other calling open to women, that they can but make a poor livelihood in their youth, and can save nothing for their old age. Now, suppose you let them work at your own trade, what will happen? Why, you and your mates will have to look round you for some other employment for your boys; that will be all. And you know that there are plenty of trades your boys can enter, quite as good as your own: and that there is the best trade of all, that of going to foreign parts, where they will secure a competence, possibly a fortune, before you yourselves are grey-headed. Meantime your girls will be provided for honestly, each becoming able to make for herself as good wages as you are now making for all your family. Put this to your own minds, and you cannot doubt which course is the best. Then put the case, as frankly and fairly, to those of your fellows who do not happen to have girls of their own to provide for, and do not doubt that they will see as well as you that what is best for women in general must be, in the long run, best for men too.

What can be said to Trades' Unions, and what will, sooner or later, be listened to and acted upon by them, is not, in anything but detail, different from what ought to be accepted and recognised by the upper professions. Whether women are fit or not to compete on terms of equality with men in such professions it is not my present purpose to argue. Other Essays in this volume will no doubt discuss that point. For the sake of argument I should be perfectly ready to concede the average inferiority of female intellect, but the man must be indeed besotted in his self-conceit who does not acknowledge that there are many women who are intellectually the superiors of some men. Now, what we have to ask is, Whether it can be right or reasonable that all these intellectual women should be debarred from doing service to the world, merely because they would force some men of more than average stupidity to abandon occupations for which they have no aptitude, and to take to other occupations in which they can really be useful? But who, it will be said, is to be the judge of this? Why, that same authority which is the judge between stupid and clever men—the public. Nobody asks for women that they should have favour shown them in any profession. It is a fact, of which we are always reminded, that women are weak, of delicate health, and subject to the interruptions of marriage and childbirth. These disadvantages weight them heavily in the race for professional employment, even against stupid men; for the public, in giving employment, will always have regard to such liabilities. Let it be noted also, that the competition in any of these higher walks can hardly ever come to be that of one sex against the other. It can only be as individual women against the whole race of men. For such pursuits are of a character which few women's minds naturally incline to, and they are all more or less of a public nature, which is itself a deterring influence, even when women have the strength and freedom from domestic duties which would enable them to enter into the competition.

But if, in spite of all the disadvantages which attend women in so competing, there should be any among them who have so clear a vocation to any branch of study or art as to be willing to undergo the labour and face the annoyances of such pursuits, who is there that can think without shame that there should be laws, either of the nation or of society, to prevent them? The laws indeed are powerless against the higher natures. Miss Carpenter's and Miss Martineau's words are quoted with respect in Parliament, though we may forbid them to have the same voice as an illiterate boor in sending a representative there. A Michael Faraday confesses with pleasure his debt to Mrs. Marcet or Mrs. Somerville, though we may exclude these ladies from even the lowest rewards of Science. Rosa Bonheur's pictures will attract crowds, in spite of the Academy rules which place obstacles in the way of women studying Art. Not less do those ladies who have qualified themselves as Doctors obtain practice, though the medical profession has done its best to shut the door against their obtaining a degree. Against the power of genuine ability class jealousy is impotent. Men are beaten by such women, and they know it. It is a mean revenge that denies the name and privileges of equality when the fact of superiority is conceded. It is a yet more humiliating avowal that men maintain rules to save themselves from such competition on a wider, though still it would always necessarily be on a limited, scale. It is a confession that but for the rules they would be beaten more often.

But the public has an interest, not merely in supporting exceptional genius, but in giving all ability its fair chance. We all suffer a loss whencver a clever woman is kept out of work to which she is willing to devote herself. We lose the value of her work, and we lose by the degradation of her whole sex through her enforced idleness, or through her resorting to the few overstocked professions to which she is admitted. In these she competes with other women, and so cuts down in a degree the remuneration of all. So every father, whose daughter may ever possibly need to support herself, has the strongest interest in combating whatever professional rules contract the sphere of women's honourable employment. His own daughter may perhaps be never fit for higher work than that of a nursery-governess; but he should remember that every other woman who is driven to be a governess because she cannot gain admission to the ranks of clerks, doctors, or artists, eats a portion of his own child's scanty bread.

As to the argument that if women were admitted to trades or professions it would take them from domestic duties and make them unwomanly, little need be said; for both points, I think, we can pretty safely leave to themselves. Their own instincts in these matters are too strong to need any guardianship from us. The husband, the household, and the children will always be the first, must often be the exclusive, care of women to whom such care belongs. The demand for liberty to work for themselves or for others is made only on behalf of the unmarried, or of the married whose home-lives still afford some leisure. And the fear of their adopting unwomanly employments cannot be better dissipated than by leaving to them the choice. Whatever business is essentially unwomanly they will of themselves avoid; and whatever is only unwomanly because at present coarse men make it so, they will by their mere presence refine. But we must not let our prejudices take the place of our judgment in such matters. The Turks lock their women up; the French hardly allow a girl to speak to a man till she is married: we lay down no such rules, yet who shall say that our women are unwomanly? It is possible that fashion with us also may err in thinking that some things would be unwomanly which are not so. Fifty years ago it was hardly womanly to write a book; in less than fifty years we may not think it unwomanly to give a lecture. Public opinion varies; but, except in some very depraved states of society, it never errs on the side of too great laxity as regards women's public conduct. Nor do women go against public opinion, unless they feel that they can ultimately carry it with them. We may leave, then, the question, whether any employment is womanly, to be settled by the women who may wish to adopt it, and by the public which may judge them.

Up to this point we have been considering the question of women's work only as it bears on the question of their subsistence. Incidentally, in the course of that argument, we have seen that the world would be the better for their work, whether it be merely physical, or whether it be mental. But we are bound to look at the matter in a broader aspect. The women who are forced to work for livelihood are after all a minority. What ought the majority to do, those who are not forced by poverty to do anything? and what position ought society to expect them, and help them, to take up?

The most prevalent understanding at present undoubtedly is, that women should do as little as possible of any active, any outside work. Let them become wives and mothers, it is said—these are their natural functions; and let them leave the business of the world to men. We concede grudgingly, and under a sort of protest, that they may do a little charity, visit some selected poor, decorate churches, and teach, under the clergyman, in Sunday Schools. All beyond that is thought exceptional, if not odd.

And yet it ought to startle us into doubt of the soundness of our notions when we find, ever and anon, how infinitely obliged we are to women when they dare to be even more than odd. The country was more grateful than it has been to any man since the Duke of Wellington, when Miss Nightingale took the extraordinary step of going out to Scutari, and bringing order and decency into the chaos of neglect that had grown up around medical men and staff officers. On a more limited scale there is many a parish that owes the deepest thankfulness to some good woman who has quietly organized its Schools, or broken down the cruel routine of its Workhouse. If it is well when these things are done, can we deprecate their being done more often; and still insist that women are out of their sphere when employed in other duties than "suckling fools and chronicling small-beer?"

It is probably the case that modern social changes have indirectly operated to lower the public idea as to the duties of women, just as they have ousted women from some of the employments that were formerly appropriated to them. In the feudal times women, factitiously elevated by the notions of chivalry, and so often called on to play the part of men when left as châtelaine of the castle in their husbands' absence, or head of the family of the yeoman who had to follow his lord to the field, could hardly at any time sink back into the mere household ornament or drudge. In every rank women had their prescribed duties, and these were so large that unmarried girls were often attached to a lady's little court, that from her they might learn, and under her practise, the proper accomplishments of a gentlewoman. But girls had another resource. The Convent opened its gates to rich and poor. In these communities, whoever could not marry, and whoever did not choose to marry, was sure of an honoured and secure asylum. There they were at least not idle. Besides the regular offices of religion, there was the management of property, the acts of charity, the learning and the teaching of the literature of the time. If we think copying manuscripts, illuminating borders, or working tapestry not very profound studies or interesting amusements, yet surely they were far less vapid than the chief avocations of modern young ladies. But above all, they were at least an alternative to matrimony. While such refuges existed, no girl could be forced into a reluctant marriage, either by compulsion of parents, or because on the death of parents there would be no home for her to live in. I am far indeed from desiring the restoration of the conventual system, with its vows of perpetual celibacy and servitude; but it is right to remember that with many evils it brought at least some compensations. To be unmarried was then to be the spouse of Christ, the revered "mother," the member of a Sisterhood surrounded with all the honour and sanctity of the Church—nowadays it is to live and die in the dreary lodgings, and under the half-contemptuous title of an old maid.

Thus it has come to pass that women have, by change to times of settled peace, and by the reformation of religion, lost something of dignity, of usefulness, and of resources. And thus it has been brought about that having scarce any choice but marriage, marriage has come to be considered as the sole function to which it is right or decent they should look. This notion is heightened, among at least the upper classes, by the ideas which the law of primogeniture fosters. It is thought a father's duty to provide largely for the eldest son, consequently the daughters' portions must be pinched. They are left enough to live on, but not enough to enable them still to move in the society in which they have been brought up. Their choice lies, then, only between marrying money or abandoning all their connexions, habits, and amusements. Foreseeing such a time, a wealthy marriage becomes a matter to which they, and their mothers for them, eagerly look forward. The more luxury increases, the more urgent seems the necessity for thus securing a luxurious provision. Unluckily, at the same time and from the same causes, there grows up an increased disinclination among young men to enter into marriage. Then the efforts of the young ladies become more desperate, and being more apparent, of course still less and less successful. So matters go on from bad to worse. It is esteemed a discredit to pass the second season after they "come out" without securing an engagement. Rich young men become so valuable a prize that selection is renounced, and even barefaced vice is no disqualification to their being well received in wealthy drawing-rooms. The young men feel and improve all the privileges of their position; they are careless of hiding what is no longer reprobated, and they begin unreservedly to speak of, and to be seen talking to, the notorious harlots of the day. Young ladies, seeing that the harlots are run after, and themselves neglected, begin (God knows it may often be with innocent ignorance) to ape the style, and in some degree the manners, of the attractive harlot. It is now the harlots that set the fashion in dress, that prescribe the fashionable drives in the Park, and that still, because in some things modest women cannot vie with them, form the attraction that daily carries young men more and more away from the society of modest women. But still the fatal emulation is kept up. Whoever wants to judge of its character has only to frequent the fashionable London drive at the fashionable hour, and there he will see the richest and most shameful woman-market in the world. Men stand by the rails, criticising with perfect impartiality and equal freedom, while women drive slowly past, some for hire, some for sale—in marriage—these last with their careful mothers at their side, to reckon the value of the biddings and prevent the lots from going off below the reserved price.

Such is the pitch to which we have arrived by telling women that marriage is their sole duty. Its terrible evils are chiefly visible among the upper classes; but who can tell what mischief is done throughout every rank of society, by examples so conspicuously set? When the best sanction of social morality, the reprobation of vice by women, is cast aside in the highest circles, who can tell how widely the encouragement may act? It is happily limited as yet in our country by two checks, the purity of the Throne, and the strength of religious feeling in the middle classes. And we may hope and believe that these influences will ultimately prevail so far at least as to shame into respect for external decency those who now flaunt their defiance of morality and modesty in the public eye. But not the less is it apparent that men and women degrade each other when social opinion inculcates that life's chief aim is luxurious enjoyment, and that to secure a good establishment is the one purpose for which a girl should be brought up.

What is it, indeed, that we reduce women to, when we argue that they have no right to meddle with public affairs, no right to follow professions, no right to occupy themselves with any really intellectual pursuits, no right to take interest in aught outside their families, no right to any education save that which is devoted to showing off their charms? Do we not in truth reduce them to the mere slaves of the harem? Do we not, like those who keep such slaves, deny in fact that they have any souls? What can they do with souls, if nature means them only to be toys of our idle hours, the adornment of our ease and wealth, to be worshipped as idols but never taken for helpmates, permitted at most to gaze from afar at the battles of life—to crown the victor with a wreath, or to shed weak tears for the dead? But even those who tell us so, or use arguments that mean so, know well that in their hearts they belie the words they utter. They know that in their straits they turn to women for sympathy, because women have understood their struggles; they seek women's counsel, because they know that women are intellectually fit to advise them; and they only affect contempt for female capacity because of the pitiful pride that refuses to acknowledge a capacity that in many things is on a level with their own, and, if in some things lower, in other things is higher than theirs.

In this is summed up the fatal error of the day in the position assigned to women. We disregard, even if we do not deny, the fact that they have souls as well as bodies,—souls not only to be saved, but to be cultivated, instructed, made fit to do what work God has assigned such souls to do on earth, as well as to grow meet for the nobler duties that may await them in heaven. Herein arises no question whether they are intellectually equal with the souls of men or not. Enough that they *are* intellectual; the conclusion follows that the intellect ought to be employed. And concede only this simple, this indisputable proposition, and it will guide us through all our difficulties. Grant that we have to think of the minds of women as their chief part; and how different must be the education we give them, as well as how different the work we must expect from them. The one dependent on the other; the education to make them capable of the work, the work as the outcome of the education.

That wider usefulness which ought to be entrusted to women is craved for by themselves. It is easy for us to speak of the frivolity of their pursuits and cares, when we force them, by all the moral power we can bring to bear, to be nothing more than frivolous. But against this constraint their own higher and better nature constantly rebels. Some, of course, there are among them, as among men, who are not capable of more than triviality. But it is incontestable that the majority of women would most eagerly welcome a truer education than they are now permitted to have. The cry among the poor is hardly more strong for leave to work than it is among the rich for leave to be useful. Against every difficulty and tacit opposition, many girls of the higher classes eagerly fling themselves into such branches of parish, church, school, or other local work, as are at all allowed to them. The more active minds form Sisterhoods, in which the nursing of the sick and the tending of the poor are the principal occupations. There is no doubt that much of the encouragement which has lately been given to Ritualism may be traced back to its recognition of the longing of women to devote themselves to what they are able to think, and to what in some sort are really, active and important services. Those who know how readily recruits are found among women for all sorts of lay Mission work will bear witness to their longing to labour in fields that are not naturally inviting to the frivolous. Again, the recent establishment of Lectures for Women, on subjects often abstruse, and given by men whose position is guarantee that they will not deal with the subjects in a too popular method, has elicited proof that, in every part of the kingdom, women are anxious to avail themselves of every opportunity of cultivating their minds, and of developing faculties which have not even the attraction of any immediate application.

These evidences cannot be a surprise to any one who regards the facts of human nature. Wherever there are faculties there is an innate craving to find work for them. That women have intellectual and moral faculties no one in terms denies, however he may choose to ignore the fact. But when we admit the fact, how terrible do the consequences seem of neglecting to provide the food which Nature demands for the hunger which she creates. Perverting the healthy instincts, we pervert the whole mental constitution. We know in States what consequences follow when the Government tries to debar the people from occupying their minds in free inquiry, or criticism, or research. The energies, driven from wholesome exercise in fields of legitimate investigation, turn to refinement of luxury and ingenuity of vice. The most degraded ages of the world are those in which wealth has been fostered and thought has been stifled. Is it possible that we can apply that system to one half of the race without parallel evils? If we tell the women, who are to be the companions of this generation, the mothers of the next, that they forfeit their title to our admiration if they think of other things than amusement and adornment, can we expect a healthy moral and intellectual tone to prevail among them? Can we train them in folly, and hope that they will not better our instruction? Can we treat them as slaves, and expect other than the vices of slaves? Nay, the higher their nature originally, the more must be the evil consequences of their enforced degradation. The God-given energy must burst out, either in the service of God or of the devil. Or if by strength of moral principle it be saved from utter perversion, through what misery of slow suffering must it pine in atrophy to extinction. I have seen a procession of monks, with a nightmare of faces, wearied, dejected, purposeless, hopeless, when not brutalized with the traces of furious rebellion against their world, and in that woful panorama of debased human nature I see the figure of what we condemn women to, when we bid them grow old in listless idleness, if they fail to secure to themselves the privileges of wifedom.

But is it out of material so fashioned that we are wise to take wives and mothers? Are women, so brought up and taught, fit to rule their own households and to bring up and teach their own children? The current satires on "fashionable mothers" may in part furnish evidence of the consequences. But it is safer to appeal to what are the common complaints made of the defects of women in the management of households and families. We hear how much time and money are given to dress, to amusements, to display; and how there follow the inevitable complaints made of servants who in such things only imitate the example their mistresses set. We learn how often novel reading occupies the main part of such attention as is given in any form to literature. We are told how frequently the husband lives a life apart from his wife, because he finds that she is not interested in the things that interest him. We are bid to recognise how an imperfect moral sense at once prevents the perception and the performance of duties; and how servants and children, seeing irregularity, untruthfulness, and selfishness in the mistress and mother, acquire the same habits themselves. I do not deny the basis of truth that lies in these charges. But I ask if the results are not what would appear, probably in a worse form, in men, if their training were as defective, their education as neglected, and if they were carefully excluded from participation in labours and interests of real importance in the way that women are? And if the mischiefs are such as evidently follow from the training, our duty is to alter the training, so that the mischiefs may be averted. For that they may be averted, common experience also tells us all. It is within the knowledge of every one that families where the mother has herself had the education enabling her to bring up her daughters well are of very different character from those which furnish the common mark of journalistic sarcasm. It is to such families, taught by such mothers, that men of sense turn for wives. Is it unreasonable, then, to urge that we should make an effort to increase the number of those who are thus deserving of our true admiration and esteem?

It does not fall within the scope of this paper to enter into the details of an educational system that would remedy the defects so prevalent at present. It is enough here to point out the principles which ought to regulate such a system. The principle is the same for women as for men. That is a true education which teaches how the faculties which its Maker has implanted in the soul can be made most serviceable to our fellow-creatures. For in serving others consists self-elevation. Whatever is divine in ourselves is most fully developed by the endeavour to make it beneficial to our neighbour. Herein is scope and motive and reward for the most patient effort of self-culture. Nor is it to be overlooked that, in the wonderful scheme of God's earthly government, the doing of good to others is the direct means by which what is called success in life is achieved for ourselves. Unthinkingly often, the man of the world who by honest effort struggles to raise himself, raises hundreds around him. All science, all commerce, all industry, by which human fame or fortune is made, spread blessings around. Not less do they lead to fame and fortune if pursued for the sake of the blessings they confer. Women's education and work make no exception to this happy rule. If a woman were to try to do the very best for herself in a worldly sense, she could take no surer course than by fitting herself to confer the largest benefits on those around her. For her, then, I ask the best when I ask that she should be trained so as to be best able to do good. Beyond elementary education this process must vary in the case of every individual, according to her individual temperament and her position in life. Only let the highest faculties be in each case most regarded. The capacities for literature, for art, for industry, for government, for organizing, for instructing, for sick-nursing, with the thousand subdivisions and modifications of each, present a wide enough field, within which every girl can find some innate taste to gratify, some special aptitude to cultivate. Let her count that her duty which she can best exercise. Let fathers and mothers count it their most solemn duty to help and guide their children to render themselves thus worthy workers in their Father's vineyard, that so when the day is done they may receive every one the reward of their work.

Does any one object that in thus developing the higher nature of women, in teaching and admitting them to the performance of important duties, there is danger that any of the peculiar charms of their sex should be lost? Surely, neither in men nor in women is it found that a sense of life's deeper realities and responsibilities, and an interest in things outside themselves, are hostile to the qualities that make the delight of companionship. The struggle, indeed, which women just now have to make in order to escape from the trammels of a false position, do sometimes lead them to take up an attitude which we should not perhaps like to see them all assume. I do not admire, any more than their critics, the type of the "strong-minded" woman, as it is occasionally presented to us. I am not arguing in favour of Woman-militant, or defending any errors of taste into which some may occasionally fall. But, on the other hand, we all have the happiness of knowing a far greater number of examples of women, intelligent and cultivated, active in every good work, interested in all that is worthy of interest, who by such development of their faculties have added additional grace and lustre to their natural attractions. Even men who look only for agreeable companions acknowledge that they are to be found rather among the educated than the uneducated. What further answer is needed to the apprehensions which only silly men venture to express, that learning and employment would make women bores and destroy the pleasures of society?

And the world has room and need for all the higher work of which women are capable. In cities and in villages, in prisons and in workhouses, in art-galleries and in letters, in all branches of industry and in every field of benevolence, the world will be grateful to the women who can do it service. In many things the world gropes and stumbles, because it has not enough of women's hands to guide it. In many other things in which men and women may labour together, there is a cry for more labour. In some things even men's work is less perfect than it would be if they had women's work to compare with their own. For women, I again say, I do not call the same as men, but different—their complement, the necessary element to the completeness of human nature. Even in our highest public duties we should be incalculably helped by admitting the directness, the simplicity, the instinctive honesty of a woman's unperverted mind. Often, their counsel would be less cowardly than men's, simply because they would more regard what is ultimately right, and less what is probably and immediately profitable. And in thus counselling us, women would save us from many disasters into which our own selfish and short-sighted policy is daily leading us, because we choose to forget that what is not right cannot be profitable ultimately, whatever the promise of safety or wealth it may hold out for the moment. Therefore even in those matters which seem furthest removed from the domestic life, the relations between States, the foreign policy of the country, we place ourselves at wilful disadvantage, because we do not invite the clear sense of women, not to direct or dictate our course, but to suggest to us views which it is immeasurably important we should consider, and which, left to ourselves, we are apt to overlook.

But in matters affecting our home administration, surely no candid mind can dispute the fact that women's opinions would be a most valuable corrective of our own. I leave out of sight all the questions which peculiarly affect women, either as regards their property or their persons, for every day we concede to them, as individuals, rights of self-government which the surviving barbarism of our laws still denies to them as a section of the community. But looking to the matters in which, as members of the community, women have an interest as great as men have, it is obvious that we should reap incalculable advantage from their considering, along with us, the national questions of Education of the young, of the management of the Poor, of the treatment of Criminals, and of the guidance of Emigration. Whoever thinks that on these topics women would be less careful, cautious, and judicious counsellors than men are, simply betrays that he takes for his type of womanhood "the girl of the period," as he has helped to make her, and knows nothing of the number of women who have thought out and watched the working of all these most difficult problems of social humanity.

But in narrower spheres than those that belong to the domain of politics we equally want the recognised help of women. Whatever the nation resolves on, each locality must administer, and in the administration there is need for all the experience and all the wisdom that both sexes can contribute. Those very questions, Education, Poor Relief, Prisons, Hospitals, and Emigration, are local questions. In every one of them there are departments which scarcely any but women are competent to deal with. Why do we not, I will not say merely admit, but why do we not urge, women to help us with the classification and redemption of female paupers and pauper children and prisoners? How can we with our rough reasoning and generalization ever attempt to deal with what a cultivated woman's intuition can alone discriminate and appreciate? Once again, for fear of being, perhaps wilfully, misunderstood, I repeat that I do not assert that every woman would be of value in such work: I certainly could still less say so of every man. But I do say, that there are thousands of women in every district who are competent to help in such work, to help in a way in which no male help would avail.

For the sake, then, of the country and of its dearest interests, we ought to invite women to bear part with us in the great Christian duty of doing good to our neighbour: for the sake of women themselves we ought so to train them that they may understand that duty and do it. Think of a woman's empty life, as too often now public opinion makes it,—her training in a few showy gifts, almost avowedly to help her in husband-hunting,—

her seclusion from all that interests the best men,—her incapacity to rule even her own household and her own children, because, alas! she has never been taught how to do either;—think of her life, but half useful if she does marry, and an utter blank if she does not,—and then say how great the loss, the pity, and the shame of an up-bringing that has such results. Women and men alike the losers, but if the pity be for the women, the shame is for the men; for it is by the indifference and misjudgment of men that women are so brought up. It is because fathers do not think of their daughters' future,—because they too often regard them as only so much goods to be got rid of in the market, and therefore only to be dressed and adapted for the market,—that the daughters are so unfit for any higher function. When we cry out about women's frivolity, or vanity, or luxury, we impeach the education which has cultivated these failings, and has not been directed to develop any of the higher and nobler faculties with which women are endowed.

I appeal then to men, because by their strength they are the masters; I appeal to women, because even now their domestic influence is so great; I appeal to all that mass of thought which forms the public opinion by which we are governed, to give to the women of the present and of coming generations only a fair chance! Let us think of them and deal with them as fellow-workers with us, it may be in different departments, but at least in the one great duty of doing some good on earth. Let us teach them and train them so that they can work with us in that duty. Shall we in doing so make them unmaidenly, unwifely, unmotherly? No; rather, more perfect in all womanly gifts and graces, of which those will first enjoy the happiness who are nearest to them in their homes. We cannot unsex women by cultivating more highly the qualities that are the especial glory of their sex. We shall not make them masterful by teaching them how best they can serve. The purity, the charity, the tenderness that is in them, we now corrupt and crush by misdirection, and by forbidding them any object save that which a possible husband and children may supply. Allowed only to expand,—allowed to be bestowed on a wider circle of sympathies,—allowed to seek out a sphere beyond the range of self-interest, these qualities will be enhanced in strength, and will become to us the richer blessings. Women and men will be drawn the closer in the bonds of mutual service, and love, and comfort, when we seek women's aid, and train them to give their aid, no longer only in our idleness and amusements, but in the daily round of duties which makes the noblest portion of our lives.

THE END.

Manufactured by Amazon.ca
Bolton, ON

35790798R00254